SENSORCOMM 2017

The Eleventh International Conference on Sensor Technologies and Applications

September 10 - 14, 2017

Rome, Italy

SENSORCOMM 2017 Editors

Manuela Vieira, ISEL-CTS/UNINOVA, Portugal
Sergey Yurish, IFSA, Spain
Brendan O'Flynn, Tyndall National Institute | University College Cork, Ireland
Dongsoo Har, Korea Advanced Institute of Science and Technology (KAIST), Daejeon, Korea
Abdallah Makhoul, University of Franche-Comté, Besançon / Institute FEMTO-ST, France
Hesham H. Ali, University of Nebraska at Omaha, USA

Printed from e-media with permission by:

Curran Associates, Inc.
57 Morehouse Lane
Red Hook, NY 12571

Some format issues inherent in the e-media version may also appear in this print version.

Printed by Curran Associates, Inc. (2017)

International Academy, Research, and Industry Association (IARIA)
412 Derby Way
Wilmington, DE 19810

Phone: (408) 893-6407
Fax: (408) 527-6351

petre@iaria.org

Additional copies of this publication are available from:

Curran Associates, Inc.
57 Morehouse Lane
Red Hook, NY 12571 USA
Phone: 845-758-0400
Fax: 845-758-2633
Email: curran@proceedings.com
Web: www.proceedings.com

Table of Contents

SENSORCOMM 2017

Forward

The Eleventh International Conference on Sensor Technologies and Applications (SENSORCOMM 2017), held between September 10-14, 2017 in Rome, Italy, was a multi-track event covering related topics on theory and practice on wired and wireless sensors and sensor networks.

Sensors and sensor networks have become a highly active research area because of their potential of providing diverse services to broad range of applications, not only on science and engineering, but equally importantly on issues related to critical infrastructure protection and security, health care, the environment, energy, food safety, and the potential impact on the quality of all areas of life.

In wireless sensor and micro-sensor networks energy consumption is a key factor for the sensor lifetime and accuracy of information. Protocols and mechanisms have been proposed for energy optimization considering various communication factors and types of applications. Conserving energy and optimizing energy consumption are challenges in wireless sensor networks, requiring energy-adaptive protocols, self-organization, and balanced forwarding mechanisms.

The conference had the following tracks:

- Deployments and implementations of sensor networks
- Performance, simulation and modelling of sensor networks
- Architectures, protocols and algorithms of sensor networks
- Sensor circuits and sensor devices
- Software, applications and programming of sensor networks
- Wireless sensor networks
- Wireless Body Sensor Networks and e-Health

We take here the opportunity to warmly thank all the members of the SENSORCOMM 2017 technical program committee, as well as all the reviewers. The creation of such a high quality conference program would not have been possible without their involvement. We also kindly thank all the authors that dedicated much of their time and effort to contribute to SENSORCOMM 2017. We truly believe that, thanks to all these efforts, the final conference program consisted of top quality contributions.

We also gratefully thank the members of the SENSORCOMM 2017 organizing committee for their help in handling the logistics and for their work that made this professional meeting a success.

We hope that SENSORCOMM 2017 was a successful international forum for the exchange of ideas and results between academia and industry and to promote further progress in the area of sensors and sensor networks. We also hope that Rome, Italy provided a pleasant environment during the conference and everyone found some time to enjoy the historic charm of the city.

SENSORCOMM 2017 Chairs

SENSORCOMM Steering Committee

Sergey Yurish, IFSA, Spain
Brendan O'Flynn, Tyndall National Institute | University College Cork, Ireland
Elad Schiller, Chalmers University of Technology, Sweden
Jiannan Zhai, Florida Atlantic University, USA
Stefano Mariani, Politecnico di Milano, Italy
Manuela Vieira, ISEL-CTS/UNINOVA, Portugal
Tadashi Okoshi, Keio University, Japan
Jerker Delsing, Lulea University of Technology, Sweden

SENSORCOMM Industry/Research Advisory Committee

Sarfraz Khokhar, Cisco Systems, Inc., USA
Shaohan Hu, IBM Research, USA

SENSORCOMM 2017
Committee

SENSORCOMM Steering Committee

Sergey Yurish, IFSA, Spain
Brendan O'Flynn, Tyndall National Institute | University College Cork, Ireland
Elad Schiller, Chalmers University of Technology, Sweden
Jiannan Zhai, Florida Atlantic University, USA
Stefano Mariani, Politecnico di Milano, Italy
Manuela Vieira, ISEL-CTS/UNINOVA, Portugal
Tadashi Okoshi, Keio University, Japan
Jerker Delsing, Lulea University of Technology, Sweden

SENSORCOMM Industry/Research Advisory Committee

Sarfraz Khokhar, Cisco Systems, Inc., USA
Shaohan Hu, IBM Research, USA

SENSORCOMM 2017 Technical Program Committee

Maykel Alonso Arce, CEIT and Tecnun (University of Navarra), Spain
Majid Bayani Abbasy, National University of Costa Rica, Costa Rica
Mário Alves, Politécnico do Porto (ISEP/IPP), Portugal
Paolo Bellavista, University of Bologna, Italy
An Braeken, Vrije Universiteit Brussel, Belgium
Erik Buchmann, Hochschule für Telekommunikation Leipzig, Germany
Maria-Dolores Cano, Universidad Politécnica de Cartagena, Spain
Juan-Vicente Capella-Hernández, Universitat Politècnica de València, Spain
Marco Cattani, Graz University of Technology, Austria
Luca Caviglione, National Research Council of Italy (CNR), Italy
Matteo Ceriotti, University of Duisburg-Essen, Germany
Amitava Chatterjee, Jadavpur University, India
Bill Chen, University of Macau, Macau
Sungrae Cho, Chung-Ang University, South Korea
Mario Cifrek, University of Zagreb, Croatia
Victor Cionca, Cork Institute of Technology, Ireland
Gautam K. Das, Indian Institute of Technology Guwahati, India
Francesco G. Della Corte, Università degli Studi Mediterranea, Italy
Jerker Delsing, Lulea University of Technology, Sweden
Dulce Domingos, University of Lisbon, Portugal
Paulo Felisberto, LARSys | University of Algarve, Portugal

Stefan Fischer, University of Lübeck, Germany
Yann Garcia, Université catholique de Louvain, Belgium
Matthieu Gautier, IRISA | University of Rennes 1, France
Paulo Gil, University of Coimbra, Portugal
Arda Gumusalan, George Mason University, USA
Malka N. Halgamuge, University of Melbourne, Australia
Jason O. Hallstrom, Florida Atlantic University, USA
David Hasenfratz, Sensirion AG, Staefa, Switzerland
Shaohan Hu, IBM Research, USA
Chao Huang, University of Notre Dame, USA
Raúl Igual, University of Zaragoza, Teruel, Spain
Tarikul Islam, Jamia Millia Islamia (University), India
Miao Jin, University of Louisiana at Lafayette, USA
Abdelmajid Khelil, Landshut University, Germany
Sarfraz Khokhar, Cisco Systems Inc., USA
Young-Jin Kim, Ajou University, Republic of Korea
Sisil Kumarawadu, University of Moratuwa, Sri Lanka
Andrew Kusiak, University of Iowa, USA
Seongsoo Lee, Soongsil University, Korea
Shen Li, IBM Research, USA
Chiu-Kuo Liang, Chung Hua University, Hsinchu, Taiwan
Tiong Hoo Lim, Universiti Teknologi Brunei, Brunei
Thomas Lindh, School of Technology and Health - KTH, Sweden
Jaime Lloret Mauri, Polytechnic University of Valencia, Spain
Benny Lo, The Hamlyn Centre for Robotic Surgery | Imperial College London, UK
Beatriz López, University of Girona, Spain
Flaminia Luccio, University Ca' Foscari of Venice, Italy
Boushra Maala, Tishreen University, Syria
Elsa María Macías López, University of Las Palmas de Gran Canaria, Spain
Abdallah Makhoul, University of Bourgogne Franche-Comté, France
Ramona Marfievici, Cork Institute of Technology, Ireland
Stefano Mariani, Politecnico di Milano, Italy
Michał Marks, Research and Academic Computer Network (NASK), Warsaw, Poland
Francisco Martins, University of Lisbon, Portugal
Natarajan Meghanathan, Jackson State University, USA
Lei Mei,California Research Center - Agilent Technologies, USA
Fabien Mieyeville, University Claude Bernard Lyon 1 | Polytech Lyon, France
Umair N. Mughal, UiT The Arctic University of Norway - Campus Narvik, Norway
Amy L. Murphy, Bruno Kessler Foundation (FBK-ICT), Italy
Mir Mohammad Navidi, West Virginia University, USA
Michael Niedermayer, Beuth University of Applied Sciences - Berlin, Germany
Shahriar Nirjon, UNC Chapel Hill, USA
Claro Noda, Mid Sweden University, Sweden
Brendan O'Flynn, Tyndall National Institute | University College Cork, Ireland

Copyright Information

A Management Strategy for Centralized Wireless Sensor Networks Applied to Small and Medium Sized Manufacturing Enterprises

Pedro Chaves and Omar C Branquinho
CEATEC
PUC Campinas
Campinas, Brazil
e-mail: pedrochaves@hotmail.co.uk
e-mail: branquinho@puc-campinas.edu.br

Fabiano Fruett
FEEC
UNICAMP
Campinas, Brazil
e-mail: fabiano@ dsif.fee.unicamp.br

Abstract—The demand for Wireless Sensor Networks (WSN) applied to industrial process monitoring and control is increasing as the forth industrial revolution (Industry 4.0) gathers pace. Flexibility and low cost make WSN the perfect choice for these modern 21st century manufacturing plants. Small and Medium Sized Enterprises (SMEs) have an important role in the growth of developing economies as they account for approximately 60% of all private sector employment, but are currently finding it difficult to take advantage of new sensor technologies. This paper describes the tests carried out with a WSN in order to ascertain the relationship between the Received Signal Strength Indicator (RSSI) and the Packet Error Rate (PER). Subsequently, a new RSSI based network management strategy is presented; it includes two RSSI tracking indices that guarantee an early warning in case the radio signal deteriorates. Both indices are generated in real time; the first estimates the RSSI tendency allowing for the mapping of a sample position in the set and its value, while the second compares the current RSSI to a preconfigured reference value. This article ends with the implementation and testing of the strategy on the ScadaBR Supervisory System.

Keywords-Wireless Sensor Networks; WSN; PER; RSSI; Network Management.

I. INTRODUCTION

Small and Medium Sized Enterprises (SMEs) contribute decisively for the advancement of developing countries. Worldwide, SMEs account for about 52% of private sector value added, varying from 16% of the gross domestic product (GDP) in low-income countries to 51% of GDP in high-income ones. SMEs dominate the world business stage; estimates suggest that more than 95% of enterprises across the world are SMEs, accounting for approximately 60% of all private sector employment [1].

If compared to wired networks, Wireless Sensor Networks (WSN) can offer substantial advantages regarding deployment, commissioning, and maintenance [2]. These networks can cover areas that are out of reach for wired networks allowing for the improvement of the processes.

The WSN currently offered by large solution providers tend to be complex, non-centralized and expensive [3] putting these solutions out of the reach of most SMEs considering that, differently from large corporations, these companies have neither the capital to acquire nor the dedicated departments to manage these new communication technologies [4].

The *raison d'être* of a WSN is to monitor and control processes and environments. A manufacturing process can be defined as a systematic series of operations executed to produce something. The more critical the process is, the more reliable the link needs to be [5]. The management of a WSN must define a set of functions that will integrate configuration, monitoring, operation and maintenance of the network services and devices [6].

Table I compiles the service classes for industrial environments, according to the International Society of Automation (ISA) [z].

TABLE I. SERVICE CLASSES (ISA)

Use	Class	Description	Characteristic
Safety	0	Emergency Action	Always Critical
Control	1	Control (Closed Loop)	Usually Critical
	2	Supervision Control (Closed Loop)	Usually not Critical
	3	Open Control (Open Loop)	Human Action
Monitoring	4	Alert	Few Consequences
	5	*Logging, up e download*	No immediate Consequences

The processes criticality and the characterization of the signal and medium generate subsidies to the network management system. The International Organization for Standardization (ISO) divides the network management into five distinct areas. This classification was developed for the Open System Interconnection (OSI) model:

- Configuration management - controls, identifies and collects from and supplies data to managed objects.
- Performance management - evaluates the behaviour of managed objects and the effectiveness of the communication.
- Fault management - enables the detection, isolation and correction of abnormal operation of the OSI environment.

- Security management - addresses aspects essential to the safe operation and protection of managed objects.
- Account management - enables charges to be established and costs to be identified [7].

In wireless communications, the received signal strength is media dependent [6]. A strategy that assists in estimating the Received Signal Strength Indicator (RSSI) tendency with relation to a threshold would be relevant to the performance and configuration management, as actions could be taken before that threshold is reached.

Supervisory Data Acquisition and Control Systems (SCADA) are industrial control systems used in the monitoring and control of remote devices. These systems collect data from remote sensor nodes in real time in order to monitor and control communication networks, including alarm monitoring, data processing, and equipment and conditions control. Based on the information from remote sensor nodes, manual or automatic commands can be executed on remote devices [8].

Big WSN suppliers tend to offer solutions for the needs of large enterprisers, with prices that can reach millions of dollars. These suppliers offer large, noncentralized networks that grant the routing decisions to the nodes [9][10][11], effectively rendering the network hostage of the topology, impacting in its control. This reality does not really attend the necessities of SMEs regarding cost, control and complexity, as, usually, these plants are small in area, demanding cheaper, less complex network solutions. Centralized solutions also allow for full network control.

For the tests in this paper, we use a low cost, centralized WSN approach geared towards SMEs, where the network manager has total control over its running.

We also identified a shortage of low-complexity network summarization solutions that can be used by non-technical operators working in SMEs. For that reason, in this paper, we present a management strategy that uses the RSSI as the main metric.

This paper is organized into eleven sections: in Section II we compare different WSN solutions, in Section III we explain the relation between RSSI and Packet Error Rate (PER), in Section IV we present the Radiuino Platform, in Section V we specify the testing set up, in Section VI we show the benchmarking test results, in Section VII we introduce the indices management strategy, in Section VIII we describe the tests done with the strategy, in Section IX we show the strategy implementation on a supervisory system, in Section X we show the tests done and in Section XI we present our conclusions and future work.

II. WSN in the Industrial Environment

Since WLANs, Bluetooth, WiFi, WirelessHart and Zigbee, to mention just some, were introduced, a lot of the effort was focused on the non-licensed Industrial, Scientific and Medical (ISM) band of 2.4 GHz as some systems can require higher data rates. However, in some cases, this band may get overcrowded, degrading the signal. There are, however, other non-licensed bands reserved for ISM applications that can be used for wireless communication [12].

The 915 MHz ISM band is narrow and limits the maximum data rates. Applications such as SCADA, where the data requirements are lower than applications found in the 2.4 GHz frequency band, can use the 915 MHz band.

In this paper, we use a platform which operates on the 915 MHz band as there are no restrictions for the use of this ISM band regarding the application type [12].

III. The RSSI-PER Relation

The RSSI is chosen as the main metric in this study since link quality monitoring methods based on hardware, e.g., Link Quality Indicator (LQI), Signal to Noise Ratio (SNR) and RSSI, make use of basic metrics provided by the chip that, if compared to software solutions, require far less overhead allowing for a better response to changes on the link [13].

As indicated by [14], for a given scenario, there is a clear relation between the RSSI and the PER as the latter tends to go up as the RSSI goes down. In this paper, we propose a strategy that takes advantage of this relation.

IV. The Radiuino Platform

All measurements in this work are done using the low cost, open software, open hardware Radiuino platform [15]. The firmware used in the transceivers was developed using the Radiuino Integrated Development Environment (IDE). The Radiuino platform is structured in layers of protocol akin to the Transmission Control Protocol/Internet Protocol (TCP/IP).

The RSSI and PER monitoring applications were developed in Python 2.6 [16] and the supervisory system used for the management was the open software ScadaBR [17].

V. Benchmarking and Test Set Up

Benchmarking tests were carried out on all modules before any tests with the strategy were carried out.

The module BE990 was the transceiver used in all nodes. All were configured with a data rate of 38.38 Kbps, operating in the ISM band of 915 MHz and using frequency shift keying (FSK) modulation. The BE990 complies with the Brazilian National Telecommunications Agency (ANATEL) regulations; it carries an Atmega 328 micro controller, a Texas CC1101 transceiver and a Texas CC1190 radio frequency (RF) amplifier [18].

Each sensor node was constituted of a module BE990 mounted on a DK104 development board. The module on the sink node was mounted on a UartSBee board [15]. We used 12 volts batteries to power the nodes during tests.

For the benchmarking tests, the wireless communication link between the sink node and each remote sensor node was emulated using a coaxial cable.

In order to avoid saturation, Mini-Circuit attenuators [19] were placed between the module in the sink node and the modules in each sensor node, as indicated in Figure 1.

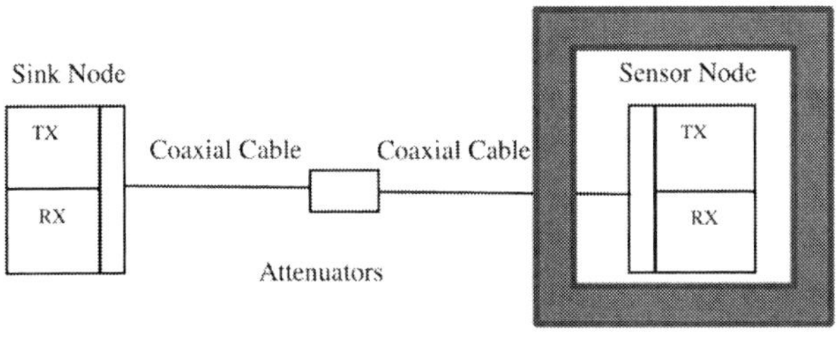

Figure 1. Emulation Setup Diagram.

The modules in each sensor node were placed in a sealed RF test chamber to check their normalization and assess their PER and RSSI results with minimum electromagnetic interference (EMI).

VI. Benchmarking and Correlation Tests Results

The results of the benchmarking tests are summarized in Table II. It shows that all modules were conforming, returning very similar values of RSSI and PER for the same attenuation scenario, in this case 90 dB. The highest standard deviation was just 0.13 dBm and the highest PER only 1.6%, indicating good stability of all modules. We concluded that the modules could be considered normalized and could be used in the correlation tests.

TABLE II. Benchmarking Results

Sensor	RSSI (average)	S.D. (dBm)	PER (%)
S1	- 42.50 dBm	0	0
S2	- 42.50 dBm	0.13	1.6
S3	- 42.00 dBm	0	0

The same set up shown in Figure 1 was used again to collect the information that allowed correlating the RSSI to the PER. This time, the attenuation was gradually increased, thus reducing the RSSI level at the sensor node and consequently increasing the PER, so to find the RSSI level corresponding to the 5% PER reference level suggested by [20]. In order to guarantee the reliability of the results, three series of 200 packets each were sent to each sensor node. The data presented in Table III shows the average results of the three test series.

TABLE III. Correlation RSSI - PER

RSSI Average (dBm)	PER (%)	RSSI SD (dBm)
-45.0	0	0.11
-52.0	0	0.31
-63.0	0	0.38
-69.5	0	0.64
-70.0	2.0	0.57
-71.5	2.5	0.69
-72.0	4.5	0.76
-75.0	5.0	0.57
-77.5	12.5	1.15
-80.0	38	4.41

The results indicate that -72 dBm is the maximum RSSI before the PER reaches the 5% reference level.

VII. Indices Zr and Zt

Indices aid in the monitoring work since they simplify the comparison of a current state with a past or predefined one.

This paper presents a management strategy that includes two indices, both generated in real time. The first estimates the trend of RSSI allowing for the mapping of a sample position in the set and its value, while the second compares the current RSSI to a preconfigured reference one.

These indices are loosely based on the Box Plot diagram and therefore present benefits such as the low complexity calculations required to obtain them, thus ensuring their easy implementation in supervisory systems.

In order to evaluate the trend of the RSSI based on the signal dispersion, we propose the index Zr composed by the ratio of the average RSSI values of a large, configurable, sliding time window (Zb) expressed by (1), which can also be understood as the historical average, by the average of the RSSI values of a small, configurable, sliding time window (Zs) expressed by (2).

$$Zb = \bar{x} = \frac{x1+x2+\cdots+xm}{m} \quad (1)$$

$$Zs = \bar{x} = \frac{x1+x2+\cdots+xn}{n} \quad (2)$$

Where m > n.

The index Zr, expressed by (3), shows how far Zs departs from the historical average Zb indicating the dispersion and, more importantly, the RSSI trend, with the advantage of returning values around 1. This index is independent of the signal strength in which the sensor node operates. This feature allows for its easy implementation in the monitoring of wireless sensor networks; since these sensor nodes are usually positioned in different areas, they tend to present different RSSI levels.

The index Zr will tend to 1 as Zs approaches Zb.

$$Zr = Zb / Zs \quad (3)$$

The second index, Zt, expressed by (4) tracks the value of Zs in relation to a reference value Rv correlated to a PER threshold and tends to 1 as Zs approaches this reference value. This index is dependent on the signal strength at which the sensor node operates.

$$Zt = Rv / Zs \quad (4)$$

The observation of these two indices gives the operative in charge of the network a clear vision of the sensor nodes current situation with respect to the RSSI and, consequently, the PER.

VIII. Indices Testing

For the preliminary tests of the strategy, a WSN as specified in Section V, comprising a sink node and a single sensor node was setup with the sensor node operating with a RSSI above the reference level of -72dBm, as established in Section VI, allowing for the mapping of the RSSI variation to the increase of the PER. From this data, the indices Zr and Zt were extracted and compared to the RSSI behavior. The choice of the sliding time window for the tests was based on the Quality of Service (QoS) we expect industrial processes will demand from a WSN, so the sliding time window used for Zb was 60 minutes and for Zs it was 1 minute. However, these values are still subject of research.

To validate the results, graphical comparisons between the variation of RSSI and Zr, RSSI and Zt and Zr and PER were done.

Figure 2 shows the RSSI with values in dBm on the primary vertical axis against the index Zr with values on the secondary vertical axis and the number of packets on the horizontal axis.

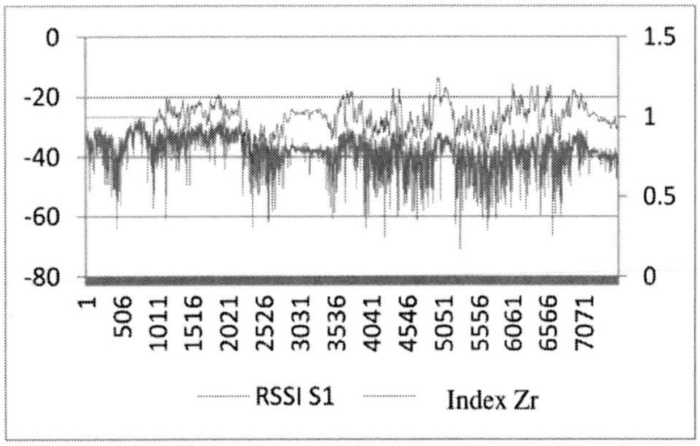

Figure 2. RSSI x Index Zr.

The graph shows that the index Zr was equal to 1 up to approximately the packet 1000, which is equivalent to the 60 minutes required for Zb to be established. From that point on, the index tracks the variation of RSSI, always centred on 1 and differs from the RSSI as it considers the averages of the last 1 and 60 minutes sliding windows. This feature dilutes the impact of possible extreme and discrepant samples.

The graphs in Figure 3 show the RSSI with values in dBm on the primary vertical axis against the index Zt with values on the secondary vertical axis, and the number of packets on the horizontal axis. The index Zt tracked the RSSI variation with respect to the reference level of -72 dBm that was never reached.

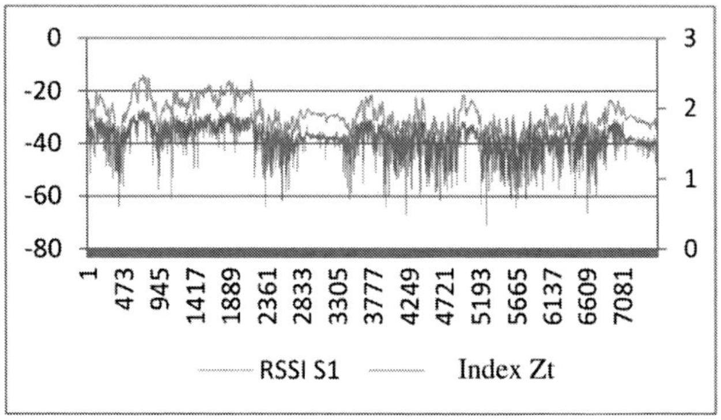

Figure 3. RSSI x Index Zt.

The index Zt acts as an alarm that is triggered whenever the RSSI reaches the pre-defined reference value, since its permanence at or below this threshold indicates an increase in the PER.

Figure 4 presents the index Zr with values on the primary vertical axis against the PER with values on the secondary vertical axis and the number of packets on the horizontal axis.

The graphs show that although the PER was consistently very low, it was higher at the times when the index Zr was below 1, that is, when the RSSI was below its historical average. It is important to observe that the graph of the PER is shown as the hourly average of its values.

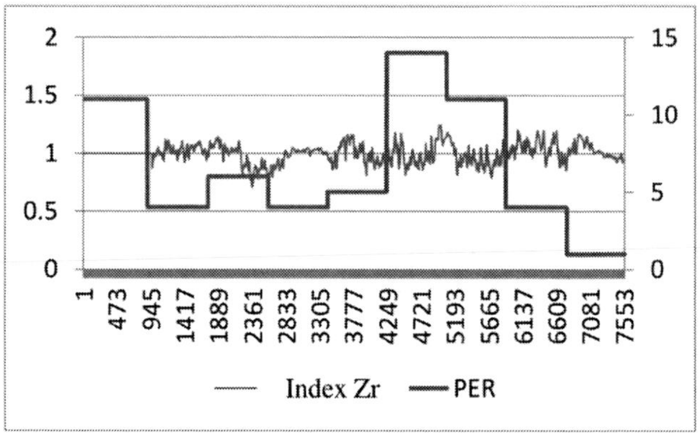

Figure 4. Index Zr x PER.

The results shown on the graphs confirm the robustness of the indices Zr and Zt and their applicability as a wireless network management strategy.

IX. Implementation on Supervisory System

The strategy was implemented on the ScadaBR Supervisory System. For the tests, a WSN as specified in Section V, consisting of a sink node and three sensor nodes using a point-to-multipoint topology was set up, as shown in Figure 5. The supervisory system was configured to collect the downlink RSSI data from each sensor node, calculate Zs for the last minute and Zb for the last 60 minutes.

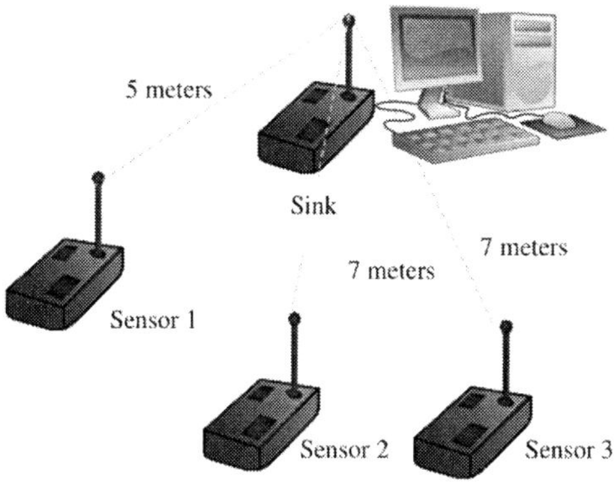

Figure 5. Point-to-Multipoint Topology.

Monitoring via supervisory system allows the construction of graphical interfaces in which different levels of information can be presented, contemplating different levels of knowledge. Figures 6, 7, 8 and 9 show the ScadaBR screen. In each figure, the bottom chart on the right, "RSSI Sensors 1,2 and 3" brings information that will be appreciated by a technically qualified person, the network manager, for example. The upper chart on the right, "Indices Sensors 1, 2 and 3" will be of great value for a person that is interested in the network but not necessarily technical, such as the production manager. The most concise information appears on the left side of the dashboard, with the Limit and Tendency light emitting diodes (LEDs) that are intended to alert a person that is not necessarily interested in the network, but dependent on it, such as a machine operator. Figure 6 shows a snapshot of the graphs obtained with sensor nodes 1, 2 and 3.

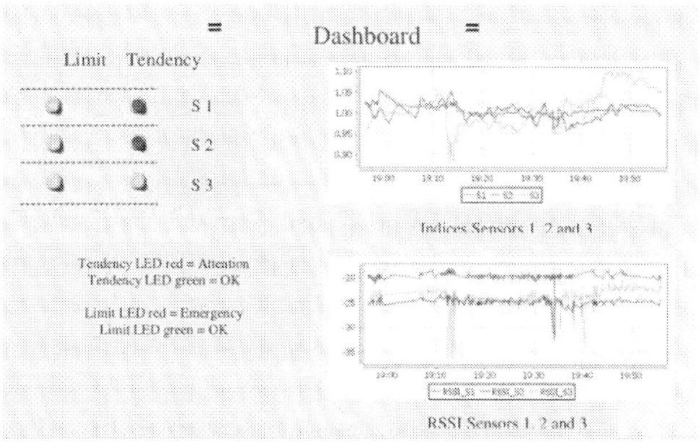

Figure 6. Supervisory System Dashboard.

The chart "Indices Sensors 1, 2 and 3" shows the variation of the index Zr for each sensor node while the chart "RSSI Sensors 1,2 and 3" brings the variation of RSSI. On the left, the Limit LEDs flash green while the index Zt is above the reference value, in this case -72 dBm, and red when Zt is at or below it, and the Tendency LEDs that indicate the position of the index Zr, flashing green while it is above 1 or red when it's below. For the sake of screen simplicity, we chose not to present graphs with the Zt index variation. It can be seen that the Tendency LEDs for sensor nodes 1 and 2 were red indicating that RSSI on these two nodes were in a downward trend. This fact can be confirmed by the graph "Indices Sensor nodes 1, 2 and 3" as the trend lines for sensor nodes 1 and 2 (red and blue lines) end below 1.

X. Stress Testing

To validate the use of the indices strategy on the ScadaBR Supervisory System, we extended the use of the test setup described in Section VIII. Tests introducing unexpected situations of use were carried out. These tests were useful to reveal any potential problems with the strategy on the supervisory system, such as performance or behavior issues, errors on startup, shutdown or on the interface.

The first test, shown in Figure 7, was done in order to ascertain what would be the supervisory system behavior in case one of the sensor nodes became unavailable.

The network was started and the 60 minutes needed for Zb to be established were observed. To simulate unavailability, the sensor node 3 was purposely disconnected from power.

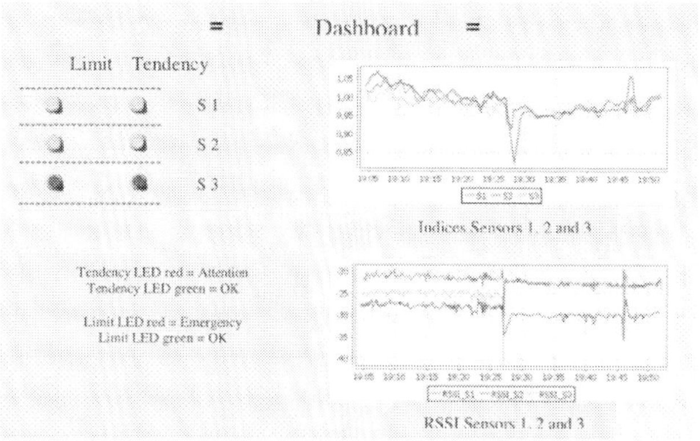

Figure 7. Supervisory System Dashboard - First Test.

The Limit and Tendency LEDs for the sensor node 3 immediately lit up in red and the green trend lines for the sensor node 3 on graphs "Indices Sensors 1,2 and 3" and "RSSI Sensors 1,2 and 3" disappear. We conclude that the strategy in the supervisory system behaved as expected.

The second test, shown in Figure 8, investigated the behavior of the indices strategy on a supervisory system in case of sudden signal deterioration. For this test, the sensor node 3 was distanced from the sink node, simulating signal deterioration. Again, it can be seen that the Tendency LED for sensor node 3 lights up in red and the green line in the "RSSI Sensors 1,2 and 3" graph reaches values below -40 dBm, reflecting accurately the node situation.

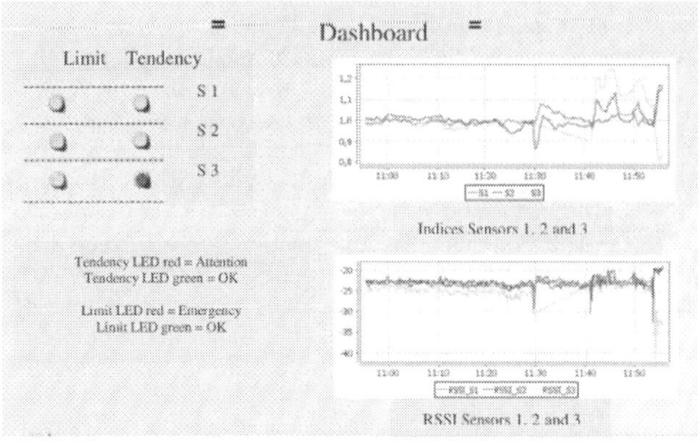

Figure 8. Supervisory System Dashboard - Second Test.

The third test, shown in Figure 9, investigated the supervisory system behavior in case of acute signal deterioration. For this test, the sensor node 3 was moved even further away from the sink node to a point where the RSSI reached and exceeded the reference value of -72 dBm, established in Section VI.

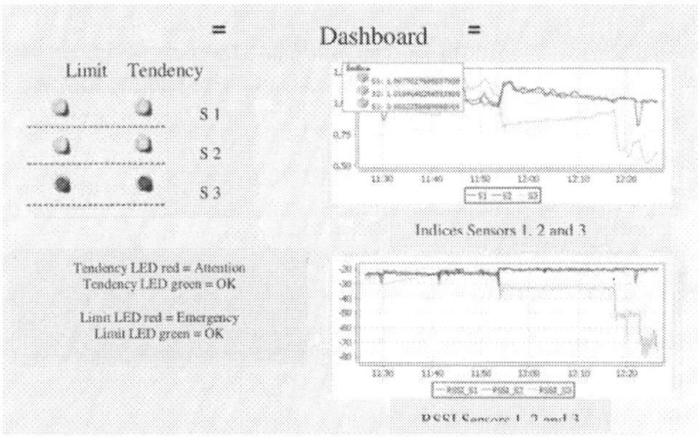

Figure 9. Supervisory System Dashboard - Third Test.

In this test, the dashboard shows the sensor node 3 Limit LED in red, indicating that the RSSI on that sensor node was below the reference value, which can lead to a PER above 5%. This condition was confirmed by the graph "RSSI Sensors 1, 2 and 3" as the green trend line for sensor node 3 reaches values below -80 dBm. The Tendency LED for that node also lights up in red indicating a RSSI deterioration which can be confirmed by the graph "Indices Sensors 1, 2 and 3" where the sensor node 3 green trend line shows the drop of the index Zr.

In order to carry out the last and most extensive test, all nodes were connected to mains power, in order to guarantee the uninterrupted supply of power. The test consisted of a continuous and uninterrupted use of the indices strategy on the ScadaBR for a whole week, in order to ascertain any possible system locking. At the end of that period, the tests pointed out that the system did not present any faults. The tests results with the indices strategy on the ScadaBR Supervisory System confirm the robustness of the solution.

XI. Conclusion and Future Work

This paper objective was to demonstrate the feasibility of employing a new network management strategy based on indices that use the RSSI as the only metric, as this solution requires far less overhead allowing for a better response to changes on the link. For that, a testing set up using the Radiuino platform was assembled so data could be collected.

The preliminary tests with the indices strategy indicated that, when compared to the RSSI readings, the strategy presents an easier interpretation of the data as the impact of extreme and discrepant samples were diluted by it.

The strategy was also implemented on the ScadaBR Supervisory System where an interface that attended the needs of different levels of network expertise was created. The stress tests carried out then returned results that also confirmed that the strategy was stable and robust enough to be employed in the monitoring of WSN in SMEs and thus help these companies to take full advantage of the Industry 4.0 possibilities.

There are still a number of topics following from our findings that would benefit from more research, including the further development of the supervisory system, as other open source network and application monitoring software like the Zabbix could be tested and evaluated, and the development of a methodology for the choice of the sliding time window for the indices Zb and Zs, according to the different industrial plant environments and requirement settings.

Also, the deployment of the indices strategy in a real SME environment with sensors distributed across the plant, where adverse conditions like propagation issues and interferences in the spectrum are the norm, would allow for a better understanding of the real capabilities of the strategy.

References

[1] The Edinburgh Group, "Growing the global economy through SMEs Contents," Available: http://edinburgh-group.org/media/2776/edinburgh_group_research_-_growing_the_global_economy_through_smes.pdf. Accessed May 2017.

[2] ISA 100 Wireless, "Control Over Wireless: Current Applications and Future Opportunities," Available: http//:www.nivis.com/resources/WCI_auto_Week_2012_%20Paper_v18Sep.pdf. Accessed May 2016.

[3] O. Branquinho,"Wireless Networks Technologies," ISBN 97885-63630-49-0. Available: http://pt.scribd.com/doc/206659698/Tecnologias-de-Redes-sem-Fio#. Accessed Octobre 2016.

[4] W. Peres and G. Stumpo, Small and medium-sized manufacturing enterprises in Latin America and the Caribbean under the new economic model, World Dev., vol. 28, no. 9, pp. 1643–1655, 2000.

[5] International Society of Automation, Available: https://www.isa.org/isa100/. Accessed Decembre 2016.

[6] Emerson Process Management, "Wireless Training," Available: http://www2.emersonprocess.com/enUS/plantweb/wireless/WirelessTraining/Pages/index.aspx. Accessed Decembre 2015.

[7] W. Stallings, "SNMP, SNMPv2, SNMPv3, and RMON 1 and 2" (3rd Edition). 1999

[8] Guide to Supervisory Control and Data Acquisition (SCADA) and Industrial Control Systems Security. Available: https://www.dhs.gov/sites/default/files/publications/csd-nist-guidetosupervisoryanddataccquisition-scadaandindustrialcontrolsystemssecurity-2007.pdf. Accessed August 2016.

[9] Emerson Web Page. Available: http://www.emerson.com/en-us/expertise/automation/industrial-internet-things/pervasive-sensing-solutions/wireless-technology. Accessed July 2017.

[10] Banner Web Page. Available: https://www.bannerengineering.com/us/en/products/wireless-sensor-networks.html. Accessed July 2017.

[11] Siemens Web Page. Available: http://w3.siemens.com/mcms/industrial-communication/en/industrial-wireless-communication/iwlan-industrial-wireless-lan/Pages/iwlan.aspx. Accessed July 2017.

[12] J. Shandle. "Unlicensed 915-MHz Band Fits Many Applications and Allows Higher Transmit Power," Available: http://www.digikey.com/en/articles/techzone/2011/may/unlicensed-915-mhz-band-fits-many-applications-and-allows-higher-transmit-power Accessed August 2015.

[13] C. Wei, L. Jian. "An Improved LQI- based Link Quality Estimation Mechanism for Wireless Sensor Networks," Available: http://www.atlantispress.com/php/pub.php?publication=csss14&frame=http%3A//www.atlantispress.com/php/paperdetails.php%3Ffrom%3Dsession+results%26id%3D12655%26querystr%3Did%253D222 Accessed Jyly 2016.

[14] V. Pereira, "PER Estimate, RSSI Reading Protocol and WSN Best Routes Determination," Available: http://tede.bibliotecadigital.puc-campinas.edu.br:8080/jspui/handle/tede/889. Accessed Setember 2016.

[15] Radiuino Site. Available: http://radiuino.cc/. Accessed August 2015.

[16] Python Software Foundation. Available: https://www.python.org/downloads/. Accessed May 2015.

[17] ScadaBR Forum. Available: http://www.scadabr.com.br. Accessed August 2016.

[18] CC1101 Low-Power Sub-1 GHz RF Transceiver. Available: http://www.ti.com/lit/ds/symlink/cc1101.pdf. Accessed July 2016.

[19] Minicircuits Data sheet. Available: https://www.minicircuits.com/pdfs/ZFRSC-123+.pdf Accessed August 2016.

[20] H. Karl, A. Hillig, Protocols and Architectures for Wireless Sensor Networks. Hoboken, NJ: Willey, 2005.

Robust Network Models for using Mobility Parameters for Health Assessment

Abhilash Patolla, Ik-Hyun Youn, and Hesham H. Ali
College of Information Science and Technology
University of Nebraska at Omaha
Omaha, NE 68116, USA
{apatolla, iyoun, hali}@unomaha.edu

Abstract — **With the recent development of wearable mobility devices, researchers are pressed to develop advanced models to take advantage of these devices. Although wearable devices produce a large volume of raw data, the process of extracting useful knowledge from the data collected from such devices remains limited. In particular, not as much has been established on how mobility parameters can be used to develop mobility patterns to assess health levels and predict potential health hazards. In this work, we develop a robust model, based on a population analysis, to utilize mobility data and extract useful information related to health assessment. We propose the use of correlation networks as one of population based analytics to consider variability and analyze mobility. The proposed approach aims at identifying patterns associated with changes in health levels that can lead to medical intervention at the early stages of a potential emerging health hazard as part of a risk management plan. We show examples to illustrate how to identify potential risk at work and provide an application of correlation network approaches using simulated mobility data.**

Keywords – Mobility parameters; network models; Data analytics; Population based analysis; Health Assessment.

I. INTRODUCTION

Human mobility has been studied extensively over many years because of its clinical significance. The impact of mobility on a number of medical and physical properties has been established in various studies. For example, variability associated with muscle fatigue, joint problems, or neurological problems has been correlated to mobility characteristics, and mobility has been used as an efficient indicator of such conditions in various studies [1, 2]. Specifically, capturing abnormal movement patterns is typically used to capture mobility impairment in the domain of mobility monitoring. For example, falling risk has been widely monitored by the variability of mobility pattern in elderly, and cumulated fatigue has been determined by capturing decline of physical activity level [3, 4]. Although Habib et al. and Gravina et al. have tried to integrate heterogeneous physiological data from wearable sensors to make informative decisions [5, 6], the importance of mobility was not significantly considered. This is the motivation behind this study, in which we employ network modeling methodology to analyze human mobility patterns.

Mobility data have at least two natural characteristics that have to be considered when analyzed. First, researchers have to consider a variation of mobility as mobility patterns contains natural variability along subject's internal and external conditions [7]. Deterministic approaches such as Manhattan and Euclidean distance methods are not always appropriate to comprehensively handle the variations of mobility. Secondly, there is a need to establish an objective mobility-based criteria to determine whether a certain pattern is problematic or not. We argue that such decision needs to be flexibly reached using population based approaches. In this paper, we propose correlation analysis, modeled by correlation networks, as one of population based analytics to take into account variation of mobility data and analyze individual's mobility patterns based on their characteristics as related to a given population.

Correlation analysis measures the statistical relationship among items. Using correlation analysis, we are able to see embedded associations among subject mobility patterns. Although correlation analysis cannot establish a causal relationship between mobility patterns, it can examine how each mobility patterns are compared with each other. In order to understand association among different mobility signatures, it is important not only to be aware of mobility patterns that enable us to compare mobility in different environments but also to be able to consider levels of mobility that correlated with various levels of physical activities.

In this study, we introduce the notion of correlation networks as the basic tool for modeling and analyzing mobility data. In addition, we show how such model can be used for prediction of mobility related risk. The proposed approach aims to identify various mobility signatures such as a sudden increase or decrease of mobility or a sudden rise in variability. Such changes in mobility signatures can then be used as part of a comprehensive preventive mobility-based risk management plan.

The methodology of this study introduces three mobility modeling versions. They are the same except that they use different ways to assign weights on the edges connecting elements while building the correlation network. Pattern-based modeling is used when several mobility samples obtained under different conditions are collected. It is based on using Pearson correlation coefficient to define the relationships between elements in the correlation network. The magnitude-based option is primarily utilized when the mobility data is collected under identical or very similar circumstances. In this case, the weights on the edges in the network are derived from the difference of magnitude of the used mobility parameters. The hybrid option is used when both magnitude and correlation are integrated into building the network. This option is primarily utilized when data is collected under conditions that slightly are different or when information about the conditions samples collected is not well defined.

This paper is organized as follows: Section II provides the descriptions of networking methodology including how the network is constructed using three different methods; pattern-based, magnitude-based, and hybrid modeling. Section III includes a practical example to highlight how the network model is used to identify potential risk. Conclusions are briefly summarized in Section IV.

II. METHODOLOGY

Based on the nature of the parameters used for collecting the data, this paper discusses three mobility models which can be used under different conditions for further analysis.

A. *Pattern-Based Mobility Model*

The subjects are represented by the nodes and the connecting edge between them represents the similarity in mobility using correlation coefficient. Correlational networks are already built using the genome data in Bioinformatics [8]. By applying a specific threshold, only some of the subjects are shown in the network. The highly connected nodes of the network have similar mobility.

This model is built using the pattern of the mobility parameter values obtained from the subjects. The correlation coefficient calculated for any two subjects can be in the scale -1 to +1. -1 means perfect negative correlation, and +1 means perfect positive correlation. In the real world, it is hard to observe either of these two. The chance that the correlation coefficient between two subjects is trivial is determined by the statistical significance parameter (P). The value of the statistical significance should be less than 0.05 to make the correlation significant. In the pattern based analysis, statistical significance plays a vital part.

Using this model, it is possible to perform analysis by using mobility samples of different granularity like hours, days, weeks, months, etc. Aggregating the mobility samples to higher granularity will result in the generalization of the subject's characteristics.

The pattern based mobility network modelling can be used in the situations where the mobility parameter samples from the subjects are collected from different environments like hard floor, carpet, marble floor, sand, before the accident, during the phase of recovery, after the accident or in the conditions where the habitat or locality changes with time. In all these different environments, we can analyze the change in subject's mobility. These changes can be visualized using the pattern based mobility model.

The pattern based mobility models can only be applied if the samples are collected from different environments. These conditions make the network more efficient when built using the pattern based mobility model. This paper claims that the pattern based correlational model can be used to build the correlational network only if the samples are known to be from a different environment.

B. *Magnitude-Based Mobility Model*

The subjects are represented by the nodes and the connecting edge between them represents the similarity in mobility using weighted magnitude difference. Table I shows the mobility samples and the weighted magnitude difference between the subjects. The desired threshold can be defined as the weighted magnitude difference. The mathematical expression used to calculate the weighted magnitude difference between two subjects A and B is as shown below:

$$\Delta\, Weighted\ Mag_{A-B} = \frac{|Mag_A - Mag_B|}{Max\,(Mag_A, Mag_B)} \times 100 \qquad (1)$$

Consider two subjects where subject one makes 200 steps on day one and 3000 steps on day two. And the second subject makes 3000 steps and 200 steps on these two days. By building the network using a pattern based model, these two subjects end up in different clusters since they have a negative correlation among them. The two subjects are similar in mobility except that they have different mobility properties on these two days due to their work timings, religious commitments or habits. Construction of correlational networks requires a mobility model that will eliminate these discrepancies.

The magnitude based mobility model can be used if the mobility parameter values collected from the subjects are from a similar environment. In a similar environment, the nature of human mobility shows a similar pattern, but the parameter collected from the subjects may be of different magnitudes. This weighted magnitude difference between the subjects is captured and represented as the edge in a correlational network. The paper says that this model can be applied if we have the knowledge that the mobility samples of the subjects are from a similar environment.

Using a magnitude based model, we can build the correlational network for the concurrent weeks and observe the change in the size of clusters and the movement of a particular subject from one cluster to another in a network.

TABLE I. MAGNITUDE BASED MOBILITY MODEL (LEFT: INPUT, RIGHT: OUTPUT)

	Sub1	Sub2	…	Sub n
Day1	42.3	…	…	84.0
Day2	80.1	…	…	61.6
Day3	28.1	…	…	89.4
Day4	46.3	…	…	47.5

Subject	Subject	Magnitude Difference
Subj 1	Subj 2	0.17
Subj 1	Subj 3	0.08
…	…	…
Subj m	Subj n	0.15

This also assists in the predictive analysis of health through the correlational network. The level of aggregation of the mobility samples results in different networks and cluster formations.

It is vital that the health status of a subject should be assessed based on their mobility samples in different environments. For illustration, consider a subject having an ailment may have good mobility levels in the normal environment, but when the subject goes to higher altitudes or uneven terrains his/her mobility levels may fall down when compared to a healthy subject. In other cases, some subjects may have better mobility levels when they are active but may completely decline when they are tired or having fatigue which shows an abnormality. In these situations, it is better to analyze the mobility levels of the subjects by building up the correlational network using other models using samples from different environments.

C. *Hybrid Mobility Model*

Both the pattern and magnitude based mobility model have limitations in their own way to build the correlational networks efficiently. They can be used in certain situations where the mobility samples are collected from similar or different environments. Based on this observation, the paper states that if we have limited knowledge about the environment of mobility samples, then the hybrid based mobility model can be used to develop the correlational network.

In the hybrid based mobility, due to unavailability of complete knowledge of mobility samples, we use both the correlational coefficient and weighted magnitude difference to develop the correlational network. First, the network is built using the correlation coefficient between the subjects as the connecting edge between them. Later, within each identified cluster, the weighted magnitude difference between the subjects is calculated, and the subjects in that specific cluster are again clustered based on their weighted magnitude difference [7, 8]. This can be done in the other way by applying the weighted magnitude difference followed by the correlation coefficient. This method can be widely related to the phenomenon called overlaying in the networks.

This paper states that the hybrid model can be applied when the knowledge about the mobility samples collected is not well known. By considering both the pattern and the magnitude, the resultant correlational network has the most important edges and the model can include all the vital mobility characteristics in it [10].

The pattern or the weighted magnitude difference between the subjects in the two sets of clusters should be significant enough to improve the model by overlaying. Otherwise, this may result in minimal information gain from the correlational network. Table 2 summarizes important characteristics of the three models.

III. EXPERIMENTAL STUDY

In this section, we illustrate the advantages of using the correlation network approach to model and analyze mobility data. The seamless monitoring of the subjects will be ensured by using a simple wearable sensor such as a Shimmer. Shimmers are wireless devices that capture the accelerometer reading on three different axes. Using the activity classification algorithm embedded in the sensor, the different times for which the particular activity performed is calculated. Based on the metabolic equivalents of each of these activities, the mobility of the subject can be calculated. The wireless sensor required for this seamless mobility capture is still under development, and a lot of research is going on to improve the efficiency and longevity of data capture. We are in the process of obtaining approval to collect mobility data of various groups to validate the effectiveness of the proposed approach. In the meantime, in this paper, we are providing a scenario using simulated data to illustrate how a correlation network can be used to analyze mobility data in a specific case study.

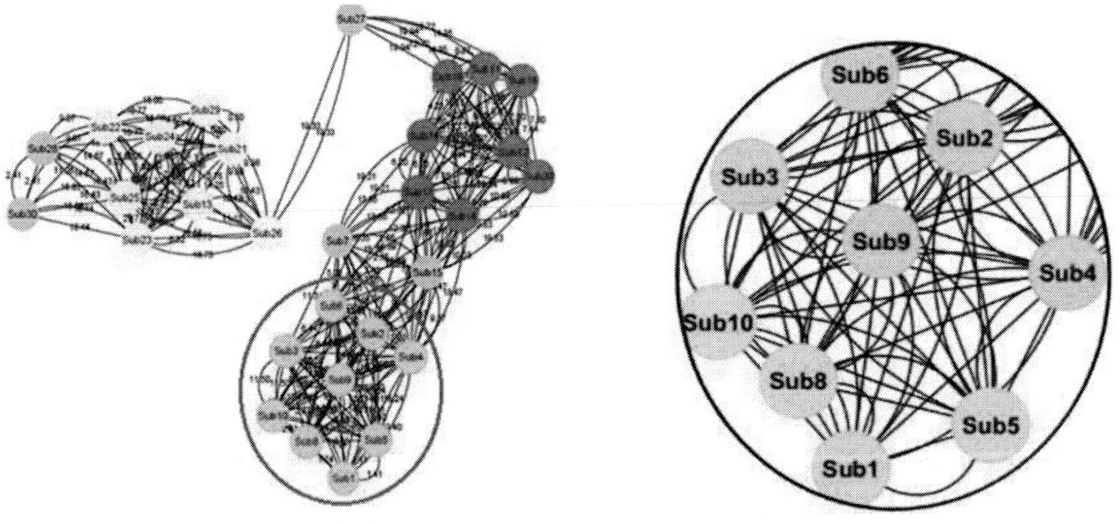

Figure 1. Hybrid Network Before and After Clustering

TABLE II. METHODOLOGY COMPARISON

	Pattern Based Mobility Model	**Magnitude based Mobility Model**	**Hybrid based Mobility Model**
Meaning of weight	Correlation coefficient between nodes	Magnitude difference between nodes	Combinatorial meaning
Sampling condition	Need to control each experimental condition	Same experimental condition is fine	Need to control experimental condition
Treatment in Experiment	Heterogeneous experimental conditions	Homogeneous experimental condition	Heterogeneous experimental conditions
Effect of Sample Size	Larger sample size is better to get robust correlation coefficient	Will not affect the robustness of network	Partial effect within clusters
Advantages	Robust population-oriented analysis	Comprehensive correlation analysis	Enable to conduct an in-depth mobility mining
Shortcomings	Difficult to control heterogeneous experimental settings	Mobility characteristics can be excessively aggregated	Need to have heterogeneous experimental conditions

In the simulated scenario, we consider a mobility monitoring of thirty nurses in a hospital environment and a correlation network is constructed using the magnitude based model. Using the activity classification model, the time periods for different activities like walking, standing, brisk walking and climbing stairs, etc. are recorded and are assigned equivalent points based on the metabolic equivalents of the activities. Considering the limitations mentioned above, this paper focuses on using the scientifically manufactured mobility data which satisfies a normal distribution which is close to real the time nature of human mobility.

The main goal of this experiment is to analyze the correlation between the different subjects and how the cluster formation changes during different sampling periods. The second goal is to observe changes in mobility behaviors of the subjects at different times during the day.

The first samples of different subjects are generated using the normal distribution with a mean value of 500 and a standard deviation '15.86%' according to the 68–95–99.7 rule. In order to show the useful nature of developing a correlational network to analyze the mobility, certain features of subjects are included in the manufactured data. The first ten nurse subjects express a decrease of mobility by ten percent for every sampling period, the next ten subjects by twenty, and the last subjects by thirty percent, as shown in Table 3.

TABLE III. MOBILITY SAMPLE OF NURSE SUBJECTS

	Sub1	Sub2	...	Sub30
Work start	553.78	...	...	384.85
2nd hours	498.40	...	...	269.40
4th hours	448.56	...	...	188.58
6th hours	403.71	...	...	132.01
Work end	363.34	...	...	92.40

Since the mobility samples are collected from a similar environment, the magnitude based mobility model is used to develop the correlational network. The weighted magnitude difference between these thirty nurse subjects is calculated for periodic time intervals, as shown in Table 3. By using a weighted magnitude difference threshold of 20%, the networks are constructed as shown in Figures 2, 3, 4 and 5. The first ten subjects are shown in green, next ten in pink and last ten in red color.

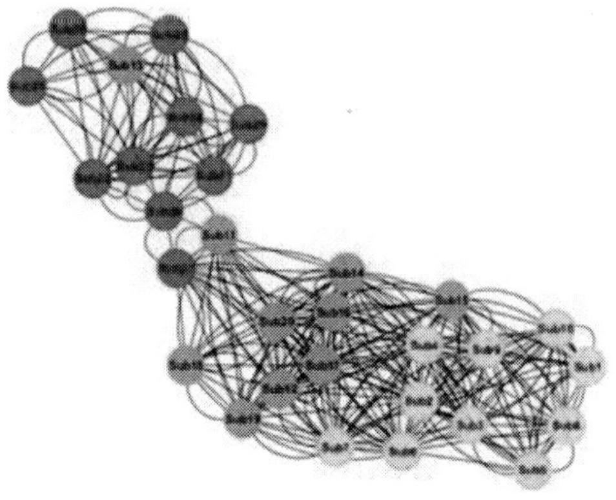

Figure 2. Mobility Network (Work Start)

Figure 3. Mobility Network (2 Hours)

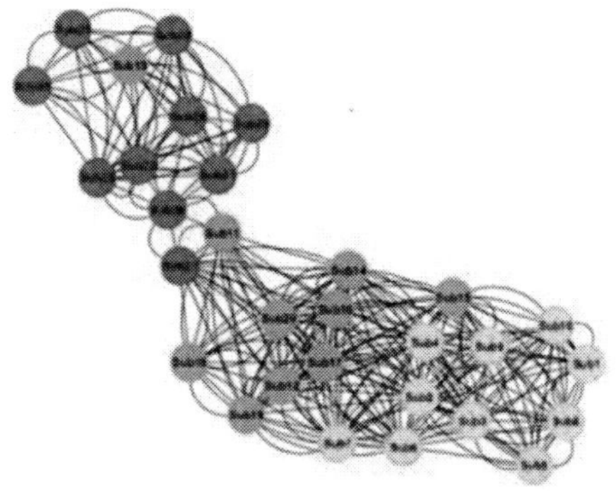

Figure 4. Mobility Network (6 Hours)

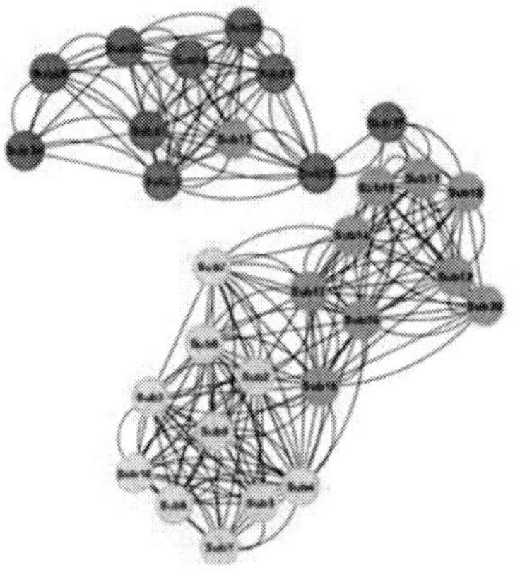

Figure 5. Mobility Network (Work End)

The correlational network shown in Figure 4 reveals that during the initial part of the day all the nurse subjects show a similar mobility. After building a new correlational network using the second sampling mobility values, in Figure 5, we can observe that all the subjects except the subjects 13, 28 and 30 show a similar mobility. In Figures 4 and 5 by observing the subjects and their colors, we can see a clear formation of clusters and the developing relation between the different subjects based on the mobility values collected from the subjects. The final correlational network developed in Figure 5 clearly shows that there are three clusters formed. By analyzing the nature of the mobility data of the subjects, a cluster containing subject 1 through subject 10 in green color shows the higher mobility. The remaining two clusters show a lesser mobility. The cluster with red color nodes shows the least mobility. Some subjects like subject 7, 15, 27, 28 and 30 show an erratic mobility because they are outliers of the normal distribution used to generate mobility data.

All the correlational networks constructed above show how the mobility behavior of the subjects changes over the time. The subjects from one to ten show relatively a better mobility than the subjects from eleven to thirty. Similarly, the subjects from eleven to thirty show a better mobility than the subjects twenty one to thirty. In addition, we can see the correlation between the subjects and how these correlations among the subjects change as the time progresses. The final correlational network in Figure 5 shows us the clear mobility nature of different nurse subjects as high, medium and relatively low. So, in order to stay cautioned and to reduce the chances of any health hazards for the nurses, we would require the correlational networks to extract this unknown hidden information. The larger the number of subjects, additional analysis and extraction of hidden knowledge can be performed from the correlational networks.

IV. CONCLUSIONS

With the recent development of devices that measure the number of steps, distance covered, number of active minutes, among other mobility data, attention continues to be heavily biased in favor of data collection tools. In order to take full advantage of the tools, attention needs to be placed on data integration and data analysis, rather than just data collection. In this work, we try to focus on how to utilize the collected data in building a robust model based on correlation models to extract useful information from the raw mobility data.

The main contribution of this study is to provide a novel approach to analyze mobility data for predicting health hazards. We proposed a correlation network model to structure the raw data and allow for extracting meaningful information that could be used to identify patterns associated with health hazards. Since, unlike mobility monitoring in the laboratory setting, more limitations exist to administrate gait monitoring in the free-living condition. Hence, robust models need be flexible in order to analyze mobility parameters. The proposed analytical model and associated methodology provide an important step in that direction. Moreover, empirical value of this study is supported by a typical scenario. The obtained results show the validity of the proposed approaches. Additional experiments using genuine data will need to be conducted to validate the network models and the proposed approach.

REFERENCES

[1] L.I. Iezzoni, E.P. McCarthy, R.B. Davis and H. Siebens, "Mobility difficulties are not only a problem of old age," Journal of General Internal Medicine, vol. 16, pp. 235-243, 2001.

[2] I.H. Youn, D. Khazanchi, J.H. Youn, & K.C. Siu, "Multidimensional Mobility Metric for Continuous Gait Monitoring using a Single Accelerometer." In Int'l Conf. Health Informatics and Medical Systems (HIMS), pp. 3-8, 2016.

[3] N. Cortes, J. Onate and S. Morrison, "Differential effects of fatigue on movement variability," Gait Posture, vol. 39, pp. 888-893, 2014.

[4] N. Stergiou and L.M. Decker, "Human movement variability, nonlinear dynamics, and pathology: is there a connection?" Human Movement Science, vol. 30, pp. 869-888, 2011.

[5] R. Gravina, P. Alinia, H. Ghasemzadeh and G. Fortino, "Multi-sensor fusion in body sensor networks: State-of-the-art and research challenges," Information Fusion, vol. 35, pp. 68-80, 2017.

[6] C. Habib, A. Makhoul, R. Darazi and C. Salim, "Self-adaptive data collection and fusion for health monitoring based on body sensor networks," IEEE Transactions on Industrial Informatics, vol. 12, pp. 2342-2352, 2016.

[7] N. Giladi, J. Hausdorff and Y. Balash, "Episodic and continuous gait disturbances in Parkinson's disease 22," Scientific Basis for the Treatment of Parkinson's Disease, pp. 417, 2013.

[8] K. Dempsey, B. Currall, R. Hallworth and H. Ali, "A new approach for sequence analysis: Illustrating an expanded bioinformatics view through exploring properties of the prestin protein," in Bioinformatics: Concepts, Methodologies, Tools, and Applications, IGI Global, 2013, pp. 1536-1556.

[9] K. Dempsey and H. Ali, "Evaluation of essential genes in correlation networks using measures of centrality," in 2011 IEEE International Conference on Bioinformatics and Biomedicine Workshops (BIBMW), pp. 509-515, 2011.

[10] K. Dempsey, S. Bonasera, D. Bastola and H. Ali, "A novel correlation networks approach for the identification of gene targets," 2011 Hawaii International Conference on System Sciences (HICSS 44), pp. 1-8, 2011.

Simulating Collaborative Sensor Calibration: Convergence and Cost

Léo Le Taro and Hervé Rivano

Univ. Lyon, INSA Lyon, INRIA, CITI
F-69621 Villeurbanne, France
{fname.lname}@inria.fr

***Abstract*—Air pollution is an increasingly concerning issue in urban areas because of its impact on citizens' health. To tackle pollution effectively, accurate monitoring is a must. Precise stations managed by governmental or specialised institutions do exist, but they are both costly and bulky, which limits the potential to deploy them densely. However, recent progress in micro, connected sensors brings new alternative deployment schemes for dense monitoring by low-cost, imprecise sensors. For such a deployment to be relevant relative to urban air quality monitoring aspects, we are concerned with maintaining the system's properties over time. Indeed, one of the major drawbacks of cheap sensors is their drift: chemical properties degrade over time and alter the measurement accuracy. We challenge this issue by designing distributed, online recalibration procedures. We present a simulation framework modelling a mobile wireless sensor network (WSN) and we assess the system's measurement confidence using trust propagation paradigms. As WSN calibrations translate to information exchange between sensors, we also study means of limiting the number of such transmissions by skipping the calibrations deemed least profitable to the system.**

Keywords—Wireless Sensor Networks; Air Pollution Monitoring; Distributed Algorithms; Sensor Calibration.

I. Introduction

Urban pollution monitoring is traditionally carried out using governmental air quality stations, precise but costly and sparsely deployed. In large cities, this limits monitoring resolution to neighbourhood level, actual estimation being computed by numerical models. Recent advances in nanotechnologies is giving birth to small, affordable electrochemical sensors. One of the major research challenges is to achieve a higher spatial resolution with dense and mobile deployments of such low-cost sensors. To keep an exploitable measurement accuracy, sensor calibration must be considered [1]. However, low-cost electrochemical sensors such as ones we use to measure NO_2 concentrations degrade over time [2], hence recalibration is required if the system is to remain usable over a long deployment. Recalibrating nodes in-place is called non-blind calibration [3]. Ground truths, i.e., reference measurements, are needed to adjust the gain and offset of the low-cost nodes. However, such an approach does not scale because it is infeasible to move a high-quality reference to periodically visit hundreds of sensors.

Another paradigm, denoted blind calibration, assumes unknown ground truths and develops techniques to predict and compensate errors in measurements. Blind calibration methods rely on the underlying signal of interest being either band-limited (i.e., varying smoothly in time and space) [4][5][6] or sparse [7]. Yet NO_2 fields prove to be neither, exhibiting large spatiotemporal variations [8], thus negating the possibility to exploit such properties.

Mobile sensing is gaining more attention as recent studies found that a few mobile nodes on well-selected routes can reflect data as accurately as many static ones [9]. On top of it, mobile sensor networks offer opportunities for multihop calibration, i.e., freshly calibrated sensors may in turn calibrate others. Work has been conducted to minimise error propagation in multihop calibration [10].

II. Problem Statement

Given a heterogeneous set of sensing units, comprised of precise base stations and low quality sensors, assuming all low quality sensors are initially uncalibrated, we are wondering whether the system converges to an exploitable state, if so, we are concerned with the time required to reach a permanent regime.

Secondly, we are interested in limiting the number of energy-hungry transmissions between sensors, and wonder how saving data exchanges would affect the system's accuracy.

In Section III, we present the model upon which we based our simulation framework. In Section IV, we detail the algorithm that the framework implements. Section V presents mathematical analyses of binary calibration in our model. Simulation results are laid out in Section VI. We then conclude the paper in Section VII, suggesting future work ideas as well.

III. Model

We model our system as a discrete time and space process in which sensors follow a stochastic mobility pattern. There are $S = \{1..s\}$ initially uncalibrated mobile sensors randomly moving within a space of $P = \{1..p\}$ positions.
For convenience, mobile sensors move following a uniform distribution: at any given time, a sensor moves to $x \in P$ with probability $1/p$. Several sensors may share the same position.

To simulate the presence of precise institutional or governmental air quality stations in a real-life urban scenario, let $R \subset P$ be the subset of r positions featuring a static reference station, assumed perfectly calibrated and reliable.

Each mobile sensor a is assigned a trust value $C_a \in [0..1]$, 0 meaning completely inaccurate and 1 meaning completely accurate. Unless recalibrated, mobile sensors degrade and lower their trust following an exponential decay of rate $\gamma \in [0..1]$: $C_a(t) = C_a(0) \cdot e^{-\gamma t}$.
Reference stations retain a constant trust of 1. Initially, all mobile sensors start with a trust of 0.

Mobile sensors are said to have a *rendez-vous* with a reference station or another mobile sensor when, at the same time instant, they stand at the same position as, respectively, a reference station or another mobile sensor.

Finally, we introduce the recalibration threshold q which conditions calibrations between mobile sensors. The rationale behind this parameter is detailed in Section IV.

IV. Implementation

Each sensor executes the following pseudo-code algorithm at every time step:

```
Data: γ, q
C ← C · e^{-γ};
foreach n in find_neighbours(p, t) do
    if n is a reference station then
        C ← 1;
    else if n is a mobile sensor and C + q < n.C then
        C ← n.C;
    end
end
```

Figure 1. Sensor trust updating process

We can observe that mobile sensors unconditionally recalibrate to reference stations, however calibration to a peer is conditioned by the variable q. In the real world, each calibration means wirelessly exchanging information. We wish to carry out only meaningful calibrations, with a high benefit. This threshold q allows skipping the calibrations deemed not worthwhile, as they would not lead to a noticeable increase of the trust.

As a corollary, a q of 1 means mobile sensors do not cooperate between each other and only recalibrate to reference stations. Conversely, a q of 0 means that a sensor will always upgrade its trust to the maximum of its neighbors'.

V. Binary Calibration: Analytic Evaluation

Binary calibration is the concept of considering either fully uncalibrated or fully calibrated sensors, with trust values being respectively 0 or 1. In our framework, binary calibration is equivalent to letting γ be zero. Let the random variable T represent the date of a sensor's first calibration.

A. Sensors do not cooperate

Each sensor has probability r/p at each time step to encounter a reference station, independently of other sensors. The probability for such a sensor to remain uncalibrated at t follows a geometric progression of rate $1 - r/p$: $P(T > t) = (1 - r/p)^t$.

The system's global average trust can be derived: $\overline{C}(t) = 1 - P(T > t) = 1 - (1 - r/p)^t$

B. Sensors cooperate

Being calibrated at t means:

- either having calibrated between 1 and $t - 1$ (noted $T \leq t - 1$);
- or *not* having calibrated between 1 and $t - 1$ *but* having a rendez-vous at exactly t (noted $T = t$).

Both cases are mutually exclusive, let us sum their probabilities, keeping in mind sensors start the simulation uncalibrated (time step 0):

$$P(T = 0) = 0$$

$$P(T = t) = 1 - (1 - \frac{1}{p})^{r + sP(T \leq t-1)}$$

$$P(T \leq t) = P(T \leq t - 1) + (1 - P(T \leq t - 1))P(T = t)$$

The rest of this paper presents results of our simulation framework whose purposes are to validate our binary calibration analysis, as well as study cases of non-binary calibration, with $\gamma > 0$.

VI. Non-binary Calibration: Performance Evaluation

In our system, individual sensors' trust occasionally jump when they recalibrate, then continuously variate to lower values because of decay. This behaviour is illustrated by the results of a simple simulation plotted in Figure 2 with a reduced number of sensors and grid positions to preserve readability. This figure hints at the possibility of a permanent regime, because after an initial period of 250 steps no sensor seems to fall below a trust of 0.8. How does the average trust of all sensors behave over a longer period of time and with different parameters?

Figure 3 shows that after a short hysteresis-shaped transient phase, the system's average trust converges to a permanent regime where the trust remains stable. Almost all sensors' trusts evolve between 0.5 and 0.95 despite a pessimistic decay rate $\gamma = 10^{-3}$. Cooperative recalibration is therefore able to maintain the accuracy of the system.

The existence of a permanent regime raises the question of how much time is necessary to reach it. We define the time to converge $t_{0.9}$ as the time by which the average trust of the system $\overline{C}(t_{0.9})$ exceeds 0.9. $t_{0.9}$ is plotted against r in Figure 4, which validates our framework against the analytic evaluations conducted in in Section V for binary calibration schemes ($\gamma = 0$). It shows that cooperation between sensors

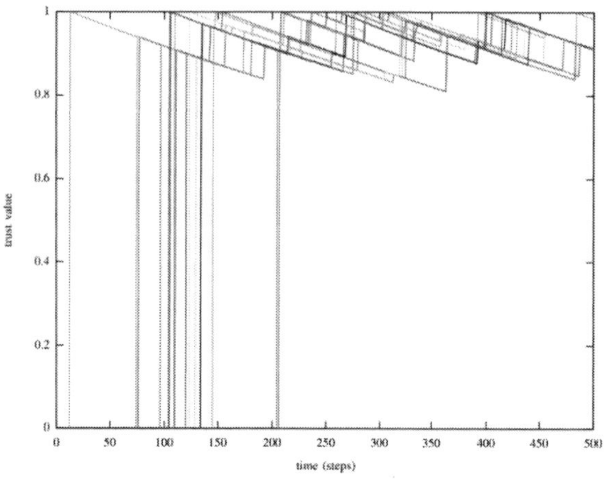

Figure 2. Sensor trust overview
($p = 400, s = 15, r = 1, \gamma = 10^{-3}, q = 0$)

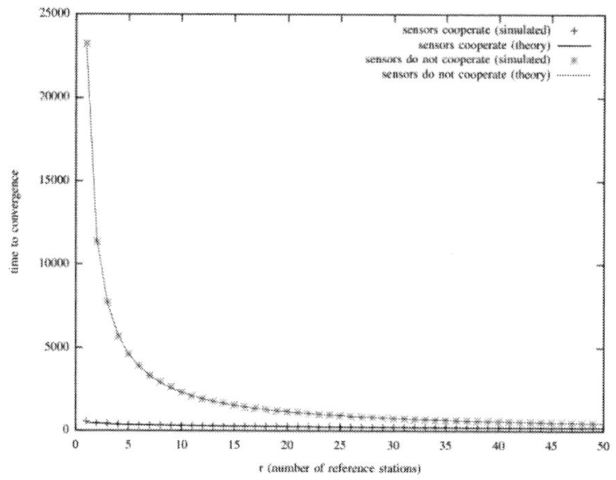

Figure 4. Time to converge
($p = 10000, s = 150, \gamma = 0$)

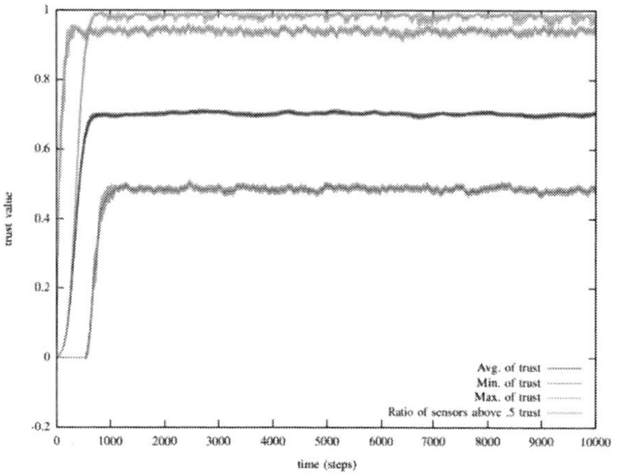

Figure 3. System state over time
($p = 10000, s = 150, r = 1, \gamma = 10^{-3}, q = 0$)
Curves represent a 95% confidence interval over 100 simulations.

have a much stronger impact on the convergence speed than the number of reference stations.

We illustrate the impact of the decay γ on the system's average trust, as well as the maximal and minimal trusts achieved by non-reference sensors in Figure 5. We also consider the ratio of sensors above a trust of 0.5.

We can observe than for $\gamma = 0.002$, the average trust is close to 0.5, which is also the median trust with 50 percent of sensors lying above that value.

Like all others, this simulation was run 100 times and results were aggregated to mitigate the stochastic nature of the results. Nevertheless, we notice that the strongest sensor's trust plot (in light blue) has a quite random aspect, explained by the fact that it depends a lot on its "luck" with rendez-vous rather than exclusively the values of simulation parameters. We deduce that while the average trust we can expect from our system is quite predictable, we cannot guarantee the reliability of a given sensor. Hence, in a real-world urban situation, areas where monitoring is critical (e.g., school or retirement home neighbourhoods) should be covered by many fixed sensors, and/or reference stations.

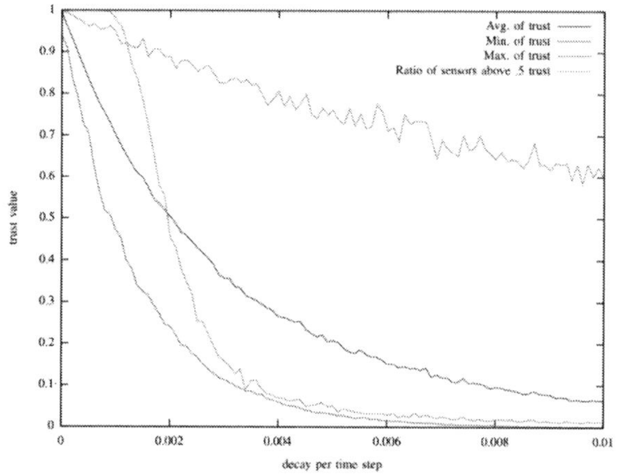

Figure 5. System state versus Gamma
($p = 10000, s = 150, r = 1, q = 0$)

Assuming sensors exchange information once for each recalibration, neglecting the cost of polling one's neighbour's trust, Figures 6 and 7 depict the trade-off between the number of wireless transmissions and the accuracy of the system, i.e., the average trust. The recalibration threshold q is the parameter that restricts transmissions to the case of "*useful*" recalibrations. Numbers were gathered during the permanent regime. An increase of q degrades the system's trust as expected. However, using even a low q dramatically limits the number of wireless transmissions while sacrificing very little trust.

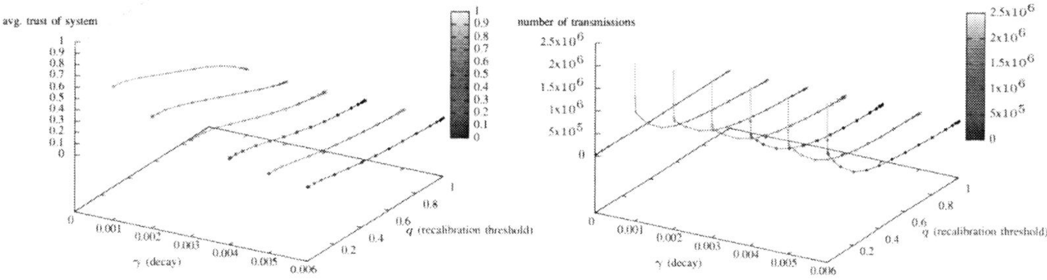

Figure 6. Tradeoff between trust and transmission cost
($p = 10000$, $s = 150$, $r = 1$)

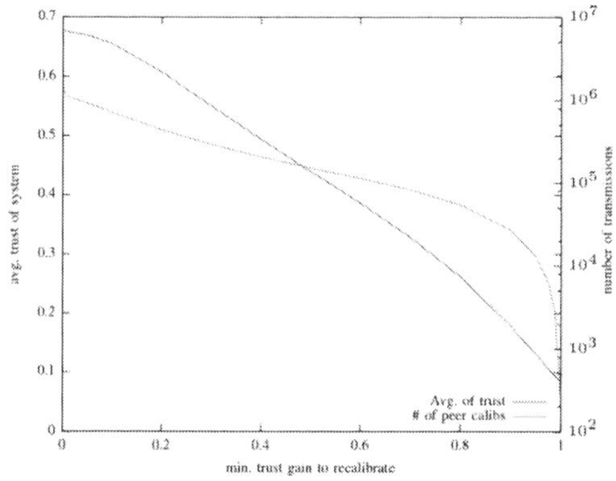

Figure 7. System trust and number of transmissions versus q
($p = 10000$, $s = 150$, $r = 1$, $\gamma = 10^{-3}$)

VII. Conclusion and Perspectives

In this paper, we have presented a simulation framework capable of providing insight on what we can expect from auto-calibrating low-cost electrochemical sensor networks. Cooperation between sensors make the system converge quickly and maintain a steady average accuracy despite the individual decay of the sensors, without requiring many reference stations. It is also shown that many wireless transmissions are spent on a very marginal improvement of the accuracy.

Adjusting certain parameters, we were able to make optimistic predictions of certain metrics like the measurement confidence of the system, its convergence time and the number of transmissions required to calibrate nodes.

Current and future work shall integrate more realistic mobility patterns into the model. One could expect that an urban mobility pattern induce correlation between subsets of sensors, hence a less stable "permanent" regime. The impact of the mobility model and the deployment of reference stations on the spatial mapping of trust values should then be investigated. Besides, realistic mobility models should take into account the distance between calibrating and calibrated nodes into the trust propagation function. Finally, calibration theory requires a non-correlated set of simultaneous calibrating and calibrated measurements. Such a set could be collected over a sequence of rendez-vous, at the cost of a more complex interpretation of the trust.

Acknowledgement

This work has been supported by the "LABEX IMU" (ANR-10-LABX-0088) and the "Programme Avenir Lyon Saint-Etienne" of Université de Lyon, within the program "Investissements d'Avenir" (ANR-11-IDEX-0007) operated by the French National Research Agency (ANR).

References

[1] G. Tolle *et al.*, "A macroscope in the redwoods," in *Proceedings of the 3rd international conference on Embedded networked sensor systems.* ACM, 2005, pp. 51–63.

[2] P. Kumar *et al.*, "The rise of low-cost sensing for managing air pollution in cities," *Environment international*, vol. 75, pp. 199–205, 2015.

[3] N. Ramanathan *et al.*, "Rapid deployment with confidence: Calibration and fault detection in environmental sensor networks," *Center for Embedded Network Sensing*, 2006.

[4] V. Bychkovskiy, S. Megerian, D. Estrin, and M. Potkonjak, "A collaborative approach to in-place sensor calibration," in *Information Processing in Sensor Networks.* Springer, 2003, pp. 301–316.

[5] L. Balzano and R. Nowak, "Blind calibration of sensor networks," in *Proceedings of the 6th international conference on Information processing in sensor networks.* ACM, 2007, pp. 79–88.

[6] J. Lipor and L. Balzano, "Robust blind calibration via total least squares," in *2014 IEEE International Conference on Acoustics, Speech and Signal Processing (ICASSP).* IEEE, 2014, pp. 4244–4248.

[7] S. Ling and T. Strohmer, "Self-calibration and biconvex compressive sensing," *Inverse Problems*, vol. 31, no. 11, p. 115002, 2015.

[8] S. Moltchanov *et al.*, "On the feasibility of measuring urban air pollution by wireless distributed sensor networks," *Science of The Total Environment*, vol. 502, pp. 537–547, 2015.

[9] C. T. Calafate and B. Ducourthial, "On the use of mobile sensors for estimating city-wide pollution levels," in *2015 International Wireless Communications and Mobile Computing Conference (IWCMC)*. IEEE, 2015, pp. 262–267.

[10] O. Saukh, D. Hasenfratz, and L. Thiele, "Reducing multi-hop calibration errors in large-scale mobile sensor networks," in *Proceedings of the 14th International Conference on Information Processing in Sensor Networks*. ACM, 2015, pp. 274–285.

[11] D. Hasenfratz, T. Arn, I. de Concini, O. Saukh, and L. Thiele, "Health-optimal routing in urban areas," in *Proceedings of the 14th International Conference on Information Processing in Sensor Networks*. ACM, 2015, pp. 398–399.

[12] W. Tsujita, A. Yoshino, H. Ishida, and T. Moriizumi, "Gas sensor network for air-pollution monitoring," *Sensors and Actuators B: Chemical*, vol. 110, no. 2, pp. 304–311, 2005.

[13] P. Buonadonna, D. Gay, J. M. Hellerstein, W. Hong, and S. Madden, "Task: Sensor network in a box," in *Proceeedings of the Second European Workshop on Wireless Sensor Networks, 2005*. IEEE, 2005, pp. 133–144.

An Electromyography Signal Conditioning Circuit Simulation Experience

Jorge R. B. Garay[1,2], Arshpreet Singh[2], Moacyr Martucci[2], Hugo D. H. Herrera[2,3], Gustavo M. Calixto[2], Stelvio I. Barbosa[2], Sergio T. Kofuji[2],
[1] University of Mogi das Cruzes - UMC, São Paulo - Brazil
[2]University of São Paulo - EPUSP, São Paulo - Brazil
[3] Federal University of Mato Grosso - UFMT - Brazil
jorgegaray@umc.br, {Arshpreet.singh, mmartucc}@usp.br, {hugo, calixto}@lsi.usp.br, {stelvio, kofuji@pad.lsi.usp.br}

Abstract - **This paper deals with concepts about the electromyography signal (EMG), which is a record of action potentials presented by muscles, and presents the software simulation of a low-cost conditioning circuit for electromyography signals including component blocks capable of signal processing and adaptation for micro-controlling devices. The low cost and high sensitivity make the developed EMG, a good choice in medical applications, such as sleep disorders.**

Keywords — *EMG; Conditioning Circuit for EMG Signals; Circuit Simulation; Instrumentation.*

I. INTRODUCTION

The EMG spectrum includes signals with frequencies varying from 10 Hz to 1 kHz, primarily between 50 and 150 Hz, and voltage peaks going from 1 μV to 100 mV, mainly between 50 μV and 9 mV. While acquiring an EMG signal, some high levels of interference and noise can be noted, requiring a carefully projected conditioning circuit to enable the signal's analysis. The main noise sources involved in this analysis are the environmental noise and the transducer noise, even though the noise from other sources can not be discarded. The environmental noise results from electromagnetic wave generators present, mainly, the frequency of 60 Hz (line frequency). It should be noted that the 60 Hz frequency is part of the EMG spectrum and should not be ruled out of the analysis. The transducer noise, on the other hand, results from the electrode-skin junction during the conversion of ionic current to electrical current, presenting DC portion (from the impedance gradient present between the skin and the electrode) and an AC portion (impedance fluctuations). Finally, there are other noises involved in the analysis, such as electromagnetic interference and cardiac noise.

Each muscle's EMG signal involves many action potentials resulting in the various MUAP (Motor Unit Action Potential) of each motor unit. In this way, it is possible to distinguish the muscle's spectrum in function of the distance between the electrodes and the contractions intensity level. The whole process involves some challenges surrounding signal processing and noise treatment, with the intention of allowing a more accurate measure and a greater sensitivity level, considering the kind of application given to the EMG [2][3][4][6].

In this paper, the surface EMG's development process is described with a special emphasis on noise treatment. The simulation analysis involves the inputs signal's processing and amplification, verifying the signal's accuracy for frequencies of 10 Hz, 250 Hz, 600 Hz and 10 kHz.

II. THE ELECTROMYOGRAPHIC SIGNAL

The electromyography signal is a small amplitude signal, with high noise levels and frequencies ranging between ± 50 and ± 500 Hz. In order to allow this signal to be interpreted by a micro-controlling device, it must be amplified, filtered and rectified, as well as the noise levels must be reduced.

The first amplification stage requires the use of an instrumentation amplifier. This amplifier is specifically made for noise attenuation at small amplitudes. For this work, and bench experiments, we used the instrumentation amplifier INA129 [1], whose details will be described in the following sections. The instrumentation amplifier works according to the principles of a differential amplifier, involving the CMRR (Common Mode Rejection Rate) properties [1]. The rejection rate, in general, is the amplification of a potential difference, which, in this case, is the difference between the two electrodes positioned over the muscle surface. Considering that the existing level of noise in both electrodes is similar, a fact that results from their similar exposure conditions, the amplification of the potential difference would eliminate much of the external noise [1].

III. THE AMPLIFIER'S DETAILS

The instrument amplifier (INA129) is a variable gain and high precision amplifier, especially designed for low voltages. With a resistor in the input, the unit gain can vary from 1 to 10,000 approximately: the output voltage can be from 1 to 10,000 times the input voltage. The internal circuitry is designed to withstand voltages up to ± 40V without damage in operation. The operation can be made with feeds of at least ± 2.25 V, with a quiescent current of only 700μA, making it suitable for battery powered systems (Figure 1).

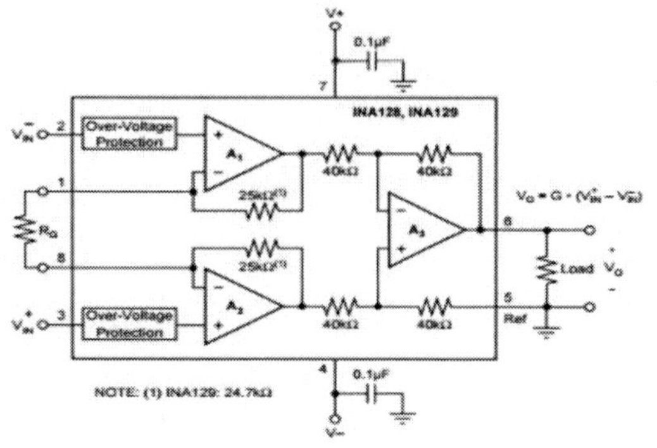

Figure 1: INA129 Instrumentation Amplifier's Internal Circuit

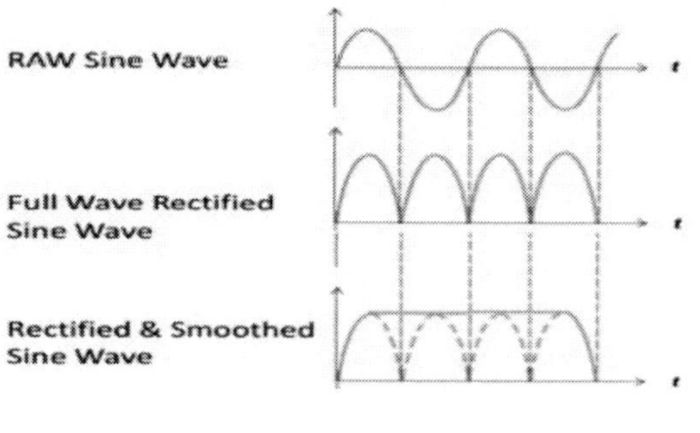

Figure 2: Circuit 1 Input Signal

The internal circuitry of the instrumentation amplifier involves three amplifiers and a combination of resistors, so the total gain obeys equation (1). Using a resistor of 240Ω, for example, the circuit obtains a gain of 206.83 (With 200Ω, it obtains a gain of 248). It is noteworthy that the main function of this amplifier, however, is to ensure a significant reduction in the input noise of the electromyography signal.

$$G = 1\frac{49.9\Omega}{R_G} \qquad (1)$$

After the first amplification, the signal is filtered using initially a high-pass filter with a cutoff frequency of 500 Hz. Then, the signal travels through (with) a low-pass filter with a cutoff frequency of 50 Hz. Therefore, the most significant part of the EMG signal proceeds to the rectification stage, in order to achieve the appropriate values for the microcontroller.

Upon conclusion of the simulation, using the National Instruments software Multisim, the circuit is printed in a PCB, substituting the equivalent circuit for SMD components.

IV. SIMULATION AND EXPERIMENTS

The first circuit consists of four functional blocks: a) the primary amplifier, b) filter, c) rectifier and d) smoother. Using a sinusoidal signal as input (assuming that the signal has a frequency within the filter passband), the wave output is rectified and smoothed. In other words, the signal is adjusted to positive, the negative portions are kept in amplitude but are transformed into positive portions and then the signal peaks are used as DC stretches. Thus, the DC output is proportional to the amplitude of input signal: by increasing the intensity of the muscle contractions detected by surface electrodes, the circuit's output signal is higher (Figure 2).

The circuit, in this way, fulfills the objective of detecting the muscle contraction at different intensity levels and condition the detected signal to an electrical signal that is compatible with a microcontroller device, so that the final output is between 0 and 5V. Thus, the simulation circuit is shown in Figure 3.

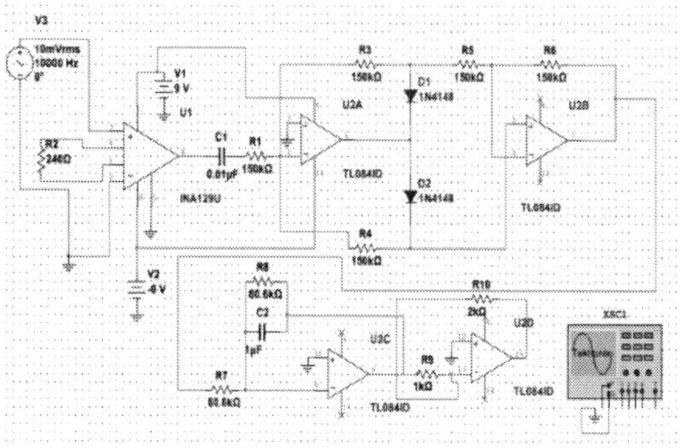
Figure 3: Simulation Circuit Configuration

The sinusoidal signal generator is used as the input of the circuit and an oscilloscope (Tektronix brand) is used at the output. Thus, in order to confirm the basic operation of the circuit, the simulation should provide four measurements: the initial amplification (made by INA129U), the filtering (attenuation of signals outside the range 50-500Hz), the rectification (final results entirely positive) and the smoothing of the output waveform. Only the noise reduction can't be verified by simulation with sine waves, since the generated signal is ideal.

Firstly, the circuit is mounted in a way of analyzing the instrumentation amplifier, as shown in Figure 4 and viewed on an oscilloscope (Figure 5):

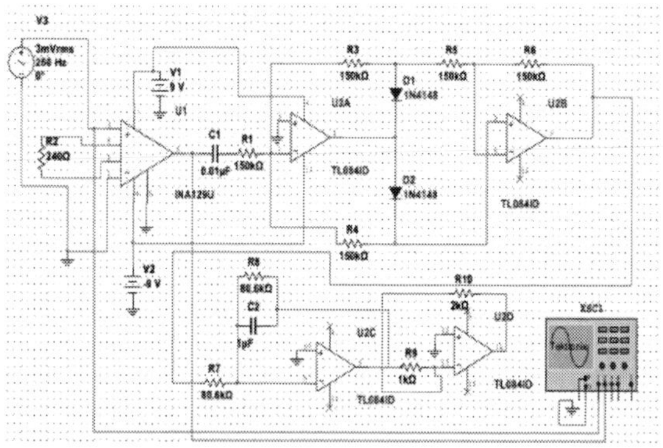
Figure 4: Simulation Circuit Configuration for Instrumentation Amplifier Analysis

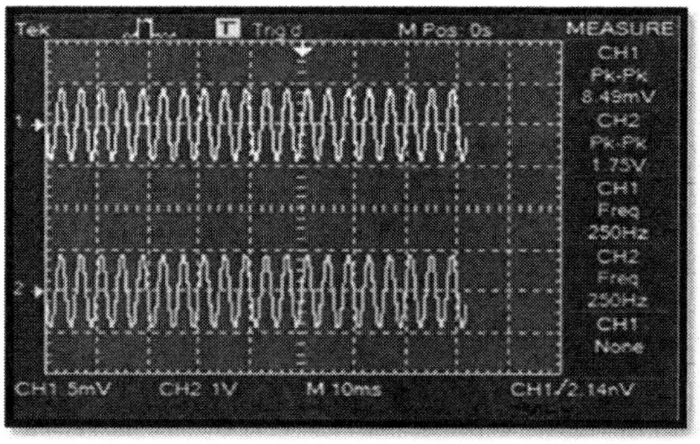

Figure 5: Results of Instrumentation Amplifier Analysis

Analyzing the results, there was a gain of nearly 206, as expected for a resistor of 240Ω. It is noteworthy that the input signal has 3mVrms, a value compatible with the EMG signal. It can also be inferred that there were no changes regarding the input signal's frequency or phase.

After checking the operation of INA129U, the filter must be analyzed. The circuit's final output must be checked for four input frequencies: 10Hz, 250Hz, 600Hz and 10 kHz. The analysis will be done by checking a possible output signal attenuation (the signal's amplitude values will be checked). It is important or remarkable that the signal frequency is changed in the rectification and smoothing process, as the negative portion of the signal is bounced to the positive voltage range, amplifying or magnifying the signal repetition (doubling its frequency). Figure 6 displays the oscilloscope positioning.

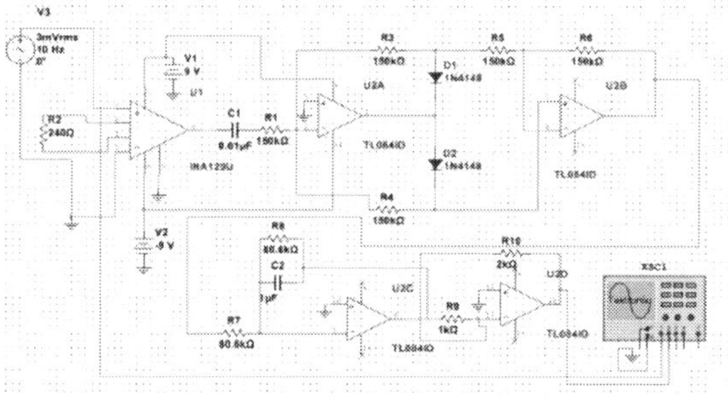

Figure 6: Simulation Circuit Configuration for Filter Analysis

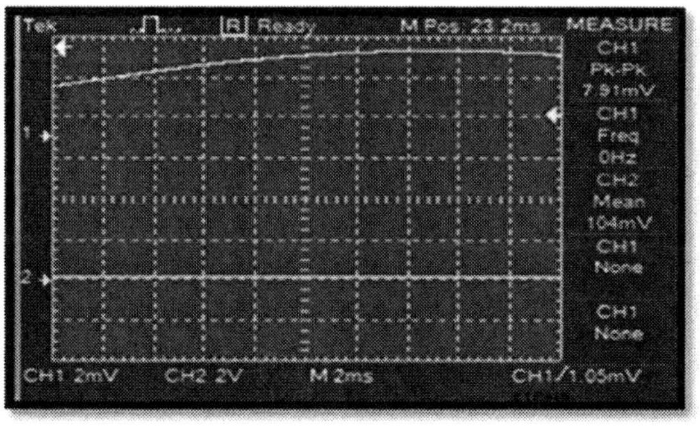

Figure 7: Results for 10 Hz input

For an input frequency of 10 Hz (Figure 7), it appears that the oscilloscope shows only a portion of the signal (the rising of the sinusoid), since the sample period chosen is too large. The circuit's output, on the other hand, has a very low value (within the range of 0 to 5V). Then, the signal, despite of being amplified, was attenuated in the circuit, since the frequency is not suitable for an EMG signal. In other words: the signal which was not detected, as an EMG signal, was filtered by the conditioning circuit.

For an input of 250Hz (Figure 8), with an amplitude close to the maximum of a typical EMG signal, a 2.39V output can be seen. As such, voltage values within 0 to 5V are proportional to the input value, so, it could be concluded that the signal is not attenuated, i.e., was not filtered. In fact, as the frequency is in the appropriate range for electromyography signal, the circuit must keep the amplifications and let the signal passes to the exit without suffering attenuation.

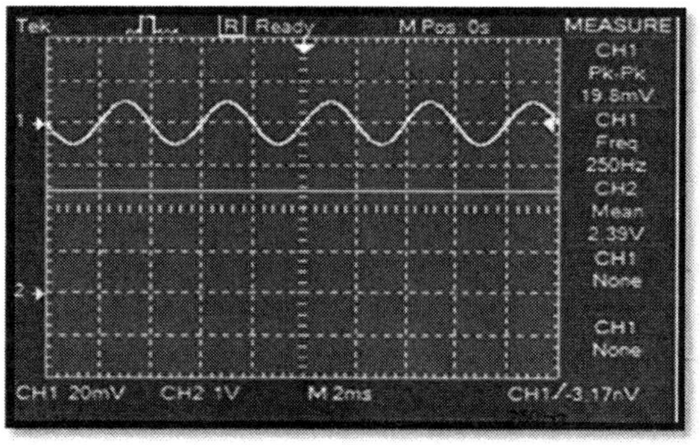

Figure 8: Results for 250 Hz input

For an input of 600 Hz (Figure 9), the attenuation is still unclear, although the frequency is already outside the range of the EMG signal. Because the value is close to the 500Hz filter cutoff frequency, the signal is not intensely attenuated. In practice, it is impossible to design a filter able to fully attenuate signals above 500Hz, as signals near cut-off frequency will continue passing through to the circuit output. However, the actual spectrum of an EMG signal is not that precisely located in the pass band mentioned above (50 to 500Hz) and, in addition, signals near to 500Hz are not very common. Thus, it is not expected or required for the circuit to be able to filter signals with frequencies that close to the cutoff frequency.

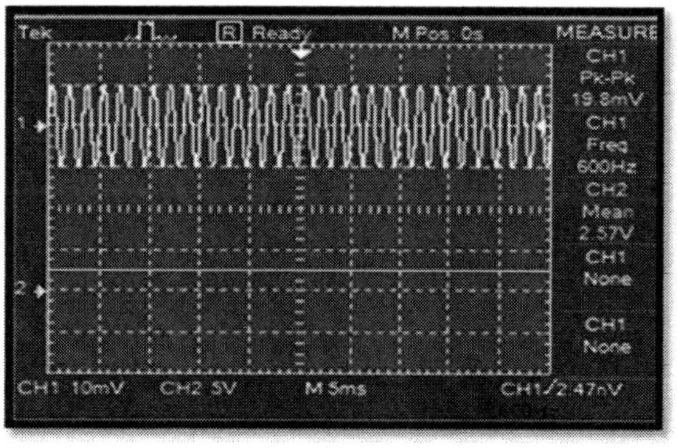

Figure 9: Results for 600 Hz Input

For an input signal of 10 kHz (Figure 10), the attenuation becomes evident. The output signal, in this case, has zero amplitude, illustrating a signal completely filtered. Unlike the previous case, the frequency of 10 kHz is distant from the circuit's cut-off frequency (500 Hz) and therefore, in a real situation, would not be part of the EMG. That frequency represents only noise, featuring as an unwanted signal. Then, the complete attenuation of the signal is indicative of a good filtering performed by the circuit.

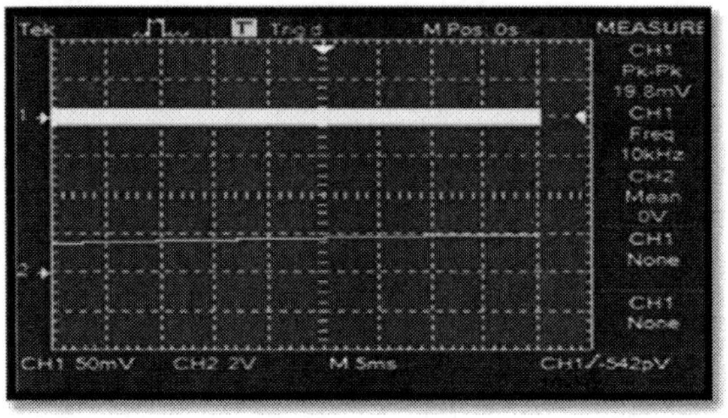

Figure 10: Results for 10 kHz input

After the filtering, the rectification and the smoothing must be verified. For that, the oscilloscope is positioned, both before and after the rectification circuit, as shown below (Figures 11-12):

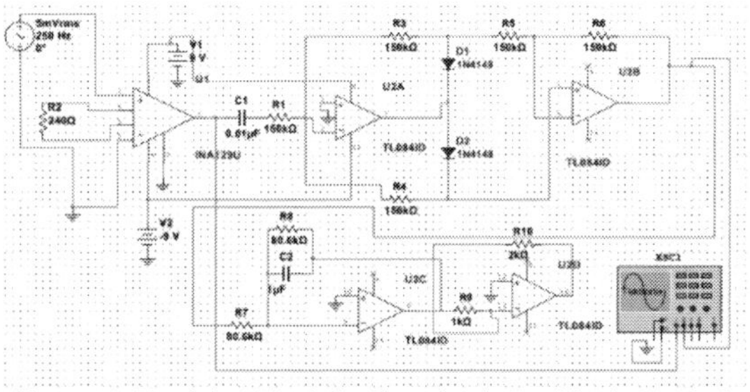

Figure. 11: Simulation Circuit Configuration for Rectification Analysis

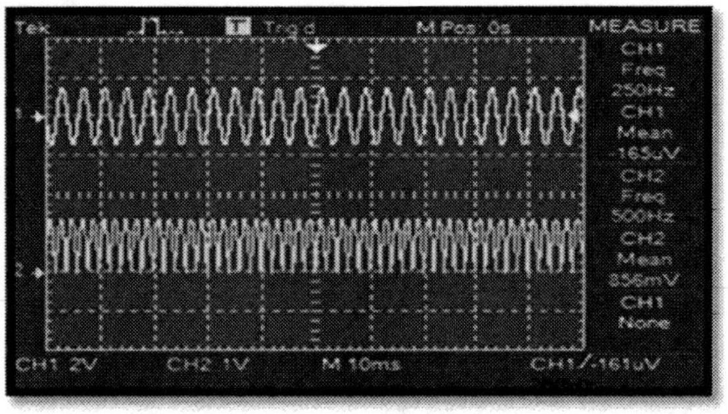

Figure 12: Results for Rectification Circuit

V. CONCLUSION AND FUTURE WORKS

The result observed on the oscilloscope evidence the frequency amplification is double and the signal's average value's rise. In fact, the full-bridge rectification results in a modular signal of the input; thus, the output presents, for a sinusoidal input, a signal with the double of the frequency and a "displacement" of the average value for a positive portion of the signal, since the negative portions were reflected upside.

The filters used in these experiments present cutoff frequencies of 50Hz and 500Hz. Using sinusoidal inputs of 10Hz, 250Hz, 600Hz and 10kHz, it could be noted the good functioning of the filters. It was observed that the circuit is able to attenuate completely the signals with 10Hz and 10 kHz (signals with frequencies too distant of the EMG spectrum), attenuate partially the input signals with 600Hz (uncommon frequency for the EMG spectrum) and not attenuate signals of 250Hz (typical frequency of the EMG spectrum).

Besides that, it should be noted that the amplified signals did not exceed 5V, such as they did not assume negative values. In this way, it can be concluded that the circuit is able to meet the conditions imposed by a micro-controlling device, which operate with input signals between 0 and 5V.

Finally, the signal's smoothing was verified. For that, it was sufficient to insert a typical signal as the input and verify the aspect of the output signal. The smoothing of an infinite sinusoidal signal is a DC voltage, since all the peaks are the same (it can be seen that the DC voltage is equal to the maximum peak value of the sinusoidal signal, already amplified, filtered and rectified).

The high sensitivity of the EMG may allow its use in several medical applications, such as studies of sleep disorders, specifically bruxism [7], even considering its low manufacturing cost.

ACKNOWLEDGMENTS

This work was funded by the Huawei Company - project number: 2994. The project is managed by the University of São Paulo Support Foundation and the Electronic Systems Department of University of São Paulo (PSI). Number of Company / Institution Agreement: OTABRA09160202003286840274.

REFERENCES

[1] Burr-Brown Corporation. Datasheet: "Precision, Low Power Instrumentation Amplifiers ". Access: http://instrumentation.obs.carnegiescience.edu/ccd/parts/INA128.pdf, Feb. 2017.

[2] J.D. Geyer, P. R. Carney, and T. Payne, "Atlas of Polysomnography," Lippincott Williams and Wilkins, 2009.

[3] S. Devuyst *et al.*, "Automatic Sleep Spindle Detection in Patients with Sleep Disorders," *2006 International Conference of the IEEE Engineering in Medicine and Biology Society*, New York, NY, 2006, pp. 3883-3886.

[4] J.F. Gagnon, R. B. Postuma, and J. Montplaisir, "Update on the pharmacology of REM sleep behavior disorder," Neurology, vol. 67, no. 5, pp. 742–747, 2006.

[5] A. Siddiqi, D. Kumar and S. Arjunan, "Surface EMG model for Tibialis Anterior muscle with experimentally based simulation parameters," *5th*

ISSNIP-IEEE Biosignals and Biorobotics Conference (2014): Biosignals and Robotics for Better and Safer Living (BRC), Salvador, 2014, pp. 1-5.

[6] M. E. G. Bigelow *et al.*, "Point-of-Care Technologies for the Advancement of Precision Medicine in Heart, Lung, Blood, and Sleep Disorders," in *IEEE Journal of Translational Engineering in Health and Medicine*, vol. 4, no., pp. 1-10, 2016.

[7] N. Jirakittayakorn and Y. Wongsawat, "An EMG instrument designed for bruxism detection on masseter muscle," *The 7th 2014 Biomedical Engineering International Conference*, Fukuoka, 2014, pp. 1-5.

FTRP: A Fault Tolerant Reliable Protocol for Wireless Sensor Networks

Islam Ahmed Moursy, Mohamed Nazih ElDerini
Computer and Systems Engineering Department
Faculty of Engineering, Alexandria University
Alexandria, Egypt
e-mail: {islam.moursy, elderini}@alexu.edu.eg

Magdy Abd-Elazim Ahmed
Vice Dean for Graduate Studies and Research
Faculty of Engineering Alexandria University
Alexandria, Egypt
e-mail: magdy@alexu.edu.eg

Abstract— **Wireless sensor networks operate in very challenging environments that make them prone to different types of faults. Hence, there is a high need for a reliable protocol that offers an acceptable functionality in the presence of faults. In this paper, we propose the Fault Tolerant Reliable Protocol (FTRP), a novel routing protocol designed to be used in wireless sensor networks. FTRP offers fault tolerance reliability for packet exchange, as well as adaptation for dynamic network changes. The key concept in this protocol is the use of node logical clustering. The protocol delegates the routing ownership to the cluster heads, where the fault tolerance functionally is implemented. FTRP utilizes cluster head nodes along with cluster head groups as intermediate storage for transient packets. In addition, FTRP utilizes broadcast in its routing messages communication. This technique substantially reduces the message overhead as compared to classical flooding mechanisms. FTRP manipulates Time to Live (TTL) values for the various routing messages in addition to utilizing jitters in messages transmission. FTRP performance has been evaluated through extensive simulations. Aggregate Throughput, Packet Delivery Ratio and End-to-End delay have been used as performance metrics. The results obtained showed that FTRP ensures high Throughput, high Packet Delivery Ratio, and acceptable End-to-End delay in the presence of changing networking conditions. FTRP performs well in dense and sparse networks while nodes are mobile. Stationary simulations represented the worst-case behavior. This is attributed to synchronized nodes, where nodes send similar messages at the same time.**

Keywords-fault tolerance; proactive routing; wireless sensor networks ; NS-3.

I. INTRODUCTION

Wireless Sensors Networks (WSNs) continue to present a lot of interest in both the research domain as well as the industry [1]. WSNs are highly adaptive to various domains, including - but not limited to - energy control systems, environmental monitoring, security, surveillance, health applications, area monitoring and Internet of Things [2].

Typical WSNs are networks composed of a large number of sensor nodes. Each node is equipped with sensors to detect various attributes of the surrounding environment. WSNs are built to operate for prolonged time and even in a hostile environment, which increases the need for fault tolerant reliable communication protocols [3].

There are many research papers on routing protocols. However, only few are adopted by the industry. The Institute of Electrical and Electronics Engineers (IEEE) had adapted the topic and introduced Low-Rate Wireless Personal Area Network (Lr-WPAN) [4] as a standard Media Access Control (MAC) layer for WSNs, which opens a great opportunity for WSNs. This paper introduces a new fault tolerant reliable routing protocol for WSNs, which is efficient under mobility conditions.

Mahmoud *et al.* [5] introduced a novel three-dimensional reference model for research in WSN reliability. The model categorizes WSN protocols into one of two techniques, which are retransmission or redundancy. Reliability is ensured within those techniques either by using a hop-by-hop or an end-to-end method to recover the lost data while maintaining either packet or event level reliability. Chouikhi *et al.* [6] classify fault tolerance techniques according to the time at which the fault tolerance is triggered (before or after the fault occurrence). According to this, these techniques are classified as preventive or curative. Hence, the proposed protocol is classified as a proactive protocol that is retransmission based, connection oriented (end-to-end), with packet level reliability and utilizing a curative technique to achieve fault tolerance.

Fault Tolerant Reliable Protocol (FTRP) operates as a table driven proactive protocol [7]. FTRP regularly exchanges topology information with selected nodes of the network. Initially, nodes are in learning mode and broadcast a status of not being in a sensor domain in preparation to join one. If no answer is received, the nodes stay in that state until an answer is received. If an answer is received, the node evaluates the answer depending on its source and its included attributes. A cluster then begins to form according to the proposed protocol.

After cluster formation, Cluster Member (CM) nodes send data messages to their designated cluster head (CH). The CH, in turn, decides how many copies of the message to be retained until an acknowledgment (ACK) is received from the destination. The CH stores that message in the cluster head group (CHG) according to the protocol-defined parameters. The proposed protocol utilizes the following main techniques:

A. *Retransmission-based reliability*

Retransmission is the traditional way of ensuring reliability [5]. This is achieved by allowing the sender node to wait for an ACK for its previously sent packets. In case no ACK is received, the packet is considered lost and retransmission takes place to ensure reliability. FTRP implementation relieves the responsibility of packet storage and retransmission to higher entity nodes (CHs, CHGs or Sinks), as will be elaborated in Section III.

B. End-to-End (connection-oriented) reliability

End-to-End reliability is a connection-oriented scheme for achieving reliability in which only the two communicating end nodes (source and destination) are responsible for ensuring reliability. FTRP implementation expands the end-to-end reliability by relieving the source node from this task, and transferring it to the CH. The CH determines, according to the replicas parameters, which CHGs to be used as storage. Whenever the destination node receives the packets, it broadcasts a message only processed by CHs or CHGs to release their locally stored corresponding replicas.

C. Packet level reliability

Packet level reliability ensures that all the packets carrying sensed data from all the related nodes are reliably transported to their destinations.

The rest of the paper is organized as follows. In Section II, the most relevant related works are presented. In Section III, the relevant FTRP protocol operations are detailed. The performance analysis of the FTRP protocol is presented in Section IV. Finally, Section VI concludes the paper and lists ongoing and future work.

II. Related Work

In this section, we review literature work addressing the same elements as our protocol, namely retransmission based, connection oriented (end-to-end) and packet level reliability.

Iyer *et al.* [8] proposed the Sensor Transmission Control Protocol (STCP), an end-to-end reliability protocol with a congestion control mechanism that is sink-centric. STCP dynamically controls the application data flow by utilizing a controlled variable reliability mechanism where the application type controls the throughput. Reliability is maintained by using ACK or Negative Acknowledgement (NACK) as end-to-end retransmission mechanisms. Packets are cached locally in each node until an ACK is received from the Sink.

Whenever the Sink receives information about congested paths, the Sink directs the downstream-congested nodes to select alternative paths. Reliability in STCP is achieved through connection-oriented explicit ACKs, which involves only the end nodes. STCP is considered scalable for a large number of nodes with high hop counts from a source node to the Sink.

STCP nodes are prone to huge end-to-end delay time [5], which results in high latency and cache overflow.

Marchi *et al.* [9] proposed a Distributed Transport for Sensor Networks (DTSN). DTSN is non-sink centric, end-to-end and an energy oriented packet reliability protocol.

DTSN is based on two mechanisms, full and differential reliability mechanisms. Full reliability is achieved via retransmission based explicit ACKs, while differential reliability is performed independently. In the full reliability mechanism, the source node keeps transmitting the packets until the number of transmitted packets equals the size of the acknowledgement window. An explicit acknowledgement request is issued from the source node to the destination to confirm message delivery. If the sequence of the packets is in order, an ACK is sent. These packets are then removed from the buffer of the source node. If a NACK is received then retransmission of the missing sequence of packets is performed. The key contribution of DTSN is the integration of mechanisms involved in achieving reliability, such as partial buffering at the source and intermediate nodes and the utilization of erasure coding. However, DTSN does not provide details on how the reliability level is maintained when network conditions change.

III. FTRP Operations

A. Protocol Overview

FTRP operations utilize a simple messaging system to communicate different protocol statuses to the participating nodes. This messaging system is used to transition the node from one state to another in order to form a logical grouping of nodes referenced later as a cluster. FTRP tries to overcome the issues in STCP [8] by utilizing a distributed cache rather than preserving the cache at the sender node. This approach allows the cluster head to control the amount of cache allocated and where to store the data packet. FTRP introduces a retry count for locally cached entries. Whenever a packet entry reaches its max retry count, (the default is six retires), it is flushed out of the cache to overcome cache overflow. In fact, FTRP is well suited for a changing environment, where its messages update the network paths and handle nodes failure well.

FTRP communicates using a unified packet format for all data related to the protocol. This provides an easy way to combine different messages in a single packet transmission. These packets are encapsulated into User Datagram Protocol (UDP) [10] datagrams. On the other hand, FTRP messages contain a sequence number, which is incremented for each message. In such case, the recipient of a control message is able to identify which information is more recent and to ignore those older unprocessed messages.

B. Definitions of main nodes status

*1) **Sink:*** The Sink is the central node of the network, having information about all nodes. Usually, it is connected to a wired network and it has access to the wireless sensor domain.

*2) **Cluster Head (CH):*** The Cluster Head can be regarded as a Sink, but for a subset of nodes. It is responsible for relaying all information from and to the nodes controlled under its domain.

*3) **Cluster Head Group (CHG):*** CHGs are normal nodes selected by the CH as per the protocol parameters to act as local cluster storage for messages in transient.

*4) **Cluster Member (CM):*** CMs are normal nodes composing the cluster and are managed by the respective CH.

*5) **Cluster Bridge Head (CBH):*** If the CH is far away from the Sink, the CBH is the node within another cluster that links the cluster with the nearest CH.

*6) **Learning:*** Initially, a node is not in a cluster or it does not know route to a Sink.

*7) **Swarm:*** A node has identified another node that is not in its domain and it has knowledge of other nodes (nonsink).

*8) **Discovered:*** A discovered node is a node that is discovered from either a Sink or another cluster.

The life cycle begins with a node in a Learning state. A few nodes who have knowledge of their respective existence can form a swarm. Few swarm nodes can then transition to a discovered state upon sensing a nearby Sink. Figure 1 depicts the state transition for nodes in FTRP.

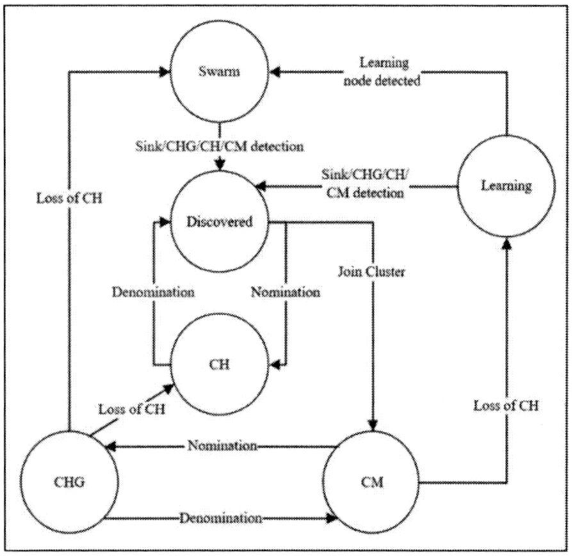

Figure 1. FTRP State Transition Diagram

The Sink nominates a discovered node to be a CH. The CH can request nearby nodes for association as CMs. Few CMs can then be nominated as CHGs, as per the predefined configuration parameters of the protocol.

C. FTRP Messaging System

1) Hello Message (HELLO)

A nonsink node lifecycle begins in a Learning state, where it periodically broadcasts a hello message exposing its status and other parameters. Hello messages have their Time to Live (TTL) [11] value set to one, in order not to flood the whole network. A Hello message is populated with the sending node known attributes, and its known existing members, if any. Hello messages are broadcasted as keep alive periodically. The behavior of each node is different upon receiving a Hello message, according to the receiving node status. A Sink node receiving a Hello message checks if the incoming node has not yet joined a domain, and if it is not a member of any other cluster. In that case, the Sink sends an association request. If the node had already been identified in a domain yet had not joined any cluster, the Sink will not take any action. This mechanism is adopted in order to control the allocation of CHs and to allow the network clustering formation to converge by favoring the node to join a cluster than to promote it to a new CH. The Sink will ignore any Hellos from other Sinks and will update the information received from any other CH.

2) Association Message (ASC)

ASCs are used to instruct nodes to join a cluster or domain. Only the Sink and the CHs are allowed to send association to other nodes. ASC messages have two classes.

a) A regular association:

A regular association messages have their TTL value set to one, so that association does not flood the network.

b) A Broadcasted Association (ASCb)

A broadcasted association messages have their TTL value set to 255 in order for a CH to be nominated when it has no direct link to the Sink. It uses its nearest CBH to reach the Sink through the distress Save-Our-Ship (SOS) mechanism.

A node populates the ASC message with its members. Having that, members of a Sink are the CHs known to that Sink and members of a CH are those nodes under the CH control as fault tolerance domain.

3) Control Message (CTL)

CTLs are used as decision-making mechanism and out of band, status updates of different protocol aspects. It has the following subclasses:

a) Reject CH promotion

Reject CH promotion is issued in the case when a Sink at some point in time decided to promote a CM to CH however, this CM was earlier acquired by another CH. In that case, rejecting the CH promotion is favored so that the CH ID pool is not depleted too fast. In return, the CM issues a Reject CH Promotion control message to notify the Sink to release the allocated CH ID.

b) Members check

A swarm node that was nominated to be CM or CH knows about the existence of other swam nodes whom with which a swarm was formed. This swarm must be checked against a high entity node (Sink in case the node is CH or CH in case the node is CM). The receiving node (Sink or CH) checks the incoming member list for local existence in its data structures, and then replies to the sender node with a

"Release swarm members" message for those members the higher entity does not know about.

c) Release swarm members

When this message is received, the node drops the sending node from its local base as swarm, and sends them swarm release notify control message.

d) Swarm release notify

This message is processed by swarm to drop the sender from its local base.

e) Swarm SOS

Whenever the swarm is about to drop its last member, it issues swarm SOS to the sender of the release notify so that the sender is treated as bridgehead and relays the SOS to the Sink. The Sink will then send an ASCb, with its TTL value set to 255, to this swarm node to be nominated as new CH.

f) Fault Tolerant message release (FT_Release)

Whenever a node successfully receives its data packet, it sends this message in broadcast mode, i.e., its TTL value set to 255, to notify CHs and CHGs to release the local copies of the messages considered for fault tolerance.

D. Routing function and fault tolerance

The default routing or forwarding scheme for a node is to direct the outgoing packets to its master (CH in case of a node, and a Sink in case of a CH). The scheme below also applies in case the CH or Sink is initiating a packet send. Upon the reception of a forward request, the routing function checks local parameters for replica count and then stores the message in the CHGs accordingly. Then, finally, the packet is forwarded normally.

CHs and CHGs are using a timed queue to store the packets. The receiving node, upon successful reception of a packet, generates an FT_Release message having the packet unique identification. Each receiving CHG, CH or Sink accepts this message and removes the requested message (if it exists) from its local queue. Upon the expiry of the queue timer, the local fault tolerance queue is checked for packets that had not exceeded their retry time, and those packets are resent. Packets having expired retry time are removed from the queue and are considered undeliverable due to unreachable destination.

IV. SIMULATION AND PERFORMANCE EVALUATION

A. Assumptions

The simulation model is based on the following assumptions:

- The Sink has infinite power source, while nodes have not.
- Each node can behave as both a client and a router.
- Each node has a single interface running the FTRP protocol on that interface.
- The nodes have the same capabilities, i.e., same coverage area and same antenna.
- The nodes are randomly placed.
- The nodes follow a 2d-walk mobility pattern in mobility scenarios and follow a constant position model for stationary simulations.
- The nodes can either receive or transmit at a time.
- There is no turn around time between transmitting and receiving. Nodes can switch between transmit and receive instantly.
- Mobility is uncorrelated among the nodes and links fail independently.

B. Performance metrics

The following performance metrics are used to analyze the behavior of FTRP.

1) Aggregate Throughput

This is the sum of the throughputs in the uplink and the downlink.

2) Packet Delivery Ratio(PDR)

This is the number of successfully delivered packets divided by the total number of transmitted packets

3) End-to-End Delay (E-2-E)

This is the sum of time taken for packets transmitted from sources to destinations divided by the total number of received packets.

C. Simulation Environment

The FTRP routing model is built using NS-3 network Simulator [12] on top of IEEE 802.11 MAC model of NS-3. Due to simulator limitations, model parameters have been tuned to match the 802.15.4 MAC layer.

TABLE I PARAMETERS FOR SIMULATION MODEL

Simulation Parameter	Value
Simulator	NS-3 (version 3.25)
Operating system	Linux (Ubuntu 14.04)
Simulation time	50 secs
Simulation Area	100m x 100m
Number of nodes	20 for sparse , 40 for dense
Node transmission range	50 meters
Movement model (for mobility tests)	Random Walk 2d Mobility Model
Stationary model (for no mobility tests)	Constant Position Mobility Model
Nodes Position allocator	Random Disc Position Allocator
Speed of mobile nodes	1m/sec and 2m/sec
Traffic type	CBR
Data payload	512 bytes
Packet rates	20 p/sec to 80 p/sec
MAC Layer	802.11 DCF with RTS/CTS
Radio Frequency	2.4 GHz
Radio Channel rate	2Mbps
Propagation loss model	Friis Propagation Loss Model
Propagation Delay Model	Constant speed propagation delay model

The Random 2d-walk model [13] was adopted for driving mobile clients. In the Random 2d-walk mobility model, each instance moves with a speed and direction chosen randomly until either a fixed distance has been walked or until a fixed amount of time has passed. If a node hits one of the boundaries (specified by a rectangle) of the model, it rebounds on the boundary with a reflexive angle and speed. This model is often identified as a Brownian motion model. The speed is varied from no mobility using a constant position model, 1m/sec to 2 m/sec. Table 1 depicts the parameters set for the simulation model that is common for all our simulations.

D. Results and analysis

FTRP is simulated using various networking scenarios with the help of the NS-3 simulator. The scenarios and results along with detailed analysis are presented in the following sections.

1) Scenario I

In this scenario, we analyze the performance of FTRP in terms of throughput, PDR and E-2-E delay in a sparse network comprising of 20 nodes. The simulation is performed by varying the number of data packets sent per second, while maintaining a constant number of flows and system load. Number of packets per flow ranged from 20 packets/sec to 80 packets/sec. The simulation was repeated using no mobility model, 1m/sec and 2 m/sec walking models. Other parameters considered for simulations are the same as shown in Table 1.

Figure 2 depicts PDR against increasing traffic load in a sparse network. It is observed that increasing the data rate beyond 280 kb/s causes PDR to begin to drop, although not significant.

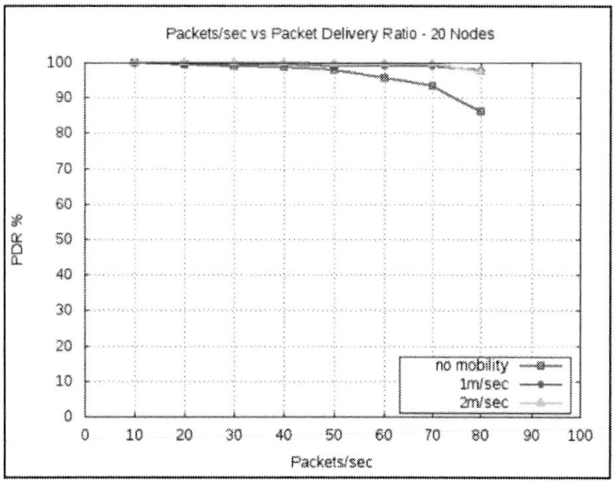

Figure 2. PDR in a sparse network

As per our simulation parameters, a data rate of 240 kb/s corresponds to 60 packets/sec and a data rate of 280 kb/s corresponds to 70 packets/sec. Mobile nodes achieve a good PDR with regard to the maximum data rate supported by Lr-WPAN [4] standard, which are 250 kb/s (approximately 63 packets/sec). While nodes are stationary, the obtained PDR results fall to above 94% at the target data rate of 60 packets/sec, which is acceptable.

Figure 3 depicts Aggregate throughput against increasing traffic load in a sparse network. It is observed that the throughput increases as the data rate increases. Both low and high mobility scenarios achieve good throughput as data rate increases even for data rates above the targeted 250 kb/s. The stationary nodes performance is lower than that of mobile ones, which can be attributed to the nodes synchronized states.

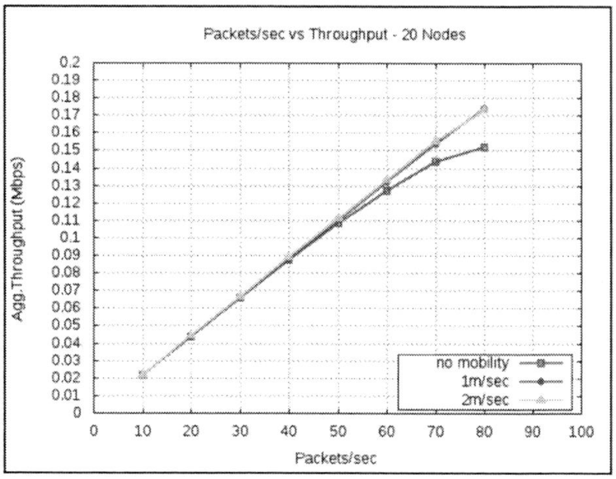

Figure 3. Aggregate Throughput in a sparse network

Figure 4 depicts E-2-E delay against increasing traffic load in a sparse network. It is observed that, as the data rate increases, the E-2-E delay increases significantly in a stationary scenario. The E-2-E delay increases within acceptable range for mobile scenarios.

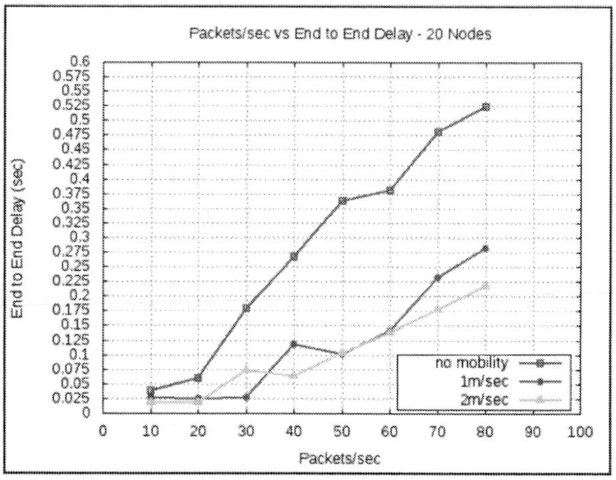

Figure 4. End to End Delay in a sparse network

The increase in E-2-E delay is expected due to the introduction of fault tolerance mechanism, which uses store and forward. In the stationary scenario, the increase is significant and can be justified by the nature of FTRP being too communicative. In the stationary scenario, the collision rate of packets can increase, while mobility helps to decrease collision. This can be attributed to the variations of node states. This variation reduces messages exchanged, reduces collisions and maintains good E-2-E delay.

2) Scenario II

In this scenario, we analyze the performance of FTRP in terms of throughput, PDR and E-2-E delay in a dense network composed of 40 nodes. The simulation is performed by varying the number of data packets sent per second, while maintaining a constant number of flows and system load. The number of packets varied per flow ranged from 20 packets/sec to 80 packets/sec. The simulation was repeated using no mobility model, 1m/sec and 2m/sec walking models. Other parameters considered for simulations are the same as depicted in Table 1. Scenario II results emphasize the results of scenario I. It is found that in a dense network with no mobility, PDR drops, Aggregate Throughput tends to saturate early and E-2-E delay increases significantly. In mobility scenarios, PDR is within acceptable ranges at 70 packet/sec rate, the Aggregate Throughput increases and E-2-E delay is within acceptable ranges. Figure 5 depicts PDR against increasing traffic load in a dense network.

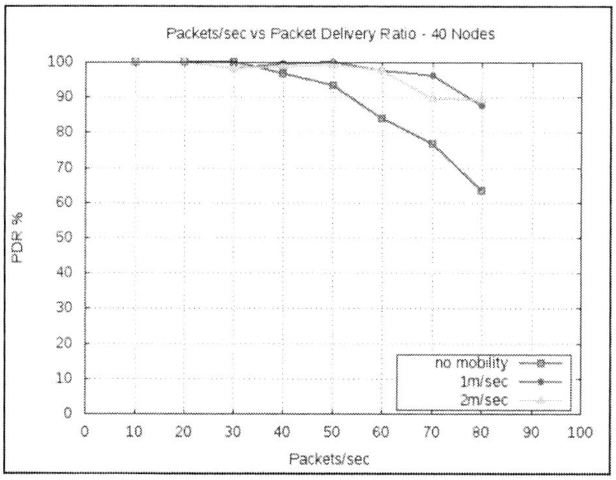

Figure 5. PDR in a dense network

It is observed that, while nodes are mobile, the PDR is almost the same. However, for data rates higher than 260 kb/s (65 packets/sec) higher mobility nodes PDR tends to saturate while for less mobile nodes PDR tends to decrease. Stationary nodes are the worst performer, result which can be attributed to synchronized nodes states.

Figure 6 depicts Aggregate Throughput against increasing traffic load in a dense network. It is observed that, while nodes are mobile, the throughput is almost the same. However, for data rates higher than 250 kb/s, higher mobility nodes' throughput tends to increase while for less mobile nodes throughput tends to saturate.

Stationary nodes are the worst performer, which can be attributed to synchronized nodes states.

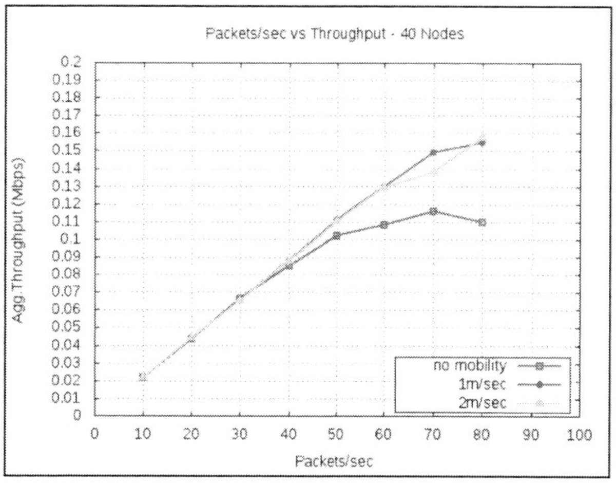

Figure 6. Aggregate Throughput ina dense network

Figure 7 depicts E-2-E delay against increasing traffic load in a dense network. It is observed that, while nodes are mobile, E-2-E is almost the same and for data rates higher than 250 kb/s all mobile nodes' E-2-E tends to increase. Stationary nodes are the worst performer, which is directly linked to the fault tolerance function, in which, for every sent packet, an ACK for reception is needed to consider a packet is delivered. This increases the time when a packet is considered successfully delivered.

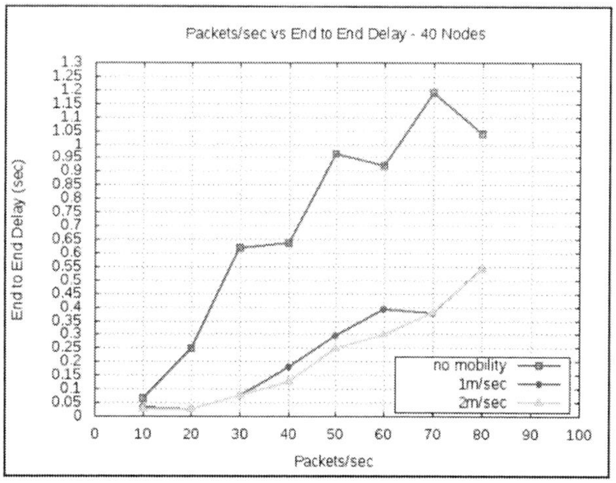

Figure 7. End to End Delay in dense network

The ACK packet as well might get lost due to network collisions and synchronized nodes states, which in turn will cause the source node to resend the packet and wait for another ACK. This significantly affects the E-2-E delay for FTRP.

V. CONCLUSION

This paper introduced a novel reliable fault tolerant routing protocol, FTRP, for wireless sensors networks. FTRP creates a communication path between source and destination nodes and forwards packets on that path.

FTRP performance has been evaluated through extensive simulations using NS-3. Aggregate throughput, Packet Delivery Ratio and End-to-End delay have been used as performance metrics. In terms of Packet Delivery Ratio and Aggregate throughput, FTRP is an excellent performer in all mobility scenarios, whether the network is sparse or dense. In stationary scenarios, FTRP performed well in sparse networks; however, in dense networks, FTRP's performance had degraded, still remaining in an acceptable range. In terms of End-to-end delay, FTRP is considered a good performer in all mobility scenarios where the network is sparse. In the sparse stationary scenario, FTRP is still considered a good performer. However, in dense stationary scenarios, FTRPs performance is considered as worst-case behavior, which can be attributed to synchronized nodes states that occur when nodes send similar messages at the same time.

There are times when properly receiving a network message carrying crucial information is more important than other costs, such as, but not limited to, energy or delay. That makes FTRP suitable for a wide range of WSNs application domains, such as military applications by monitoring soldiers' biological data and supplies while on the battle field as well as battle damage assessment. FTRP can also be used in health applications by tracking and monitoring doctors and patients inside a hospital and elderly assistance, in addition to a wide range of geo-fencing, environmental monitoring, resource monitoring, production lines monitoring, agriculture and animals tracking.

FTRP should be avoided in dense stationary deployments such as, but not limited to, scenarios where a high application response is critical and life endangering, such as biohazards detection or within intensive care units.

As future work, we plan to improve the performance of FTRP in stationary scenarios. The FTRP performance was evaluated through simulations. We plan to extend the FTRP implementation in a WSN operating system to compare the complexity of a real system against the simulation results. The effect of varying the number of attempts to retransmit a non-delivered packet (max retry count) should be investigated. Furthermore, the energy efficiency has to be evaluated for various FTRP operations.

REFERENCES

[1] A. A. Kumar, K. Øvsthus, and L. M. Kristense, "An Industrial Perspective on Wireless Sensor Networks - A Survey of Requirements, Protocols and Challenges" IEEE Communications Surveys & Tutorials, vol. 16, no. 3, pp. 1391 - 1412, 2014, doi:10.1109/SURV.2014.012114.00058.

[2] C. Alcaraz, P. Najera, J. Lopez, and R. Roman, "Wireless Sensor Networks and the Internet of Things Do We Need a Complete Integration" 1st International Workshop on the Security of the Internet of Things (SecIoT'10), Dec. 2010.

[3] S. Misra, I. Woungang, and S. C. Misra, "Guide to Wireless Sensor Networks", Springer, London, pp. 293-295, 2009.

[4] IEEE Standard for Low-Rate Wireless Networks. [Online]. Available from: http://standards.ieee.org/ 2017.07.07.

[5] M. A. Mahmood, W. K. Seah, and I. Welch, "Reliability in wireless sensor networks: A survey and challenges" The International Journal of Computer and Telecommunications Networking, vol. 79, pp. 166-187, Mar 2015, doi: 10.1016/j.comnet.2014.12.016.

[6] S. Chouikhi, I. ElKorbi, Y. Ghamri-Doudanec, and L. Azouz Saidane, "A Survey on Fault Tolerance In Small And Large Scale Wireless Sensor Networks" The International Journal for the Computer and Telecommunications Industry, vol. 69, pp. 22-37, Sep 2015, doi:10.1016/j.comcom.2015.05.007.

[7] B. D. Shivahare, C. Wahi, and S. Shivhar, "Comparison Of Proactive And Reactive Routing Protocols In Mobile Adhoc Network Using Routing Protocol Property" International Journal of Emerging Technology and Advanced Engineering, vol. 2, no. 3, pp. 356-359, Mar 2012, ISSN: 2250-2459.

[8] Y. Iyer, S. Gandham, and S. Venkatesan, "STCP: A Generic Transport Layer Protocol for Wireless Sensor Networks," The 14th International Conference on Computer Communications and Networks (ICCCN 2005) IEEE, Oct 2005, pp. 449-454, ISSN:1095-2055, ISBN:0-7803-9428-3.

[9] B. Marchil, A. Grilo, and M. Nunes, "DTSN: Distributed Transport for Sensor Networks" The 12th IEEE Symposium on Computers and Communications (ISCC 2007) IEEE, Jul 2007, ISSN: 1530-1346, ISBN: 978-1-4244-1520-5.

[10] RFC 768 - User Datagram Protocol – IETF. [Online]. Available from: https://www.ietf.org/. 2017.07.07.

[11] RFC 791 - Internet Protocol. [Online]. Available from: https://tools.ietf.org/. 2017.07.07

[12] NS-3 Overview. [Online]. Available from: http://www.nsnam.org/ 2017.07.07.

[13] NS-3 Manual. [Online]. Available from: https://www.nsnam.org/. 2017.07.07.

An Effective Voronoi-based Coverage Enhancing Algorithm in Directional Sensor Networks

Cheng-Yen Chung, Hao-Wei Chen, and Chiu-Kuo Liang
Dept. of Computer Science and Information Engineering, Chung Hua University
Hsinchu, Taiwan, R.O.C.
Email: {m10002012, m10402026, ckliang}@chu.edu.tw

***Abstract*—A directional sensor network is composed of many directional sensor nodes. Unlike conventional omni-directional sensors that always have an omni-angle of sensing range; directional sensors may have a limited angle of sensing range due to technical constraints or cost considerations. Area coverage problem is still an essential issue in directional sensor networks. In this paper, we study the area coverage problem in directional sensor networks. The problem is to maximize the area coverage of a randomly deployed directional sensor network. Each directional sensor can rotate its sensing direction in order to get better coverage in an interested region. In this study, we propose a distributed greedy algorithm that can improve the effective coverage area by using the characteristics of Voronoi diagram. The sensor field is divided into Voronoi cells by the calculation of sensors and the working direction of each sensor is evaluated based on the size and the location of the farthest Voronoi vertex of its surrounding Voronoi cell, respectively. Simulation results show that our proposed algorithm achieves around 5% to 15% better performance than that of previous proposed methods in terms of the area coverage rate.**

Keywords-Directional Sensor Networks; Rotatable Sensors; Area Coverage Problem; Voronoi Diagram.

I. INTRODUCTION *(HEADING 1)*

In recent years, wireless sensor networks have received a lot of attention due to their wide applications in military and civilian operations, such as fire detection [1], vehicle traffic monitoring [2], ocean monitoring [3], and battlefield surveillance [4]. In wireless sensor networks, many works have been done during the last decade. However, most of the past works were always based on the assumption of omni-directional sensors that has an omni-angle of sensing range. In real environment, there are many kinds of directional sensors, such as video sensors [5], ultrasonic sensors [6] and infrared sensors [7]. The omni-directional sensor node has a circular disk of sensing range. The directional sensor node has smaller sensing area (sector-like area) and sensing angle than the omni-directional one. Compared to omni-directional sensors, the coverage region of a directional sensor is determined by its location and orientation. This can be illustrated by the example in Figure 1.

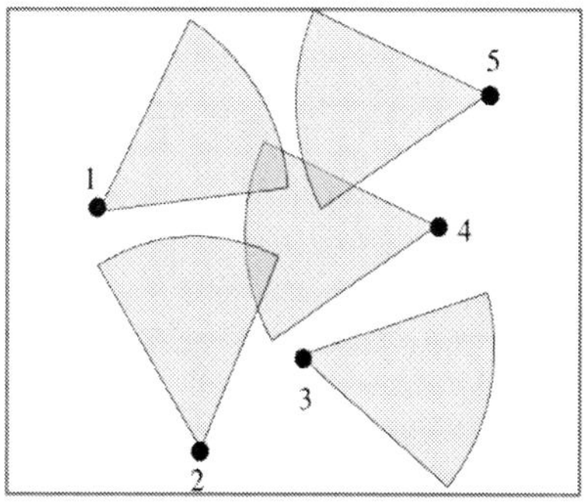

Figure 1. An example of five directional sensors deployed to cover the target region.

Area coverage is a fundamental problem in wireless sensor networks. Sensor nodes must be deployed appropriately to reach an adequate coverage level for the successful completion of the issued sensing tasks [8][9]. However, in many potential working environments, such as remote harsh fields, disaster areas, and toxic urban regions, sensor deployment cannot be performed manually. To scatter sensors by aircraft may result in the situation that the actual landing positions cannot be controlled. Consequently, the coverage may be inferior to the application requirements no matter how many sensors are dropped. For obtaining the better performance in directional sensor networks, directional sensors (e.g., cameras) may be able to rotate around a fixed axis to enhance its coverage in sensing radius [7]-[9]. Therefore, the coverage region of a directional sensor is determined by both its location and its direction of sensing radius. Those sensors that can rotate their sensing directions are called the rotatable sensors. We define the working direction of a sensor as the direction in which it is currently pointing at. We also call the sensing range of a sensor's working direction as its coverage region. The coverage region of different sensors may be overlapped with other sensors after they are randomly deployed. Thus, we need to schedule sensors to face to certain directions to maximize the covered area of the whole network.

In this paper, after sensors are randomly deployed into a target region, our goal is to maximize the total area coverage that can be achieved by rotating each sensor's working direction to proper direction. The problem of working direction scheduling to cover maximal regions, called Maximum Directional Area Coverage (MDAC) problem, has been proved to be *NP*-complete [9]. A greedy solution has also been provided through scheduling working directions of sensors. We propose a distributed greedy algorithm for MDAC problem with rotatable sensors to increase the area coverage.

The remainder of this paper is organized as follows: Related work is discussed in Section II. In Section III, the directional sensing model and some preliminaries are proposed. In Section IV, the problem statement is proposed. Section V proposes the distributed greedy algorithm for solving the problem. In Section VI, we present experimental results obtained from different perspectives on the number of sensors, the sensing radius and the sensing angle, respectively. Section VII summarizes our findings.

II. RELATED WORK

Ma and Liu [10] discussed that the number of directional sensors can be deployed to achieve coverage rate p in a distributed directional sensor network (equation (1)). Directional sensors are randomly and uniformly scattered within a given area. Here, R is the sensing radius, S is the given area, and α is the offset angle of the field of view. To be clear, $\alpha R^2/S$ indicates that a directional sensor can monitor given area that is within its sensing region. Therefore, after N directional sensors are deployed, the probability that covers a given area is represented in

$$p = 1 - (1 - \frac{\alpha R^2}{S})^N. \quad (1)$$

In other words, if the coverage rate of a given area is at least p, the number of deployed directional sensors should be represented in

$$N = \frac{\ln(1-p)}{\ln(S - \alpha R^2) - \ln S}. \quad (2)$$

Kandoth and Chellappan [11] proposed a greedy solution called the Face-Away (FA) algorithm to achieve the maximal area coverage rate in the interested region. The *FA* algorithm works in a very simple manner. Each sensor calculates a new working direction that only needs the positions of neighboring sensors. The neighboring sensors of a directional sensor, say *s*, are those sensors located within the circular area centered at *s* with sensing radius *R*. In fact, every sensor should be recognizable from its surroundings when being viewed by its neighbors. Once a sensor is recognized, each sensor must center it in view and record the current working direction.

Li et al. [12] proposed the Voronoi-based centralized approximation (VCA) algorithm and the Voronoi-based distributed approximation (VDA) algorithm of the solution to their proposed optimal coverage in directional sensor networks (OCDSN) problem for covering maximal area while activating as few sensors as possible. Their algorithms are both based upon the so-called boundary Voronoi diagram (BVD). Each sensor will rotate its working direction to cover the largest edge of its surrounding Voronoi region. Thus, the covered area will be increased. However, as the number of sensors increased and non-uniformly deployed into the region, the overlapped area among sensors increased as well.

In [13], the authors proposed two greedy schemes, namely the Intra-cell Working Direction Selection (IDS) and the Inter-cell Working Direction Adjustment (IDA) schemes, which are also based on the Voronoi diagram, to rotate the working direction of each sensor to the direction of the vertices of its corresponding Voronoi cell. The IDS scheme rotates the working direction of each sensor to the Voronoi vertex having the maximum coverage. Then, the IDA approach improves the overlapped coverage between adjacent cells to increase the overall area coverage.

In this paper, we devised a greedy approach for sensors to select their working directions to increase the area coverage. Simulation results show that our proposed algorithm outperforms than previous algorithms, including Face-Away, VDA, and IDS algorithms.

III. PRELIMINARIES

A. Directional Sensing Model

Compared to an omni-directional sensor, which has a disc-shaped sensing range, a directional sensor has a smaller sector-like sensing area and smaller sensing angle, as illustrated in Figure 2. In Figure 2, the sensing region (also called the sensing sector) of a directional sensor is a sector denoted by 4-tuple ($p(x,y)$, r, θ, α). Here, $p(x,y)$ is the location of the sensor node, r is the sensing radius, θ ($0 \leq \theta < 2\pi$) is the working direction angle and α ($0 < \alpha \leq 2\pi$) is the angle of view. The special case of this model, where $\alpha = 2\pi$ can be described as omni-sensing model.

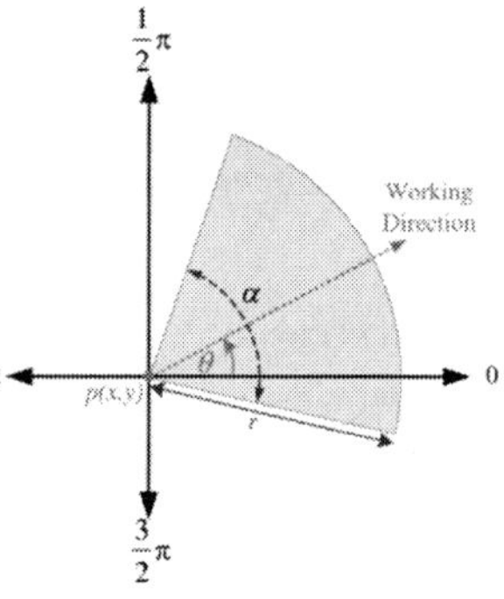

Figure 2. The directional sensing model.

We illustrate the characteristic of directional sensors:

- Each directional sensor is homogeneous, such as: sensing angle, sensing radius, and communication radius.
- Each directional sensor can sense only one limited angle of omni-direction.
- Each directional sensor is fixed and can rotate arbitrary angle in sensing region.
- The communication radius is twice than the sensing radius such that sensing neighbors can reliably communicate.

B. Voronoi Cells

Voronoi diagram, a well-known data structure in computational geometry [14], partitions a plane into a set of convex polygons such that all points inside a polygon are closest to only one site. This study used the Voronoi diagram structure and divided the sensing area into Voronoi cells according to the positions of deployed sensors, as shown in Figure 3.

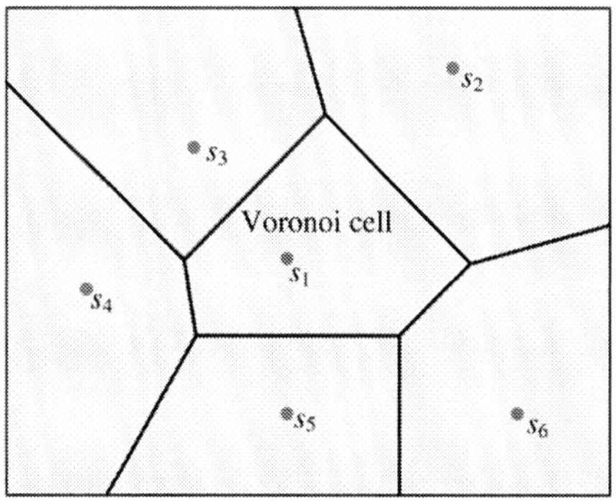

Figure 3. Dividing sensing area into Voronoi cells associated with sensors.

The construction effectively produces polygons with edges that are equidistant from neighboring sites. Those line segments that form the boundaries of Voronoi cells are called the Voronoi edges. The endpoints of these edges are called the Voronoi vertices.

IV. PROBLEM STATEMENT

Usually a numerous of sensors are randomly deployed into a target region for covering the area as much as possible in order to reach an adequate coverage level for further applications. However, it is not easy to obtain optimum coverage because of the overlapped covered area. The defect in using centralized algorithms for this problem is that a node with powerful computing resource is required for calculation. Moreover, massive node information must be transmitted to the sink node in multi-hop mode, thus consuming a lot of sensor network transmission resources. On the contrary, the distributed algorithms do not need global information but only local information gathered from neighboring sensors for calculation, thus consuming fewer calculation and network transmission resources. In addition, the distributed algorithm is more practical to implement real-time response or adjustment according to the dynamic environment change.

For numerous directional sensors randomly distributed in the sensing field, the field coverage problem is a basic and important problem without optimal solution. This study used the distributed greedy algorithm to obtain the near optimum solution. Based on the Voronoi cells structure, each sensor uses the vertices of its cell as the candidate targets of working direction. The working direction is selected and adjusted and the original direction of each sensor is changed on the two principles: (1) to enlarge the area covered by the sensor while reducing the sensors overlapped coverage with neighboring sensors as much as possible; (2) to avoid the sensor coverage being outside the sensing field as possible; so that the overall target area coverage is improved.

Now, we formally state our problem as follows:

Problem: Randomly deploying N directional sensors with sensing range R_S, communication range R_C and sensing angle α in a given target sensing region where $R_C = 2R_S$ and $0 < \alpha \leq 2\pi$, we are asked to devise a distributed algorithm for each sensor to adjust or rotate its working direction so that the total area coverage is maximized.

V. PROPOSED SENSOR DIRECTION CONTROL SCHEME

In this section, the algorithm corresponding to the two major principles of selecting working direction will be described respectively, which are Working Direction Selection scheme and Out-of-Field Coverage Recovery procedure.

A. Working Direction Selection

Although we all know that a sensor can rotate its sensing direction to increase the coverage, we still do not know which direction is the best for a sensor to rotate. Therefore, the main idea of our proposed algorithm is to determine the most possible direction of a sensor to rotate so that after the rotation, the overlapped region with other sensors is minimized. The following is our strategy for finding the rotating direction. According to [13], the sensor having the optimal sensing quality is to cover the most area within its corresponding Voronoi cell. Thus, our first step is to determine which direction is the most likely for a sensor to cover within its Voronoi cell zone. To do so, when each sensor completes the construction of its Voronoi cell, the vertices of the cell are used as preliminary working direction candidates. The sensor calculates respective coverage sizes within the cell zone of aligning direction with each vertex of its Voronoi cell and selects the vertex having the maximum coverage and the minimum overlapped with other sensors within the cell zone as its working direction. In other words, this selection will decide the most effective or non-overlapped sensing area from the position of sensor.

Obviously, the decision for a sensor of selecting the most effective or non-overlapped sensing area depends on the directions of its neighboring sensors. If the working directions of all neighboring sensors are determined, the sensor can easily determine its working direction to the direction that has no overlapped area with its neighboring sensors. However, if some neighboring sensors have not decided their working directions yet, then there may have chances to overlap with these undecided sensors. Therefore, the sequence of sensors for determining their working directions will affect the performance of reducing the overlapped area. For determining the decision sequence, we consider the average edge length of the Voronoi cell of each sensor. The average edge length of each sensor is calculated as the length of all edges in its surrounding Voronoi cell divided by the number of its neighboring sensors. Therefore, it can be seen that if the average edge length is small, the sensor may have more neighboring sensors than those with larger average edge lengths. In this case, it is better for the sensor to determine its working direction before other sensors since once it decided, all the neighboring sensors can easily determine their working directions by avoiding the area covered by the decided sensor.

Here, we describe our proposed greedy algorithm for MDAC problem. The proposed algorithm is called the *Voronoi-based Minimal Size First* (VMSF) algorithm. In our proposed algorithm, when each sensor completes the construction of its Voronoi cell, the sensor calculates the average edge length of its surrounding Voronoi cell as the priority of rotation. It should be noticed that, as we mentioned above, the smaller the average edge length is, the higher the priority will be. In other words, if the average edge length of a sensor is small, meaning that the sensor may have many neighbors, then the sensor has higher priority to be scheduled for rotation. Once a sensor has determined to rotate, the new direction can be obtained by finding the vertex of its Voronoi cell with largest uncovered and non-overlapped region.

B. Out-of-Field Coverage Recovery

The positions of a part of deployed sensors may be close to the boundary of the target region. The working direction of these sensors may face toward the boundary so that most of coverage is outside the sensing field, wasting the coverage of sensors of the sensing field. Therefore, after the working direction selection procedure, this study implements additional Out-of-Field Coverage Recovery procedure on these sensors near the boundary. Figure 4 shows an example with three cases. The working direction of an out-of-field sensor can be recovered by rotating the working direction towards the inside of sensing field, as shown in Figure 5, so that the working direction angle θ of s_i should conform to θ_1 or θ_2.

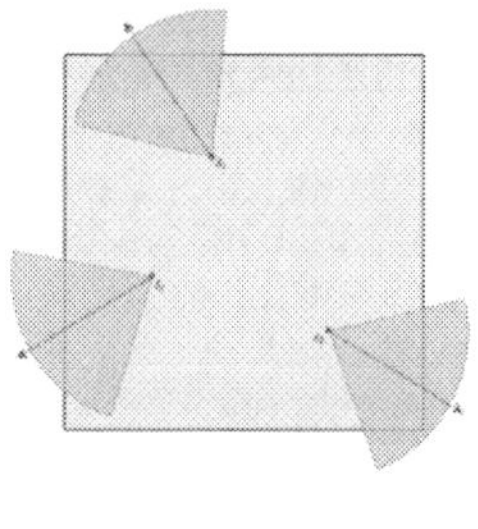

Figure 4. An example of out-of-field coverage.

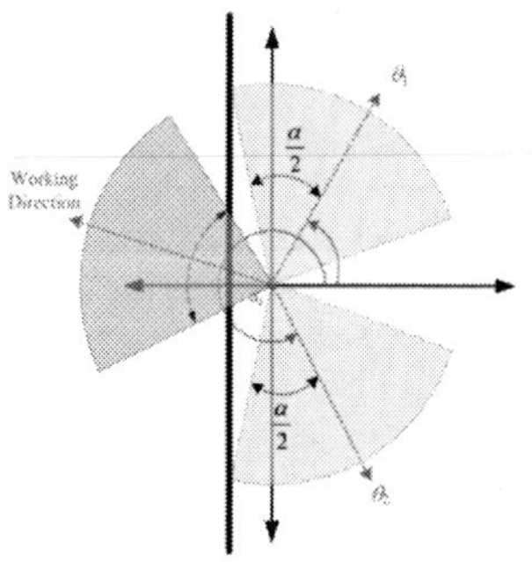

Figure 5. Direction adjustment for of Out-of-Field Coverage Recovery.

The pseudo-code of the our proposed VMSF algorithm is shown in Figure 6.

Algorithm: Voronoi-based Minimal Size First algorithm

I. Initialization Phase (only performed once)

Send a coverage message containing sensor ID, initial working direction, and location of sensor s_i and wait a period of time for collecting the information from sensing neighbors
Calculate the Voronoi diagram and determine the priority value P_i and broadcast the value
Collect the priority values from all neighboring sensors and go to the **Decision Phase**.

II. Decision Phase

while *true* **do**
  Find the highest priority values, denoted as P_{max}, among neighboring sensors
  if $P_i > P_{max}$ **then**
    Find the point, say A, on the Voronoi cell with maximal uncovered region and non-overlapped region
    Rotate its working direction to point A, set its priority value to 0 and send a scheduled message containing ID and priority value to its sensing neighbors
    Exit the while loop
  else
    if $P_i = P_{max}$ **then**
      Wait for a random duration or a scheduled message sent by a sensor, say s_j, is received
      if no scheduled message received **then**
        Find the point, say A, on the Voronoi cell with maximal uncovered and non-overlapped region
        Rotate its working direction to point A, set its priority value to 0 and send a scheduled message containing ID and priority value to its sensing neighbors.
        Exit the while loop
      end if
    else
      Wait until a scheduled message sent by a sensor, say s_j, is received
    end if
    Set the status of s_j as "scheduled" and update its priority P_i according to its remaining "unscheduled" neighboring sensors
    Send P_i to its "unscheduled" neighboring sensors
    Collect the priority values from all of its "unscheduled" neighboring sensors
  end if
end while

Figure 6. The proposed sensor direction selection algorithm.

In the next section, we will present the performance of our proposed sensor movement algorithm.

VI. SIMULATION RESULTS

This section describes the parameters and performance effects of different perspectives on our proposed algorithm, compared with previous algorithms. We conducted our experiments on a computer with 3.0 GHz CPU and 4GB memory. All experiments are done in C# on .NET platform. Our simulation network consists of 50 to 200 directional sensor nodes placed randomly within a 500 *m* x 500 *m* area. Every experiment was repeated 100 times and the recorded data was averaged over those runs. Table 1 lists the values of the common parameters used in all the experiments.

TABLE I. EXPERIMENTAL PARAMETERS

Parameters	Description
Network Size	500 × 500 (m^2)
Sensing Radius	30*m*, 35*m*, …, 60*m*
Sensing Angle	60°,80°, …, 180°
Number of Sensors	50, 75, …, 200

The main goal of our simulation is focused on the comparison of the performance of our proposed VMSF algorithm, random approach (Random) in which each sensor select its working direction randomly, FA, VDA and IDS algorithms, in terms of the coverage rate. The coverage rate p is defined as the ratio of the total covered area by all sensors over the network size. We evaluate the effects of our algorithm on three different perspectives. First, we examine the effect that the number of sensors N makes to the improvement of coverage rate p. Second, we evaluate the effect that the sensing radius improves the coverage rate p. Third, we examine the effect that the offset angle makes to the improvement of coverage rate p.

A. Coverage rate vs. Number of sensors

This experiment evaluates the effect that the number of sensors N makes to the performance of coverage rate p of Random approach, FA, VDA, IDS, and VMSF algorithms respectively. The sensing radius R is set to 50m and the sensing angle α is set to 120°. The result is shown in Figure 7.

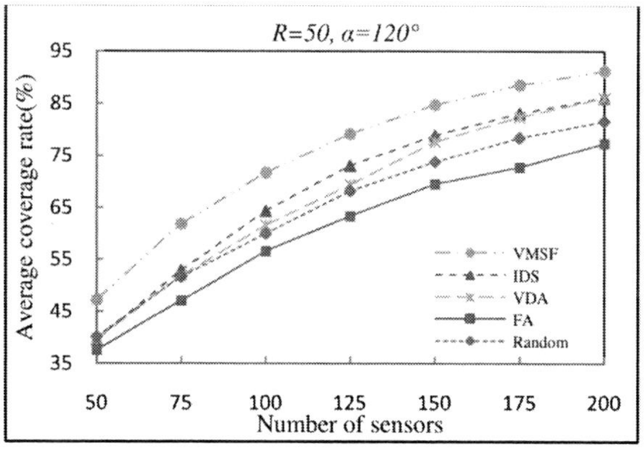

Figure 7. Coverage rate vs. number of sensors with R = 50m and α = 120°.

In Figure 7, we can see that our proposed VMSF algorithm outperforms all other approaches. For example, when the number of sensors is 200, the sensing radius is 50m and the sensing angle is 120°, the coverage rates of Random approach, FA, VDA, IDS, and VMSF algorithms are 77.31%, 74.48%, 83,18%, 84.09%, and 92.42% respectively. Thus, the VMSF algorithm outperforms other approaches. This is because that VMSF algorithm can achieve the less overlapping area and the order of sensors chosen to rotate will influence the performance of coverage rate. Therefore, our proposed VMSF algorithm can get the most improvement on coverage rate among all algorithms.

B. Coverage rate vs. Sensing radius

This experiment examines the effect that sensing radius R makes to the performance of coverage rate p of Random approach, FA, VDA, IDS, and VMSF algorithms respectively. The sensing angle is set to 120°. The number of sensors is set to 200. The result is shown in Figure 8.

In Figure 8, we can see that our proposed VMSF algorithm outperforms all other approached. For example, when the number of sensors is 200, the sensing radius is 60*m* and the sensing angle is 120°, the coverage rates of Random approach, FA, VDA, IDS, and VMSF algorithms are 86.89%, 86.12%, 90.58%, 93.23% and 96.91% respectively. Thus, the VMSF algorithm performs better than other approaches from 3.68% to 10.02%. This is because that our VMSF algorithm can achieve less overlapped region and higher coverage rate. We also note that, as the sensing radius increases, the coverage rates of all algorithms rise. This is obvious since the greater the sensing radius is, the more sensing area can be obtained.

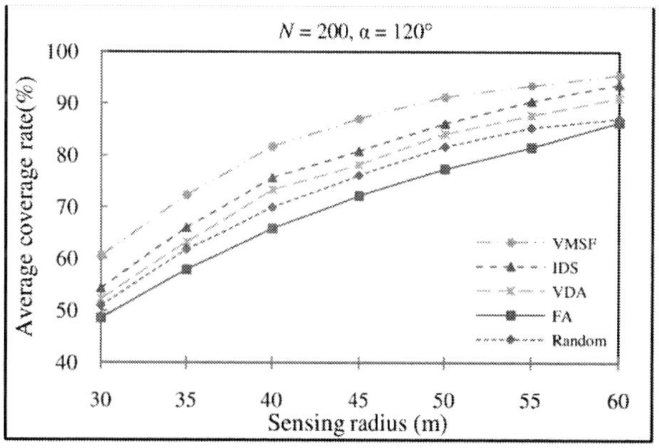

Figure 8. Coverage rate vs. sensing radius with N = 200 and α = 120°.

C. Coverage rate vs. Sensing angles

This experiment evaluates the effect that sensing angle α makes to the performance of coverage rate p of Random approach, FA, VDA, IDS, and VMSF algorithms respectively. The sensing radius is set to 50*m*. The number of sensors is set to 200. The result is shown in Figure 9.

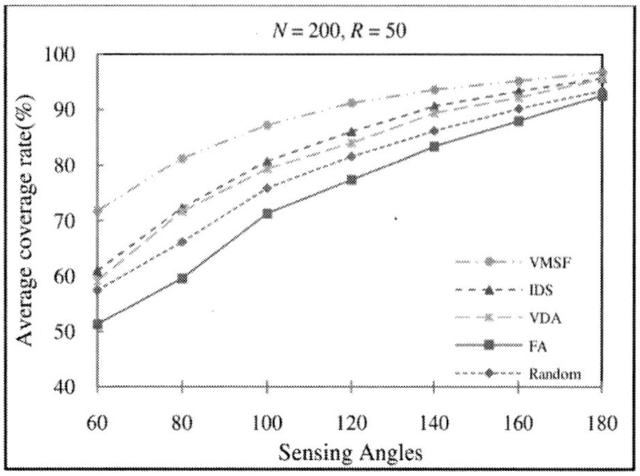

Figure 9. Coverage rate vs. sensing angles with R = 50m and N = 200.

In Figure 9, we can see that our proposed VMSF algorithm outperforms all other approaches. For example, when the number of sensors is 200, the sensing radius is $50m$ and the sensing angle is 120°, the coverage rates of Random approach, FA, VDA, IDS, and VMSF algorithms are 78.12%, 82.31%, 84.92%, 86.53%, and 91.68% respectively. Thus, the VMSF algorithm performs 5.15% better than the IDS algorithm. This is because that our proposed VMSF algorithm can achieve less overlapped area and higher coverage rate. We also note that, as the sensing angle α increases, the coverage rates of all algorithms rise. However, once the value of α exceeds a certain value ($\geq$ 140° in this experiment), the increasing coverage rate becomes flat rising. This is because, when the network density and sensing radius are fixed, the larger the sensing angle is, the smaller the possibility of uncovered area becomes.

VII. CONCLUSIONS

In this paper, we investigate the Maximum Directional Area Coverage (MDAC) problem in which we are asked to maximize the area coverage by scheduling the sensing direction or rotating the working direction of each sensor. We propose a distributed greedy algorithm, called the Voronoi-based Minimal Size First (VMSF) approach, which is based on the size of the corresponding Voronoi cell and the area of the overlapped region between directional sensors. Simulation results show that our proposed algorithm achieves better performance around 8% to 15%, 4% to 10%, and 5% to 13% than those of previous algorithms in terms of coverage rate on different number of sensors, sensing radius and sensing angles, respectively.

REFERENCES

[1] M. Hefeeda and M. Bagheri, "Randomized k-coverage algorithms for dense sensor networks", In: 26th IEEE International Conference on Computer Communications (INFOCOM '07). Anchorage, AK: IEEE Press, 2007, pp. 2376–2380.

[2] K. Chakrabarty, S. Iyengar, H. Qi, and E. Cho, "Grid coverage for surveillance and target location in distributed sensor networks", IEEE Transactions on Computers, vol.51, no.12, pp.1448–1453, 2002.

[3] S. Kininmonth et al., "The Great Barrier Reef Sensor Network", PACEM IN MARIBUS XXXI proceedings, Townsville, 2005, pp.361–369.

[4] I. F. Akyildiz, W. Su, Y. Sankarasubramaniam, and E. Cayirci, "A survey on sensor networks," ACM Trans. on Multimedia Computing, Communications and Applications, pp. 102-114, Aug 2002.

[5] M. Rahimi et al., "Cyclops: In situ image sensing and interpretation in wireless sensor networks," in ACM Conference on Embedded Networked Sensor Systems(SenSys), pp. 192-204, 2005.

[6] J. Djugash, S. Singh, G. Kantor, and W. Zhang, "Range-only SLAM for robots operating cooperatively with sensor networks," in *IEEE* International Conference on Robotics and Automation, pp. 2078-2084, 2006.

[7] R. Szewczyk, A. Mainwaring, J. Polastre, J. Anderson, and D. Culler,"An analysis of a large scale habitat monitoring application," ACM Conference on Embedded Networked Sensor Systems (SenSys), pp. 214-226, 2004.

[8] T. Clouqueur, V. Phipatanasuphorn, P. Ramanathan, and K. K. Saluja, "Sensor Deployment Strategy for Target Detection," Proc. First ACM International Workshop Wireless Sensor Networks and Applications, pp. 42-48, 2002.

[9] W. Cheng, S. Li, X. Liao, C. Chen, and H. Chen , "Maximal Coverage Scheduling in Randomly Deployed Directional Sensor Networks" in International Conference on Parallel Processing Workshops, ICPPW 2007, pp. 68-68, 2007.

[10] H. D. Ma and Y. Liu, "On coverage problems of directional sensor networks," in International Conference on Mobile Ad-hoc and Sensor Networks (MSN), pp. 721-731, 2005.

[11] C. Kandoth and S. Chellappan, "Angular Mobility Assisted Coverage in Directional Sensor Networks," *Proceedings of International Conference on Network-Based Information Systems* (NBIS 2009), pp. 376-379, 2009.

[12] J. Li, R. Wang, H. Huang, and L. Sun, "Voronoi-Based Coverage Optimization for Directional Sensor Networks," Wireless Sensor Network, Vol. 1 No. 5, 2009, pp. 417-424.

[13] Tien-Wen Sung and Chu-Sing Yang, "Voronoi-based coverage improvement approach for wireless directional sensor networks," Journal of Network and Computer Applications, Volume 39, March 2014, pp. 202–213.

[14] F. Aurenhammer, "Voronoi Diagrams: A Survey of a Fundamental Geometric Data Structure," ACM Computing Surveys, vol. 23, pp. 345-405, 1991.

[15] S. Meguerdichian, F. Koushanfar, M. Potkonjak, and M.B. Srivastava, "Coverage Problems in Wireless Ad-Hoc Sensor Network," Proc. IEEE Infocom, pp. 1380-1387, 2001.

[16] C. K. Liang, M. C. He, and C. H. Tsai, "Movement Assisted sensor deployement in directional sensor networks," Proceedings of 6th International Conference on Mobile Ad-hoc and Sensor Networks, Hangzhou, China, 2010, pp. 226-230.

[17] C. Zhu, C Zheng, L. Shu, and G. Han, "A survey on coverage and connectivity issues in wireless sensor networks," Journal of Network and Computer Applications, Volume 35, 2012, pp. 619-632.

Multi-Hop Protocol to Extend Signal Coverage

Eloísa Alexandre Nielsen Matthiesen and Omar Carvalho Branquinho
PUC Campinas
Campinas, Brazil
Email: eloisa.anm1@puccampinas.edu.br
Email: branquinho@puc-campinas.edu.br

Guilherme Lopes da Silva and Paulo Cardieri
UNICAMP
Campinas, Brazil
Email: guitalos@gmail.com
Email: cardieri@decom.fee.unicamp.br

***Abstract*—This paper describes the tests carried out with a Wireless Sensor Network in order to examine the radio coverage in the large space of a university food court. Due to the challenging environment, the development of a multi-hop protocol was necessary. The protocol deems a sensor node as a repeater to extend the signal reach. We used the Radiuino open-source platform to develop the protocol with the flexibility to design an address strategy in the packet. The preliminary results indicate that the protocol developed is feasible, stable and robust.**

Keywords-WSN; multi-hop topology; routing protocol.

I. INTRODUCTION

Wireless Sensor Networks (WSNs) play an important role in Internet of Things (IoT) applications, having low-power sensors and easy installation. Indoor WSNs will be essential in smart homes, monitoring appliances and systems, such as closing the windows automatically based on the weather forecast [1].

Usually, a WSN consists of sensing nodes that report their results to a base station node. The base station node can process the data and monitor the network [2]. If a WSN needs to cover a wide area and the sensing nodes can not communicate directly with the base station node, a change in the topology of the nodes can be a solution.

In this project, the sensing nodes were placed inside the food court of the Pontifícia Universidade Católica of Campinas in Brazil, and the base station node was placed in a laboratory. The distance between the base station node and the repeater node was 200 meters. Although is a small distance, it is in non-line-of-sight (NLOS), making the direct communication impossible.

To extend the range of the signal, a multi-hop protocol was created, using protocol stacks with five layers, akin to the Transmission Control Protocol/Internet Protocol (TCP/IP) concept.

The rest of the paper is structured as follows. In Section II, we discuss the state-of-the-art. In Section III, we present the payout of the WSN. Section IV shows preliminary results and we conclude in Section V with the outcome of the experiment.

II. STATE OF THE ART

WSNs can have a distributed or a centralized routing protocol. The majority of articles found in literature use a distributed routing protocol, such as [3], [4], [5], in which the protocol runs in a peer-to-peer mode, requiring all the nodes to possess processing power. Another used protocol is the Routing Protocol for Low Power and Lossy Networks (RPL), but it is also a distributed protocol [6], being different from the protocol shown in this project.

Although, by using the distributed protocol, the system does not depend on a centralized process unit. It also uses more energy, decreasing the equipment's lifetime. The base station node, in both cases, always needs to be connected to the Internet and to have processing power.

Another advantage of centralized routing is the simplicity of the network nodes. Only the base station node demands more complex processing capabilities. It also allows the development of the multi-hop protocol, that would not be possible with a distributed routing management.

That simplicity makes it easier to meet the Quality of Service (QoS) parameters, like changing the routing path, changing radio attributes, such as power and channel. This ability is important for WSN operators, as seen in [7]. Without a centralized routing protocol, this operator can not attest to the QoS parameters.

Further, it is possible to change priorities, for example, the information importance of the nodes can change over time. Considering those aspects, the WSN of this paper has a centralized routing protocol.

III. MATERIAL AND METHODS

In this setup, we employed seven sensor nodes using the open *Radiuino* [8] platform, a library of Arduino that allows the user to work in five layers. This platform was chosen because it allows a change of network topology, differently from other platforms like *ZigBee* [9].

The logical view of the network is shown in Fig. 1. The base station node uses the first three layers (PHY, MAC and Net) while the sensors nodes use five layers (PHY, MAC, Net, Transp and App).

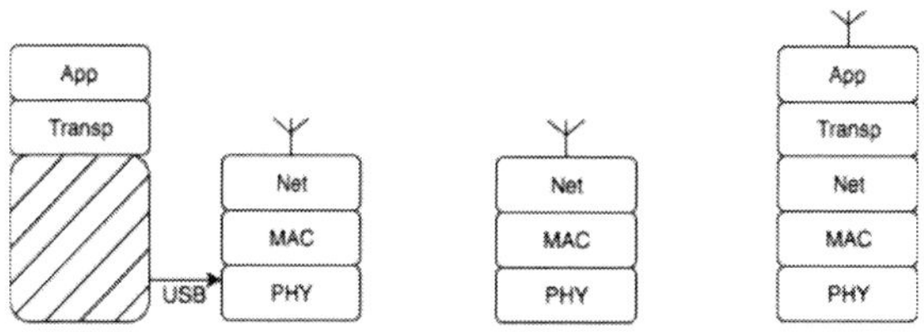

Figure 1. Logical view of the WSN layers.

The communication modules used in the set up were BE990 and BE900, both homologated by the Brazilian National Telecommunications Agency (ANATEL). These modules carry an ATMega328 processor and a CC1101 RF transceiver with a bandwidth filter, operating in the Industrial, Scientific and Medical (ISM) frequency of 915 MHz. The BE990 module also has a CC1190 that integrates a power amplifier (PA) with a low-noise amplifier (LNA) for improved wireless performance [10].

The communication module BE900 can reach up to 100 meters indoors and 500 meters outdoors. The communication module BE990 can reach up to 1000 meters indoors and 8000 meters outdoors. Those distances are considering it is in line-of-sight (LOS), which we did not have in this project.

One sensor node was programmed to work only as a repeater, receiving data from the base station node and forwarding the packet to the other five sensor nodes. For a better performance, the base station node, the repeater node and the sensor 5 node used the BE990 (16dBm) module, while sensors nodes from 1 to 4 used BE900 (10dBm).

In the layout of the system, the base station node is B, the repeater node R and the sensors are S1, S2, ..., Sn. Fig. 2 shows this layout.

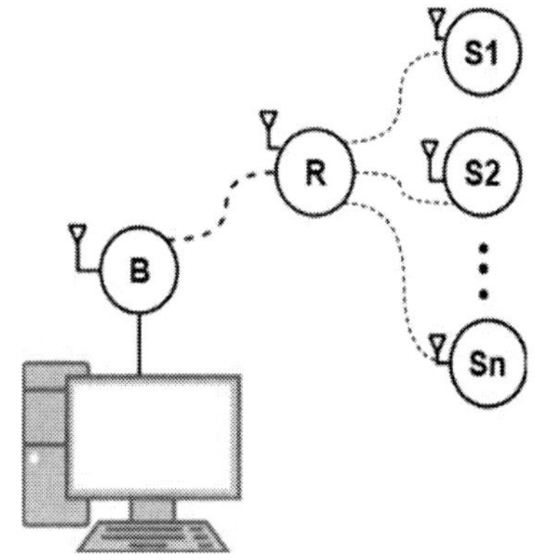

Figure 2. Layout of the system.

Radiuino packet has 52 bytes. The first 4 layers have 4 bytes each, forming a 16 bytes header. The rest of the packet belongs to the Application layer. The remaining 36 bytes are split into two halves, 18 bytes to measure proprieties and 18 bytes to control processes.

The WSNs have a centralized protocol where the base station node is responsible for the routing protocol. The routing protocol approach is hierarchical. The route is chosen trough the ID of the nodes.

The protocol algorithm uses the bytes from 8 to 11 (bytes of the Net layer header). In byte 8 is placed the address (ID) of the next node that is to receive the packet; in byte 9 goes the address of the final node in downlink; in byte 10 goes the ID of the sender in the hop and in byte 11 goes the address of the final node in uplink.

An example of the protocol where the base station node's ID is 0, the repeater node's ID is 20 and the sensor node's ID is 1 is shown in Fig. 3. The protocol was designed to work only with the message in the packet, so the node sensor reacts, changing the addresses for the next hop. The advantage of this strategy is that it allows the sensor nodes to be scalable.

The repeater node, which is predefined, works with bytes 8 and 10, it inputs the data of byte 8 in byte 10 (its address) and inputs the data of byte 9 in byte 8 (the sensor address). The sensor node swaps byte 8, for the data, in byte 10, and swaps byte 9, for the data, in byte 11. After that, it inputs its own address (ID = 1) in bytes 10 and 11.

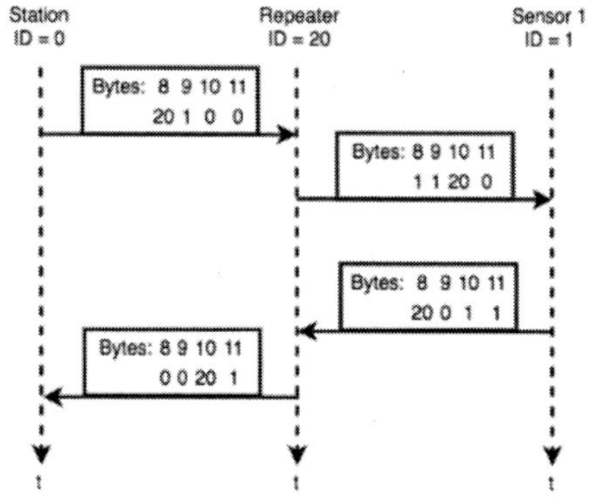

Figure 3. Sequence diagram of the packet.

IV. PRELIMINARY RESULTS

The first test lasted for six hours, from 1pm to 7pm, while the received signal strength indicator (RSSI) of down and uplink were measured. Fig. 4 shows the RSSI of sensor 3 node as a function of time. The solid line is the downlink RSSI, that is, the RSSI that the sensor is measuring. The dotted line is the uplink RSSI, that is, the RSSI measured by the repeater node.

The solid points showing in both lines are the errors, when the packet was lost in transmission.

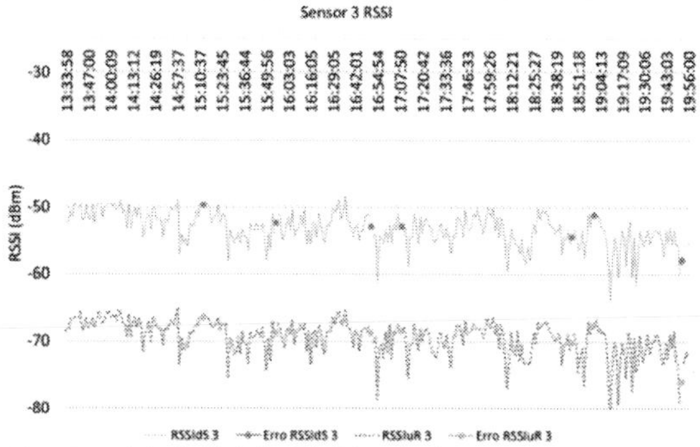

Figure 4. Chart of RSSI of Sensor 3.

The discrepancy shown is the result of different communication modules in the repeater node and in the sensor 3 node. The position of the sensor node also influences the RSSI stability. Sensor 3 node is not in the line of sight making it less susceptible to passers-by. The majority of packets lost are when the flux of people in the food court increases.

In Fig. 5, we show the RSSI for the sensor 5 node as a function of time. The downlink RSSI is overlapping the uplink RSSI.

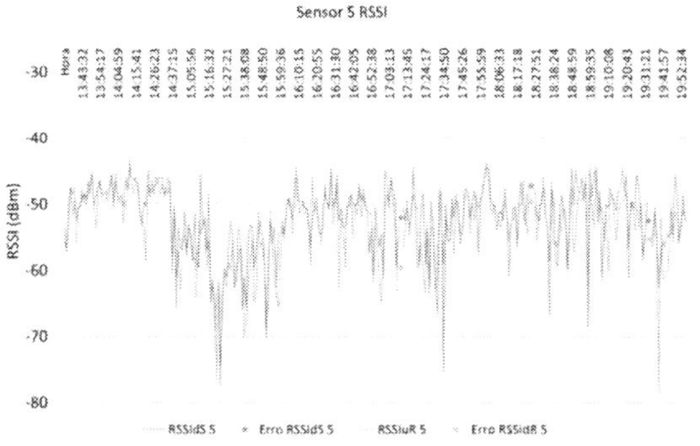

Figure 5. Chart of RSSI of Sensor 5.

The overlapping of RSSI happens because the same module BE990 was used in both the repeater node and the sensor 5 node. Its position was in LOS, making the RSSI more unstable as a result of passers-by interference.

V. CONCLUSION

The purpose of this project was to cover university's food court. A pretest was made trying the direct communication between sensor 3 node and the base station node, which was impossible due numerus obstacles between them.

After the development of the protocol and the placement of the repeater node, the communication was possible.

Sensor 3 node follows a Gaussian distribution, while sensor 5 node follows a Rayleigh distribution. This data is important to manage the WSN and take decisions about it.

The RSSI improvement that is shown in sensor 5 node can be attributed to the different location and to different communication modules.

In the future, some statistics will be compiled while the tests are running, estimating the average of the signal and its standard deviation.

REFERENCES

[1] A. Al-Fuqaha, M. Guizani, M. Mohammadi, M. Aledhari, and M. Ayyash, "Internet of Things: A Survey on Enabling Technologies, Protocols, and Applications," *IEEE Commun. Surv. Tutorials*, vol. 17, no. 4, pp. 2347–2376, 2015.

[2] L. Atzori, A. Iera, and G. Morabito, "The Internet of Things : A survey," *Comput. Networks*, vol. 54, no. 15, pp. 2787–2805, 2010.

[3] K. Cheng, K. Lui, Y. Wu, and V. Tam, "A Distributed Multihop Time Synchronization Protocol for Wireless Sensor Networks using Pairwise Broadcast Synchronization," vol. 8, no. 4, pp. 1764–1772, 2009.

[4] E. Alnawafa, "IMHT : Improved MHT-LEACH Protocol for Wireless Sensor Networks," pp. 246–251, 2017.

[5] H. Shafieirad and R. S. Adve, "Opportunistic Routing in Large-Scale Energy Harvesting Sensor Networks," 2016.

[6] M. O. Farooq, C. J. Sreenan, K. N. Brown, and T. Kunz, "RPL-based routing protocols for multi-sink wireless sensor networks," *2015 IEEE 11th Int. Conf. Wirel. Mob. Comput. Netw. Commun. WiMob 2015*, pp. 452–459, 2015.

[7] G. Gaillard, D. Barthel, F. Theoleyre, and F. Valois, "Service Level Agreements for Wireless Sensor Networks: A WSN operator's point of view," in *2014 IEEE Network Operations and Management Symposium (NOMS)*, 2014, pp. 1–8.

[8] Radiuino, "Teoria do Radiuino," 2016. [Online]. Available: http://radiuino.cc/projetos/. [Accessed: 25-May-2017].

[9] A. Elahi and A. Gschwender, *ZigBee wireless sensor and control network*. Prentice Hall, 2010.

[10] Texas Instruments, "850 – 950 MHz RF Front End." 2009.

MAC Protocol Design Requirements for Mobility-aware Wireless Sensor Networks

Adrian Kacsó and Wajahat Abbas Kazmi

Department of Electrical Engineering and Computer Science
University of Siegen, Germany
Email: [adrian.kacso, syed.kazmi]@uni-siegen.de

***Abstract*—The usage of mobile nodes is a requirement in some wireless sensor networks (WSNs) applications (wildlife or patient monitoring). They require that data packets are sent reliably, mainly as bursty traffic with low energy consumption and low latency to a base station for monitoring. Mobility of nodes introduces several communication challenges, such as frequent topological changes, intermittent connectivity, and increase in collision rate. In order to fulfill the application requirements (e.g., energy efficiency, reliable transmissions, lower end-to-end latency) low duty-cycle, mobility-aware medium access (MAC) protocols have been proposed. The paper describes the main characteristics of recent mobility-aware MAC protocols, including our protocol, highlighting their assumptions and working mechanism, their advantages and limitations. It presents concrete application constraints and protocol features for designing MAC protocols for mobility-aware WSNs. Moreover, challenges in the evaluation of the proposed MACs are discussed and prospective future directions are identified.**

Keywords–wireless sensor network; mobility-aware Mac protocols; reliable, burst traffic; mobile WSNs; simulation

I. INTRODUCTION

While the initial research on wireless sensor nodes (WSN) medium access protocols (MACs) assumed static nodes only, it becomes obvious that mobility support is necessary for many application scenarios, e.g., wildlife and patient monitoring. Thus, we analyze first the existing mobility-aware MAC protocols with their achievements and drawbacks. In this paper, we consider mobile nodes aiming to report their data with minimal delay by establishing a communication link with a static or fixed node towards the sink. We refer to WSNs containing mobile nodes as Mobile Wireless Sensor Networks (MWSNs) in this paper. The design concerns for MAC in MWSNs significantly differ from that of cellular systems and Mobile Ad-hoc Networks (MANETs) in spite of the common aspect of mobility in these networks. In cellular systems, mobile nodes are directly connected to the base station having a single hop, versus multiple hops in MWSNs. Also, energy conservation is not an important design constraint in cellular systems because the base station and mobile nodes are not energy constrained. In addition, contrary to cellular networks, the handover process in MWSNs is more complex because relay nodes in MWSNs are not resourceful like base stations in cellular networks. MANETs are also not having energy-related issues and the main focus of MAC design is on quality of service provisioning.

Research in the area of WSNs focused primarily on improving energy efficiency and prolonging network lifetime whereas factors as mobility, latency, throughput, reliability, scalability were treated as secondary concerns so far. Numerous MAC layer designs for static WSNs have been proposed by researchers. The protocols and algorithms presented in these proposals were surveyed to acquaint researchers with the state-of-the-art in the field. Apart from categorizing the protocols into different classes (synchronous, asynchronous, frame-slotted, multichannel), [1] presents the evolutionary development of MAC protocols in addressing problems that fall in the domain of these classes of protocols. In [2], Bachir et al. identify collisions, overhearing, protocol overhead and idle listening as the main sources of energy consumption on the basis of problems they intend to address. Problems that occur due to mobility in MWSNs, particularly energy and reliable delivery related issues, need to be addressed and investigated.

Synchronous MAC protocols are based on common active/sleep schedules, where the clock is used to wake up the nodes for a specific period at given synchronization points in time. Nodes having the same schedule build a cluster. Such protocols require clock synchronization among all the nodes belonging to the same cluster. Synchronous protocols can be employed in MWSNs applications, where a cluster of nodes is attached to a moving target (person, animal, device), yielding a fix network topology, where a tight synchronization between nodes can be achieved. Even here, it remains challenging to detect mobile nodes and try to ensure communication with as few as possible disconnections when moving among different clusters, while also considering energy constraints of border nodes (in charge of seamless handing over for mobile nodes).

Asynchronous MAC protocols are based on preambles to announce a transmission. They require neither time synchronization nor schedule dissemination. Each node operates distributively and can choose its active schedule independently from other nodes. Therefore, such protocols are more scalable and robust to topology changes in the network. Asynchronous protocols can be more efficient than synchronous protocols in MWSN applications, such as wildlife monitoring, where a reliable communication between energy constrained mobile and static nodes is infrequent and energy efficiency is a primary concern. Their limitations are reduced channel availability and increased competition among the nodes. Collisions can be frequent, especially in dense networks with frequent transmissions, which would imply retransmissions and increase thus the energy consumption. Due to the mobility in dense zones, mobile nodes experience high medium access delays. Therefore, the major challenges to be considered while designing asynchronous MAC protocols for MWSNs are duty cycling of mobile node, medium access contention and communication efficiency as well as handover and reconnection of mobile nodes.

In [3], Ding et al. provide a survey of MAC protocols for MWSNs proposed until 2011 and present the available mobility models and mobility estimation techniques. It discusses the characteristics, advantages and disadvantages of the following mobility-aware MAC protocols: MS-MAC [4], MMAC [5], M-TDMA [6], MA-MAC [7], MobiSense [8], and MCMAC [9]. In [10], authors presented a survey of MAC protocols for MWSNs proposed till 2013. It gives a general classification of WSN mobility based on type of mobile element, type of movement, protocol level considerations and type of mobility handling entity. It summarizes WSN mobility solutions proposed at MAC and network layer and few MAC layer protocols: MS-MAC [4], MOBMAC [11], AM-MAC [12], MD-SMAC [13], MMAC [5], CFMA-MAC[14], MoX-MAC [15], MAMAC [16] and MMH-MAC [17]. In [18], the authors highlight advantages and drawbacks of protocols proposed until 2009 besides their own protocol Machiavel [19].

The contributions of this paper are twofold: we present 1) the main contributions of some relevant MAC protocols for MWSNs (since 2013) and discuss their working mechanism, advantages and limitations to identify research achievements; 2) our Mob-MAC protocol design and identify prospective future direction on this topic. This paper is structured as follows. Section II presents a discussion of the relevant MAC protocols including our Mob-MAC protocol for MWSNs. Section III provides conclusions and future directions.

II. Design Issues in MAC Protocols for MWSNs

In this section, we investigate a group of MAC protocols for MWSNs according to their application assumptions and the existing sensor network deployment. We group them into preamble sampling (asynchronous) and cluster-based (synchronous) protocols.

TABLE I. Summary of relevant MAC protocols for MWSNs.

Protocol	A/S	Derived from	Major problem addressed
M-ContikiMac [20]	A	ContikiMAC [21]	Handling bursty traffic
ME-ContikiMAC [22]	A	ContikiMAC [21]	Handling bursty traffic
X-Machiavel [18]	A	X-MAC [23]	Delays in burst transmission and reconnection
MoX-MAC [15]	A	–	Overhead minimization
MT-MAC [24]	S	T-MAC [25]	High packet drop rate during handover
MS-SMAC [26]	S	S-MAC [27]	Mobile node disconnection due to speed variation
MobIQ [22]	A	ContikiMAC [21]	Neighbor discovery, Channel contention, Hidden terminal problem
MobiDisc [28]	A	ContikiMAC [21]	Delays in burst transmission, handover and reconnection

We consider large sensor networks, where a large number of static and mobile nodes coexist. It is assumed that static nodes build a routing backbone (convergecast communication infrastructure), e.g., a tree rooted at a sink, in which each static node has a parent. A mobile node knows (or it is able to detect) that it is mobile and does not forward data packets. A mobile node establishes communication links with (randomly) static nodes in order to inject their data in the backbone. Static nodes forward the data hop by hop to the sink. Mobile nodes are considered more energy constrained that static nodes. Due to the mobility, disconnections between mobile nodes and the static infrastructure are frequent and common use cases. Networks are dense enough (a mobile node finds at least a static node in the vicinity). The application requirements are high packet delivery ratio at sink, low end-to-end latency, energy efficient transmissions of relevant data in a burst. Our objective is to address mobility efficiently under burst traffic in high density WSNs by achieving low end-to-end and handover delays, low energy consumption and prolonged lifetime. Table I presents some relevant MAC protocols for MWSNs showing their working scheme (column *A/S*: A=Asynchronous, S=Synchronous), the protocol from which they are derived and the major problems addressed by them.

A. *Synchronous MAC Protocols for MWSNs*

Synchronous MAC protocols for MWSNs use the cluster topology to handle mobility. Schedules are propagated by broadcasting SYNC packets at the beginning of the listen phase every predefined number of cycles. When a mobile node moves out of its original cluster range, it should receive a SYNC packet from the border node, deployed between the two clusters, in order to learn as soon as possible the new schedule. The next protocols use different methods to handoff the mobile node to another cluster.

1) MT-MAC [24] : is an extension of T-MAC [25], a synchronous protocol that adopts an adaptive duty cycle according to the variation in traffic load. The mechanism of MT-MAC is divided into two phases, namely the scheduling phase and mobility handling phase.

In the scheduling phase, nodes are classified adaptively into stationary node, border node, cluster head and mobile node, where each node belongs to at least one virtual cluster.

In the mobility phase, upon receiving a SYNC packet, a static node observes the Received Signal Strength Indicator (RSSI) and Link Quality Indicator (LQI) values. In case a change in RSSI and LQI values is above a certain threshold, it is considered that the node is mobile and a timer is triggered. If a node marked as mobile stays in the same cluster more than a particular time, it is considered that the node is static. Based on the above mechanism, when a border node detects that a mobile node is approaching, it informs the node about the schedule of the next cluster. Thus, the mobile node can perform handover in an organized manner.

Limitations of the protocol are: a) Mobility estimation using RSSI and LQI is not reliable. b) MT-MAC is only suited when the mobile node is not energy constrained. If the mobile node is energy constrained, keeping the schedule of both clusters is not optimal. c) If there are more mobile nodes and the border nodes are energy constrained, the interactions with mobile nodes will consume much energy of the border nodes. The scheduling phase must be reinitiated periodically to select other border nodes.

2) MS-SMAC [26] : proposes a mechanism that reduces the probability of disconnection of mobile node with neighboring nodes when the speed of mobile node changes during movement. It is designed based on the fact that existing mobility-aware MAC protocols for WSNs do not show adaptive behavior to the change of mobile node speed.

Upon entering a new cluster, a mobile node broadcasts its speed and direction. The static nodes in the cluster acknowledge the packet sent by the mobile node, also providing information about their next sleep time and next announcement interval (when mobile node should send update about its current speed). An acknowledgment sent by border nodes contains information about sleep times of the current and the neighboring cluster.

Mobility estimation, as well as localization of mobile nodes is performed by a mechanism that makes use of the three largest RSSI values to reference neighboring nodes. The protocol also introduces a mechanism to provide up-to-date information to mobile and static nodes about active cycles of other nodes to ensure better connectivity between nodes.

Limitations of the protocol are: a) Mechanism for mobility estimation and handover decision introduce significant overhead. b) Mobility estimation and localization using RSSI is not reliable. c) The implicit assumption regarding the numbers of nodes in the cluster is not clear. The mechanism for localization needs three RSSI values, thus assuming the presence of at least three nodes in the cluster. If the number of nodes in the network, particularly mobile nodes, is high the protocol performance will be degraded due to complex computations involved in mobility estimation and handover.

B. Asynchronous MAC Protocols for MWSNs

A variety of applications involving mobility, such as patient and wildlife monitoring, require data to be transmitted in bursts. This occurs in scenarios where mobile nodes have occasional contact with different static nodes in the network and need to transmit urgently relevant sensed data. Relevant asynchronous MAC protocols send strobed preambles to notify potential receivers and use additional mechanisms to achieve better performance.

1) M-ContikiMAC [20]: is an extension of the ContikiMAC protocol [21], which is the default duty cycling mechanism in ContikiOS [29]. It is a preamble sampling protocol designed for static networks employing unicast and broadcast transmissions. It uses a special mechanism to handle bursty traffic in the network. The node intending to transmit a burst of packets informs the receiver about more packets in a row by setting a burst flag.The receiver on observing this flagged data keeps its radio *on* to receive more packets until the transmission is over. For the last packet in the burst, the flag will not be set, and, this way, efficient burst handling is achieved.

In M-ContikiMAC, a mobile node is not aware of the next hop in the rooting tree. Therefore, it cannot use unicast and must broadcast at least in the first step. It has to find out the address of a static neighbor node in the tree to communicate with it. M-ContikiMAC uses an anycast transmission, which allows the first node, the one that received the anycast packet and acknowledged it, to be the real recipient for the next packets in the burst.

If a mobile node is intending to send packets in burst, it sets besides the burst flag a byte field (*ReqHop*) to discover a static parent node. A static receiver, upon receiving an anycast packet, checks the value of the field. If the value is zero, it receives the packet and sends an acknowledgment informing the transmitter node about its address for unicast transmission. The receiver keeps its radio on to receive the burst from the sender. When the mobile sender receives the acknowledgment, it sets the byte field to the address of the receiver and unicasts the remaining packets (starting with the 2nd data packet) to it. In case of disconnection with the receiving node, the mobile sender sets the field to 0 again and repeats the same procedure to find a new potential receiver node as relay to sink.

Limitations of the protocol are: a) Useless forwarding of the 1st data packet on the route to sink. b) The collision of the ACKs. c) Mobile node disconnection from temporary parent. All these are correlated. Let us assume that two receiver nodes receive simultaneously a packet (either the 1st or one during reconnection). They will reply with an acknowledgment at (near) the same time, which collide at the sender. According to M-ContikiMAC, these nodes will keep their radio on and forward the first received data packet on several routes to the sink. The sink detects packet duplication and the useless traffic produces congestion, high latency and high energy consumption.

2) ME-ContikiMAC [22]: overcomes the limitations in M-ContikiMAC. In ME-ContikiMAC, the mobile node sends a control packet using anycast instead of the first data packet. The control packet is not forwarded by receiving nodes. Even if acknowledgements from two or more receivers collide, the control packet will not be forwarded to the sink. The mobile node will retransmit the control packet and will not initiate burst transmission until it receives an acknowledgment from any receiving node, which reduces packet duplication in the network. The same mechanism is used for reconnections.

Limitations of the protocol are: a) Receiver nodes send the acknowledgment upon receiving the control packet and switch the radio on waiting for the next packets in the burst. If the acknowledgments collide, the receivers are not aware about it and loose energy waiting for the burst. b) During bursts, a new mobile or static node can generate the hidden station problem. Moreover, an aggressive mobile mode (i.e., sending control packets without waiting the next preamble cycle) may affect the communication of the static nodes. c) For dense networks, it is necessary to avoid the collision of the ACKs; (the control packet is resent until the ACK is received). d) If the mobile node doesn't receive its expected ACK, the burst is postponed for the next preamble cycle, which increases the latency.

3) X-Machiavel [18]: takes benefit of the strobed preamble mechanism used by X-MAC to include mobile nodes in the communication. Data packets initiated by a mobile node have higher priority compared to those of static/fixed nodes. A mobile node, before a transmission, overhears the medium and 'steals' the medium from a static node already involved in a not guarded incipient communication (either with a special preamble or a flag). The idea is based on the fact that mobile nodes are energy constrained and without sending a preamble, they insert their data after overhearing a preamble of the intended static receiver. The communication between static nodes can be postponed, which may induce message buffering, retransmissions and latency in the static routing infrastructure. The protocol uses a special header that is included in the preamble, data and ACK packets. The header contains a *type* that allows to use various preambles or acknowledgements and a *flag* byte, where the M-bit informs each relay receiver that the data is from a mobile node on the way to sink, and the medium cannot be stolen by a mobile. A special preamble type prevents potential forwarders to claim the data.

Limitations of the protocol are: a) Complex implementation, special header added to each frame type. b) If the final destination of the data packet acknowledges a preamble later than a static forwarder in the same vecinity, the forwarding is not optimal and the latency increases. c) Unfairness, data initiated from a mobile node have higher priority than from a static one. d) Two or more ACKs from potential receivers may collide, which triggers a retransmission.

4) MoX-MAC [15]: allows a mobile sender to overhear an ongoing transmission between two static nodes, in order to send his own data to the static sender at the end of the ongoing transmission. Limitations of the protocol: a) Mobile nodes must be in the range of both communicating static sender and receiver. b) Since the mobile node must use the basic X-MAC scheme if no ongoing transmission is detected, the efficiency of the approach is highly dependent on the frequency of transmissions between the static nodes.

5) MobIQ [30]: proposes a mechanism to enable efficient neighbor discovery for mobile nodes, reduction of channel contention and overcoming hidden terminal problems.

Mobile nodes, due to their movement (or link disconnections), often have to change their static next-hop in order to send all the data packets of a burst. An efficient handover mechanism allows mobile nodes to maintain an uninterrupted communication with the static routing backbone. This can be achieved with a fast neighbour discovery and regular updates from the neighborhood. For discovering and selecting an appropriate neighbor, the mobile node continuously anycasts control packets for the whole preamble duration to assure that all neighbors receive them. All receivers acknowledge it by sending their ID and routing metrics (e.g., hops to sink, remaining battery) to the mobile node. Between all its potential receivers, the mobile node selects the best next forwarder node on the route to sink (the network layer provides the metrics to the link layer) and starts burst transmission in the next sampling period.

To avoid channel contention during transmission of burst packets, the mobile node informs the nodes about the queue length in every data packet. Using this queue length information, receiver nodes can adjust their sleep schedule. To avoid the hidden terminal problem, where more than one mobile node send data to the same receiver, the receiver node disseminates the queue length information of the current sender in ACK packets, by overhearing which other intending sender(s) can adjust their wait period accordingly.

Limitations of the protocol are: a) Neighbors of mobile node will come to know which node was selected by the mobile node once it starts the burst transmission; therefore, all neighbors will wake up in the next sampling period, which will result in energy consumption for nodes which were not selected. b) Since two or more ACKs from potential receivers may collide, the mobile node may select not the best forwarder.

6) MobiDisc [28]: an extension of MobIQ, introduces the First Ack Next-hop (FAN) mode, which enables reduction of delays in transmission of bursts by allowing mobile sender nodes to select a better (according to some routing metrics) forwarder node on the route to sink. Using the FAN mode, if another static forwarder samples the medium during the ongoing burst transmission of the mobile node with the first forwarder, then it will inform the mobile node about its metric using a notification packet. Later, the mobile node may decide to select the second forwarder (according to it metrics) and perform a handover.

During burst transmission, mobile node may get disconnected from its current static receiver. The Fast Recovery Mechanism (FRM) aims at reducing the handover and reconnection delays by granting priority to traffic of mobile nodes over that of static nodes. Thus, upon discovery of disconnection, the mobile node immediately starts sending control packets to search for a new potential receiver within the same preamble cycle.

Limitations of the protocol are: a) In FAN mode the energy consumption of both mobile and static nodes increases (due to extended listening time to receive the notification and more Clear Channel Assessment (CCA) slots). b) The protocol does not consider the possibility of medium access conflicts between more mobile nodes getting disconnected in the same vicinity, while discussing FRM.

7) Mob-MAC: is our proposal. We opt for a preamble based MAC approach, since, in our use cases, the mobile node is energy constrained. When a mobile node has data to send, it broadcasts a preamble as a strobe control frame, containing a *ReqHop*, a flag, and a *type* field. The *ReqHop* field is set to a default anycast address (denotes either all or a given receiver), the flag tells the receiver that the packet is from a mobile node, it is urgent, and the type grants frames different priorities. The control frame serves to inform the vicinity that the mobile node is searching a receiver as forwarder of its data. To assure that all neighbors of the mobile sender receives the control frame, it is transmitted the whole preamble period. The mobile nodes have to switch often their next hop node, due to its mobility across the static node infrastructure, link quality fluctuations and disconnections. An efficient handover mechanism allows mobile nodes to establish a communication link with the static infrastructure by switching reactively between different static forwarder nodes. The handover is implemented only in the mobile nodes, as they are known in advance. Both static and mobile nodes are designed using cross-layering, since routing or application layer information (e.g., routing metrics of a path to sink, or latency requirements) is made accessible to the MAC layer. Thus, when a static receiver as potential forwarder acknowledges a control frame, it informs the mobile node about its address and its metrics (the cost on the route to sink through this forwarder). After that, the static node switches off its radio until the next preamble sampling period. The mobile node, by comparing the metrics, selects the best forwarder and starts the burst transmission in the next preamble period. Each potential forwarder wakes up during that period and by receiving one of the packet inside the burst, concludes that was not selected and switch off its radio. During the burst transmission, the mobile node may be disconnected from its current forwarder or the neighborhood can provide info to the mobile node, suggesting it to change the forwarder if there is a most appropriate one. In case of disconnection, the mobile node starts by sending control frames. In case one of the neighbors overhears the i-th data transmission inside an ongoing burst, it informs (similar principle to FAN) the mobile node about its better metrics. In order to activate this mode of operation, the mobile node must wait a given time after the ACK reception (similar to the TA in T-MAC), in order to get the new information and later to switch the forwarder when transmitting the $(i+1)$-th data packet.

The communication initiated by a mobile node is considered having higher priority that the transmission between static nodes and therefore, a mobile node can steal the medium from an ongoing communication between two static nodes, except the case when the data was originated from a mobile node.

First results using the new Mob-MAC indicate performance improvements in our scenarios concerning increased packet delivery rate at sink and lower end-to-end delay with a very small increase in energy consumption.

We have evaluated our protocol by comparing it with implementations of mobile variants of T-MAC and X-MAC in the MiXiM/OMNeT++ Framework Simulator using a random waypoint mobility model. The mobility models specify the mobility pattern used by the mobile nodes. In random waypoint mobility model, the mobile node pauses for a fixed period and then moves from an initial to a final position by randomly choosing the speed and direction within a given time or distance. When the given time elapses or the distance has been reached, the node pauses again, adopts a new direction and speed and moves to another location. Furthermore, the model where the mobile node moves to the next destination without pausing is referred to as Random Walk model.

TABLE II. COMPARISON AND EVALUATION OF THE MAC PROTOCOLS.

Protocol	Performance compared with	Mobility model	Evaluation using
ME-ContikiMAC [22]	MoX-MAC[15], MOBINET[31], M-ContikiMAC [20]	Random waypoint	COOJA simulator
MX-MAC [32]	—	—	TinyOS (IMote2 platform)
MT-MAC [24]	MS-MAC[4], T-MAC [25]	Random walk, Random waypoint	Castalia Simulator
MS-SMAC [26]	S-MAC[27], MS-MAC [4], MMAC[5]	—	TOSSIM simulator
MobIQ [30]	MoX-MAC [15], MOBINET[31], ME-ContikiMAC[22]	Random waypoint	ContikiOS (Tmote-Sky platform), COOJA simulator
MobiDisc [28]	MoX-MAC[15], ME-ContikiMAC [22]	Random waypoint	ContikiOS (Tmote-Sky platform), COOJA simulator
Mob-MAC	MT-MAC/RB [33],	Random waypoint	MiXiM / OMNet++ Simulator

Table II presents the simulators/testbeds used for evaluation of all discussed protocols and the mobility models used. The protocols contained in the first column of the table extend and/or improve the corresponding protocols cointained in the second column.

III. CONCLUSIONS AND FUTURE DIRECTIONS

Most of the proposed MAC protocols for MWSNs extend the existing protocols designed for static nodes and therefore inherit their drawbacks. The concerns regarding the design of mobility-aware MAC protocols presented in this paper need to be addressed while designing new mobility-aware MAC protocols for WSNs. Based on our findings, we present few prospective future directions for MAC protocol design in MWSNs.

- *Reduction of the overhead on energy-constrained mobile nodes:* Most MAC protocols designed for MWSNs assume that mobile nodes are not energy constrained, which is not the case in some practical scenarios such as in wildlife or person monitoring. When designing scenarios with energy constrained mobile nodes, the aspect of overhead on mobile nodes needs to be taken into consideration.

- *Enabling reliable bursty transmission in MWSNs:* Although some solutions have been proposed for burst transmission in MWSNs, the focus is merely on enabling burst transmission rather than providing reliability. In emergency situations, such as fire monitoring or healthcare reliable burst transmission is required because providing insufficient information may cost human lives. Thusm solutions providing reliable burst transmission in MWSNs need to be designed.

- *Providing fair media access is a challenging task in dense MWSNs:* The situation becomes much more complex when mobile nodes are present in a WSN which has energy constrained static nodes having critical data. Many previously proposed MAC solutions for WSNs with mobile nodes assume that media access will be granted to mobile nodes as soon as they enter the network. Therefore, it is a design issue that depends on the application if some communication should be prioritized. If vital data need to be reported immediately there must be a mechanism that will allow to differentiate between vital and not urgent data packets.

- *Improvement of overall communication efficiency in complex scenarios:* When a mobile node moves with high speed and it has a large number of packets to send, it may not be possible to send all the packets because of the short time span available for handshaking and burst transmission. Taking energy efficiency, reliability and delay constraints into consideration, efficient schemes (e.g., handovers) to improve overall communication efficiency need to be devised.

- *Using receiver-initiated preamble sampling:* In scenarios where energy constrained mobile nodes are used, receiver-initiated preamble sampling will reduce energy consumption by reducing the communication overhead on mobile sensor nodes.

- *Develop novel scheduling schemes to reduce latency in packet forwarding to the sink:* Mobile nodes moving across dense networks of static sensor nodes suffer from long medium access delays and transient disconnection. The mobile node should be able to access the medium regardless of the level of contention on the medium in order to report its collected data in burst and with minimal delay. The transmissions of the mobile node need to be integrated in the low duty-cycle communication schedule of static nodes. In case of disconnection, a neighbor discovery mechanism is needed to allow mobile nodes to keep continuous connectivity with the static infrastructure. These aspects need to be resolved at the MAC layer (according to information provided by network or application layers).

A real energy benefit is achieved when using strobe preamble sampling MAC protocols with low duty cycles. Considering the scarce energy, communication and processing resources of the mobile nodes, a joint optimization of the MAC, network and application layers by employing a cross-layer design is a promising alternative to maximize the network performance, while reducing the global energy consumption. As future work, we continue with extensive simulations and analyze more thoroughly the performance of Mob-MAC protocol to find further possible optimizations and to validate our design.

REFERENCES

[1] P. Huang, L. Xiao, S. Soltani, M. W. Mutka, and N. Xi, "The evolution of MAC protocols in wireless sensor networks: A survey," IEEE communications surveys & tutorials, vol. 15, no. 1, 2013, pp. 101–120.

[2] A. Bachir, M. Dohler, T. Watteyne, and K. K. Leung, "MAC essentials for wireless sensor networks," IEEE Communications Surveys & Tutorials, vol. 12, no. 2, 2010, pp. 222–248.

[3] Q. Dong et al., "A survey on mobility and mobility-aware MAC protocols in wireless sensor networks," IEEE Communications Surveys and Tutorials, vol. 15, no. 1, 2013, pp. 88–100.

[4] H. Pham and S. Jha, "An adaptive mobility-aware MAC protocol for sensor networks (MS-MAC)," in International Conference on Mobile Ad-hoc and Sensor Systems. IEEE, 2004, pp. 558–560.

[5] M. Ali, T. Suleman, and Z. A. Uzmi, "MMAC: A mobility-adaptive, collision-free mac protocol for wireless sensor networks," in 24th International Performance, Computing, and Communications Conference (IPCCC). IEEE, 2005, pp. 401–407.

[6] A. Jhumka and S. Kulkarni, "On the design of mobility-tolerant TDMA-based media access control (MAC) protocol for mobile sensor networks," in International Conference on Distributed Computing and Internet Technology. Springer, 2007, pp. 42–53.

[7] T. Zhiyong and W. Dargie, "A mobility-aware medium access control protocol for wireless sensor networks," in GLOBECOM Workshops (GC Wkshps). IEEE, 2010, pp. 109–114.

[8] A. Gonga, O. Landsiedel, and M. Johansson, "MobiSense: Power-efficient micro-mobility in wireless sensor networks," in International Conference on Distributed Computing in Sensor Systems and Workshops (DCOSS). IEEE, 2011, pp. 1–8.

[9] M. Nabi, M. Geilen, T. Basten, and M. Blagojevic, "Efficient cluster mobility support for tdma-based mac protocols in wireless sensor networks," ACM Transactions on Sensor Networks (TOSN), vol. 10, no. 4, 2014, p. 65.

[10] R. Silva, J. S. Silva, and F. Boavida, "Mobility in wireless sensor networks–survey and proposal," Computer Communications, vol. 52, 2014, pp. 1–20.

[11] P. Raviraj, H. Sharif, M. Hempel, and S. Ci, "MOBMAC-an energy efficient and low latency MAC for mobile wireless sensor networks," in Proceedings Systems Communications. IEEE, 2005, pp. 370–375.

[12] S.-C. Choi, J.-W. Lee, and Y. Kim, "An adaptive mobility-supporting MAC protocol for mobile sensor networks," in Vehicular Technology Conference.VTC Spring. IEEE, 2008, pp. 168–172.

[13] S. Hameed, E. Shaaban, H. Faheem, and M. Ghoniemy, "Mobility-aware MAC protocol for delay-sensitive wireless sensor networks," in International Conference on Ultra Modern Telecommunications and Workshops (ICUMT). IEEE, 2009, pp. 1–8.

[14] B. M. Khan and F. H. Ali, "Collision free mobility adaptive (cfma) mac for wireless sensor networks," Telecomm. Systems, 2013, pp. 1–16.

[15] P. D. Ba, I. Niang, and B. Gueye, "An optimized and power savings protocol for mobility energy-aware in wireless sensor networks," Telecommunication Systems, vol. 55, no. 2, 2014, pp. 271–280.

[16] B. Liu, K. Yu, L. Zhang, and H. Zhang, "MAC performance and improvement in mobile wireless sensor networks," in Eighth ACIS International Conference on Software Engineering, Artificial Intelligence, Networking, and Parallel/Distributed Computing (SNPD), vol. 3. IEEE, 2007, pp. 109–114.

[17] L. Bernardo et al., "A mac protocol for mobile wireless sensor networks with bursty traffic," in Wireless Communications and Networking Conference (WCNC). IEEE, 2010, pp. 1–6.

[18] R. Kuntz, J. Montavont, and T. Noël, "Improving the medium access in highly mobile wireless sensor networks," Telecommunication Systems, 2013, pp. 1–22.

[19] R. Kuntz and T. Noël, "Machiavel: Accessing the medium in mobile and dense WSN," in 20th International Symposium on Personal, Indoor and Mobile Radio Communications. IEEE, 2009, pp. 1088–1092.

[20] G. Papadopoulos et al., "Enhancing ContikiMAC for bursty traffic in mobile sensor networks," in SENSORS. IEEE, 2014, pp. 257–260.

[21] A. Dunkels, "The contikimac radio duty cycling protocol," Swedish Institute of Computer Science, 2011.

[22] G. Z. Papadopoulos et al., "Wireless medium access control under mobility and bursty traffic assumptions in WSNs," Mobile Networks and Applications, vol. 20, no. 5, 2015, pp. 649–660.

[23] M. Buettner, G. V. Yee, E. Anderson, and R. Han, "X-mac: A short preamble mac protocol for duty-cycled wireless sensor networks," in Proceedings of the 4th International Conference on Embedded Networked Sensor Systems, ser. SenSys '06. New York, NY, USA: ACM, 2006, pp. 307–320.

[24] M. Zareei, A. M. Islam, A. Zeb, S. Baharun, and S. Komaki, "Mobility-aware timeout medium access control protocol for wireless sensor networks," AEU-International Journal of Electronics and Communications, vol. 68, no. 10, 2014, pp. 1000–1006.

[25] T. Van Dam and K. Langendoen, "An adaptive energy-efficient MAC protocol for wireless sensor networks," in Proceedings of the 1st international conference on Embedded networked sensor systems. ACM, 2003, pp. 171–180.

[26] F. Peng, "A novel adaptive mobility-aware MAC protocol in wireless sensor networks," Wireless Personal Communications, vol. 81, no. 2, 2015, pp. 489–501.

[27] W. Ye, J. Heidemann, and D. Estrin, "An energy-efficient MAC protocol for wireless sensor networks," in Proceedings Twenty-first annual joint conference of the computer and communications societies INFOCOM, vol. 3. IEEE, 2002, pp. 1567–1576.

[28] G. Z. Papadopoulos, V. Kotsiou, A. Gallais, P. Chatzimisios, and T. Noel, "Low-power neighbor discovery for mobility-aware wireless sensor networks," Ad Hoc Networks, vol. 48, 2016, pp. 66–79.

[29] A. Dunkels, B. Gronvall, and T. Voigt, "Contiki-a lightweight and flexible operating system for tiny networked sensors," in 29th Annual International Conference on Local Computer Networks. IEEE, 2004, pp. 455–462.

[30] G. Z. Papadopoulos et al., "A Mobility-Supporting MAC Scheme for Bursty Traffic in IoT and WSNs," in Global Communications Conference (GLOBECOM). IEEE, 2016, pp. 1–6.

[31] D. Roth, J. Montavont, and T. Noel, "MOBINET: Mobility management across different wireless sensor networks," in Wireless Communications and Networking Conference (WCNC). IEEE, 2011, pp. 351–356.

[32] W. Dargie and J. Wen, "A seamless handover for wsn using lms filter," in 39th Conference on Local Computer Networks (LCN). IEEE, 2014, pp. 442–445.

[33] A. Kacsó and U. Schipper, "Receiver-based routing service for t-mac protocol," in Proc. 4th Int. Conf. on Sensor Technologies and Applications (SENSORCOMM'10). Venice, Italy, July 18-25 2010, pp. 489–494.

A Flexible Wireless Sensor Platform with an Auto Sensor Identification Scheme

Yi-Jie Hsieh, Chih-Chyau Yang, Yi-Jun Liu, Wei-Lin Lai, Chien-Ming Wu, and Chun-Ming Huang
National Chip Implementation Center
National Applied Research Laboratories, Taiwan
Email: yjhsieh@cic.narl.org.tw; ccyang@cic.narl.org.tw; yjliu@cic.narl.org.tw; wllai@cic.narl.org.tw; wucm@cic.narl.org.tw; cmhuang@cic.narl.org.tw

Abstract—**In this paper, a flexible wireless sensor platform with an auto sensor identification scheme is presented. Our presented flexible wireless sensor platform consists of sensor modules, and each sensor module is a part of the sensor system and in charge of one job in the system, such as computation, communication, output or sensing. Users can stack multiple modules together to build a unique sensor system. Since users are able to easily replace one module with others, our platform is highly extendable and reusable. A low-cost sensor identification scheme is proposed in this paper to detect which sensor is mounted on the platform automatically. This scheme utilizes a unique I²C address to identify the sensor type. A low-cost Electrically-Erasable Programmable Read-Only Memory (EEPROM) only needs to be setup in the non-I²C sensing modules. Furthermore, a firmware initialization process is also adopted to achieve the sensor identification mechanism. To demonstrate the proposed platform, we show an ambient temperature detection application in the paper. The results show that the proposed platform is suitable for academic researches and industrial prototype verification.**

Keywords-flexible sensing platform; sensor system.

I. INTRODUCTION

The Internet of Things (IoT) development has progressed rapidly in the past few years. This concept was widely used not only for the industry and research purposes, but also in commercial products in our daily life [1][2]. The idea of IoT is to group "things" together with internet, allow "things" to communicate or interact with each other, and even, to gather their information and utilize it. Numerous IoT devices have used wireless sensors to recognize environments due to the continuously increasing availability of wireless sensors. Besides, wireless sensors are also widely used in many research fields, such as sensor networks and sensor fusion.

There are several ways to build a sensor platform. The first one is to manually compose different sensor units according to requirements. In [3], Spanbauer et al. proposed a sensor cube called MICA. Each MICA node contains multiple sensors inside. Different kinds of MICA nodes can be applied in various applications. To build up these kinds of sensor platforms, users must have enough hardware knowledge and resources. Besides, these self-made sensors are designed for specific purposes, so they have limited extendibility and reusability. The second way is to use existing sensor platforms. However, most ordinary sensor platforms are designed for sensing only one feature, so multiple sensors have to be used for multi-sensing applications. This will increase cost, lose accuracy, and cause synchronization problems. There are also products that divide a sensor node into wireless module and sensor boards, such as MicaZ [4]. For different purposes, users can stack different sensor boards on the wireless module, so the reusability is further increased. However, the architecture usually allows only one sensor board connecting with the wireless module. Although some sensor boards have multiple sensor modules, the flexibility is still confined.

To support various researches and product developments, a broad range of wireless sensors is required. In this paper, we present a flexible wireless sensor platform which enables users to arbitrarily combine different modules with few constraints, so that they can create a unique sensor system according to their requirements. For the purposes of extensibility and reusability, we divide the sensor system into six units: output, sensing, communication, processing, power, and debug unit. Each unit is in charge of one specific function in the system. To build a sensor platform, users can select required sensor modules and stack them one by one, just like building bricks. This feature makes the proposed platform highly flexible and reusable.

Since our presented platform supports a variety of sensor types and sensor interfaces, how to make the sensor system easy to use has become an important task. Normally, every time we stack a different sensing module on the processing module, we have to download the corresponding firmware code to the Micro Control Unit (MCU) in order to drive this module. This work not only increases complexity for application developers, but also brings inconvenience to common users. A sensor identification scheme is therefore inevitable to identify which sensor is mounted on the platform automatically. In [5][6], R. Morello et al. adopted the Transducer Electronic Data Sheet (TEDS) based on IEEE P1451 standard to store sensor information. This method allows microprocessors to access data through a standardized protocol and to realize the sensor self-identification. For the only purpose of the sensor identification, the hardware cost of this method is high since the TEDS memory needs to be setup in each sensing module. K. Mikhaylov et al. [7][8] proposed a sensor identification mechanism by using the Intelligent Modular Periphery Interface (IMPI). The IMPI is implemented as a daisy chain interface based on the Serial Peripheral Interface (SPI) bus. However, the bus routing complexity is high while the number of interconnections becomes large. In this paper, a sensor identification scheme is proposed to identify the sensors on the platform automatically. This scheme utilizes a unique I²C address to identify the sensor type. A low-cost EEPROM only needs to be setup in the non-I²C sensing module. Furthermore, a firmware initialization process is also adopted to enable the sensor identification mechanism.

The rest of this paper is organized as follows. In Section II, we present the idea of flexible sensor platform. Then, the hardware implementation and the proposed sensor identification scheme are described in Section III. Next, we use an example for demonstration in Section IV. Finally, the conclusions are given in Section V.

II. FLEXIBLE SENSOR PLATFORM

Our presented sensor system is divided into six units for the purposes of extensibility and reusability. Each unit is in charge of one function in the system: (1) Power unit which provides power to all other units is the key influence factor of the sensor life time and sensor size. A power unit can be, for example, Li-Po battery, button cell battery, or car charger; (2) Processing unit has to drive other units and execute firmware commands. A processing unit can be a MCU, a Field-Programmable Gate Array (FPGA), or just a controller. (3) Sensing unit is one of the main components in the sensor system to recognize surrounding environments, such as acceleration, color, image and so on. (4) Communication unit is used for communication. It can receive commands, transmit results, and relay messages. Here we focus on only wireless transmission, such as Bluetooth Smart (BLE), ZigBee, or Wi-Fi. (5) Output unit shows computational results and reminds users by screen, sound, or vibration. (6) Debug unit provides debug functions. When a sensor module is stacked on the debug unit, the designer can check signals of each pin and download images from PC.

Each unit has I/O pins to receive commands and transmit data. These pins can be standardized I/O pins such as Inter-Integrated Circuit (I^2C), Serial Peripheral Interface Bus (SPI), Inter-IC Sound (I^2S) and Universal Asynchronous Receiver/Transmitter (UART), or they may be General-Purpose Input/Output (GPIO) pins defined for the specific usage. For communication between different units, we define a universal bus that connects all units together and is implemented by connectors, as shown in Figure 1. The universal bus contains three kinds of pins, standard I/O pins, GPIO pins, and power lines. All signals from the processing unit are physically connected to the universal bus, so the processing unit can control other units through the universal bus. As for the power lines, they deliver electric power from the power unit to others.

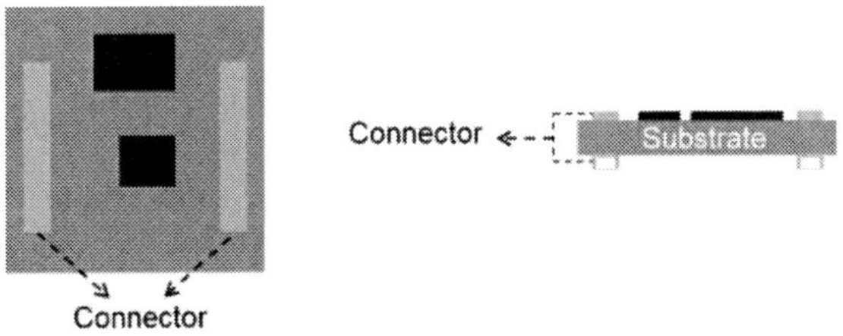

Figure 1 The top schematic view and side schematic view of a sensor module.

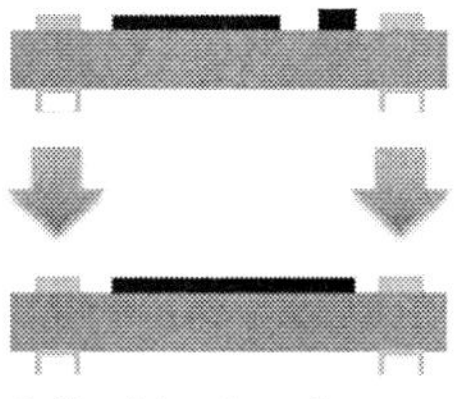

Figure 2 Combination of two modules.

Under the definition of each unit, we further classify a unit into modules. Each unit can have multiple modules. Each module is one of the implementations of the unit. For example, the transceiver unit may have BLE module and Wi-Fi module, the sensing unit may have compass module and thermometer module, and the power unit may have Li-Po battery module and button cell battery module. The reason we classify a sensor platform into units and modules is to increase flexibility. For each unit in a highly flexible platform, users should have more choices to replace one module with others. Figure 1 shows the schematic view of a sensor module in the proposed platform. The green and black areas are PCB substrate and electronic components, respectively. Each module is implemented on an equal-size PCB substrate which has connectors on both front side and back side. Thanks to the universal connector, different modules can be combined concurrently, as illustrated in Figure 2. Here, two connectors are used in order to increase the stability of the architecture. The area between two connectors on the PCB substrate is for placement of electronic components.

III. IMPLEMENTATION

In this section, we introduce the implementation of the presented sensor platform and the proposed auto sensor identification scheme.

A. *Hardware Implementation*

Our presented flexible wireless sensor platform primarily consists of (1) a power module, (2) a processing module, (3) a sensing module, (4) a communication module, (5) an output module, and (6) a debug module. The power module includes a Li-Po battery, a power management unit, a Near-Field-Communication (NFC) control, a wireless charging unit and the coils. In the current implementation, the processing module includes not only an MCU unit but also a 9-axis motion sensor and a BLE unit. The sensing module, communication module, output module or debug module can be integrated in the platform through the I^2C, SPI, UART, I^2S, and analog interfaces. Figure 3 shows the appearance of our power module, processing module, and sensing module. Each module size is 35mm × 35 mm. The processing module is a 32-bit ARM Cortex-M3 processor, supporting I^2S, I^2C, SPI, UART, and analog interfaces. The BLE communicates with the MCU by SPI interface. There are four universal connectors on each module, two on the top side and the other two on the bottom side. As mentioned in the previous section, all peripheral signals and power lines are delivered through these connectors.

Figure 3 The pictures of power module, and processing module and an temperature sensing module.

Figure 4 Packages for attachable and wearable applications.

TABLE I. PACKAGE COLORS AND SENSOR UNITS

Color	Units	Color	Units
Blue	Analog sensing unit	Orange	Processing unit
Green	Digital sensing unit	Red	Power unit
Yellow	Communication unit	Purple	Sensor mount

Another important feature of the proposed sensor platform is the mountable ability. For some applications, such as altitude detection, the sensor has to be tightly mounted on the object. For this purpose, we design packages for sensor boards. Figure 4 shows packaged sensor bricks with different colors. Each sensor unit is given a unique color. The mapping table of sensor units and their corresponding colors are described in Table 1. Besides the five colors mapping to five units, the purple ones are sensor mounts. Currently, there are mounts for bats, wrists, tripods, belts, flat surface, and magnetic surface.

B. Auto Sensor Identification Scheme

In this paper, an auto sensor identification scheme is proposed to detect which sensor is mounted on the platform automatically. The users can therefore launch the corresponding user's application according to the identified sensor type. This scheme utilizes the unique I^{2}C address to identify the sensor type. A low-cost EEPROM only needs to be setup in the non-I^{2}C sensing module. Moreover, a firmware initialization process is also adopted to enable the sensor identification mechanism.

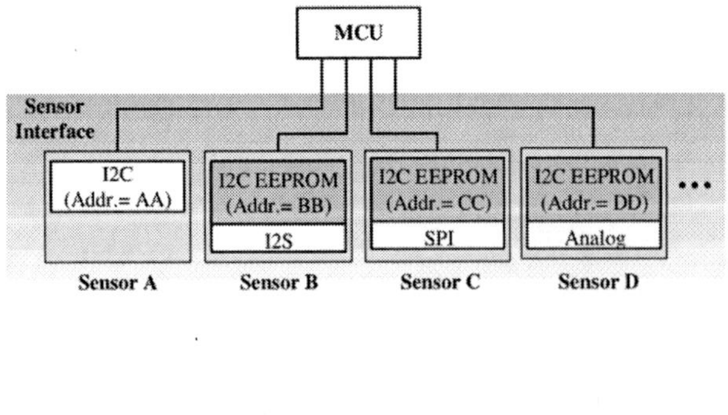

Figure 5 The hardware architecture of the sensor identification scheme.

Currently, the transmission interfaces of the sensor modules to MCU can be analog voltage output, I^{2}C, I^{2}S, UART and SPI, etc. Among these interfaces, the I^{2}C device possesses a unique 7-bit address, which is used to appoint a certain I^{2}C device to perform the operations of data write or read. Normally, the unique I^{2}C device address is configured in advance, so that the address for each I^{2}C sensor device can be different. This characteristic can thus be used to perform the sensor identification. For those non- I^{2}C sensor devices, we can just add an I^{2}C-interfaced EEPROM on the sensing module and use it to perform the sensor identification as the method used in I^{2}C sensors.

Figure 5 shows the hardware architecture of our proposed sensor identification scheme. All the sensor signals are connected directly to the MCU. Each sensor with I^{2}C interface owns its unique I^{2}C address (Addr.), and for the rest of non-I^{2}C sensing modules, we add an I^{2}C EEPROM and configure it with a unique I^{2}C address. Before the MCU starts to read sensor data, it scans the I^{2}C address of the sensor first. Since the I^{2}C address of each sensor is set to be unique, it can be used to identify the sensor type. For example, if the result of I^{2}C address scan is AA, the MCU identifies that the sensor is "Sensor A", and then starts to read the sensor data with the I^{2}C protocol; if the result of I^{2}C address scan is BB, the MCU determines that the sensor is "Sensor B". Since the interface of Sensor B is I^{2}S interface, the MCU starts to read the sensor data with the I^{2}S protocol. The same flow can be applied to the other sensors. With this kind of hardware design, we can identify the sensor type automatically by using the unique I^{2}C address.

To achieve the auto-sensor-identification function in our presented platform, the MCU needs to perform a firmware initial process, as shown in Figure 6. First, we need to turn on the power of the flexible platform. The MCU then starts to perform the hardware initialization setting (*INITIAL_HW*) which initializes required peripheral controllers. After the hardware initialization completes, MCU starts to scan the number of sensors plugged-on and the sensor IDs (*SCAN_SENSOR*). The sensor IDs are defined based on the I^{2}C address of the sensing module. When the scan process completes, MCU begins to initialize those sensors connected on it (*INIT_SENSOR*) and put the initial sensor data in the built-in table. In the following step, MCU reads the Media Access Control (MAC) address of the BLE device and writes it in the Near-field communication (NFC) Tag (*READ_NFC_TAG*). Then, the MCU enters the waiting status, and waits for the BLE connection and communication (*WAIT COMM LINK*).

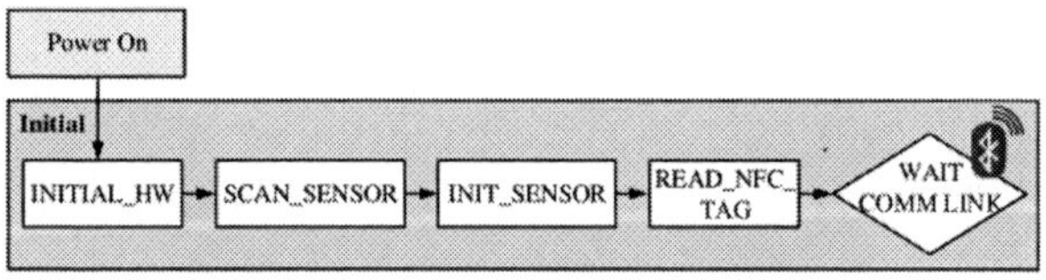

Figure 6 Firmware initialization process.

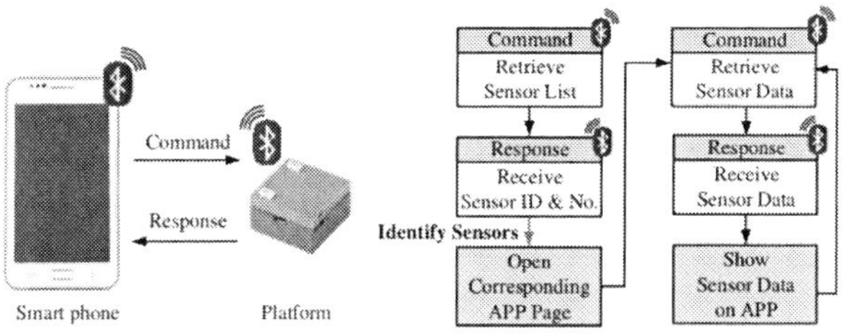

Figure 7 Communication flow path between smart phone and platform.

After the presented flexible platform finishes the firmware initialization process, it is ready to connect the smart phone App with the BLE. For now, there are two ways to establish BLE connection. Firstly, users can open the App in their smart phone and see all available proposed platforms around with different MAC addresses. Afterwards, users manually select the target device to establish the BLE connection. Secondly, users can use the NFC functions of both the smart phone and the platform to set up the connection. Once you move the NFC sensing area of the platform towards that of a smart phone, the smart phone detects the MAC address of the flexible platform through NFC tag thus knows which device to connect with. The BLE connection can thus be established automatically.

In the case of the BLE transmission between the smart phone and the platform, the smart phone acts as a master and the platform acts as a slave. After the BLE connection between the two devices is established, the smart phone starts to send commands, while the platform starts to receive and decode the commands, then responds to the smart phone. Figure 7 shows the handshaking flow for realizing auto-sensor-identification. The smart phone sends a command to be aware what sensors are plugged on the platform (*Retrieve Sensor List*), while the platform decodes the command and responds with the sensor IDs and quantity (*Receive Sensor ID & No.*). In this way, the smart phone can identify what sensors are present on the platform, and open the corresponding App page. The smart phone then sends a command to retrieve the measurement results of the sensors (*Retrieve Sensor Data*). The platform executes the command and transfers the sensor data to the smart phone (*Receive Sensor Data*). Consequently, the smart phone shows the received data on the App. Normally, the smart phone will send the *Retrieve Sensor Data* command continuously to get the latest sensor data.

IV. Applications and Results

For demonstration of the proposed platform, an ambient temperature detection application is given as an example in this section. Users can develop more applications by combining different modules together. In this application, we use an I^2C semiconductor-based temperature sensing module, a processing module, and a power module, as shown in Figure 8.

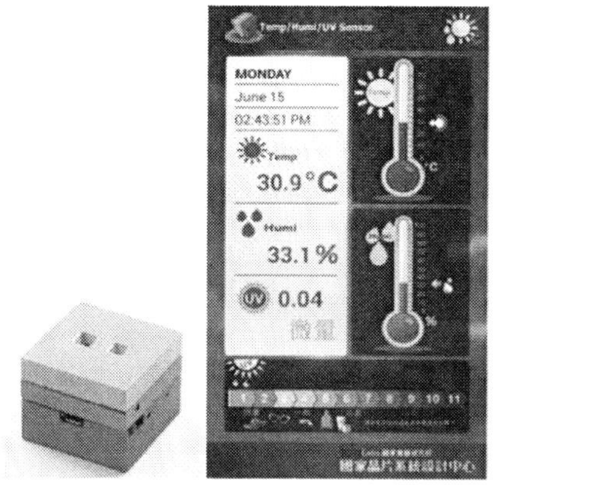

Figure 8 A temperature sensor system and its smart phone App.

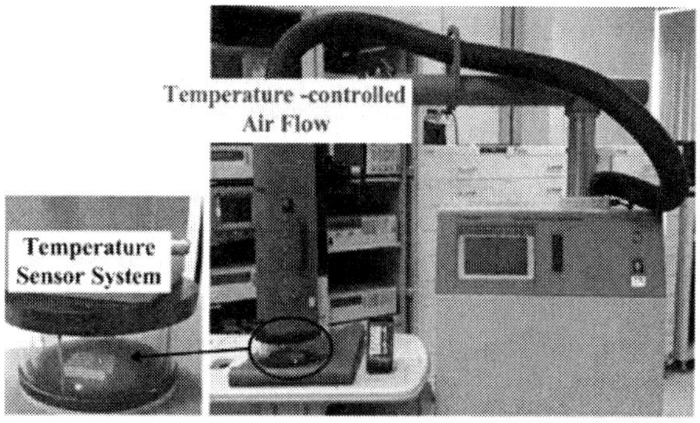

Figure 9 Experimental environment of a temperature sensor system.

The main difficulty of this application is the sensor calibration. Since each temperature sensor in the sensing module has different properties, we have to individually calibrate each sensor module. Figure 9 shows the instrument of temperature forcing chamber [9] used to perform the sensor calibration. The temperature sensor system is first setup in this temperature chamber. The corresponding sensor temperature can be recorded according to each target temperature set in the temperature chamber. In this way, we can therefore obtain the mapping table between temperature values of sensing module and the chamber.

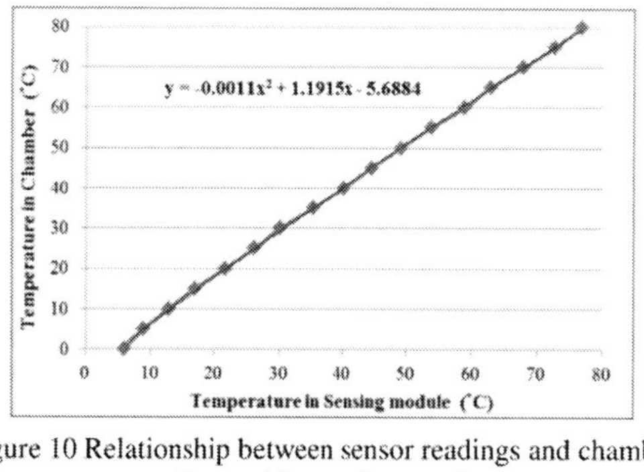

Figure 10 Relationship between sensor readings and chamber readings with transfer equation.

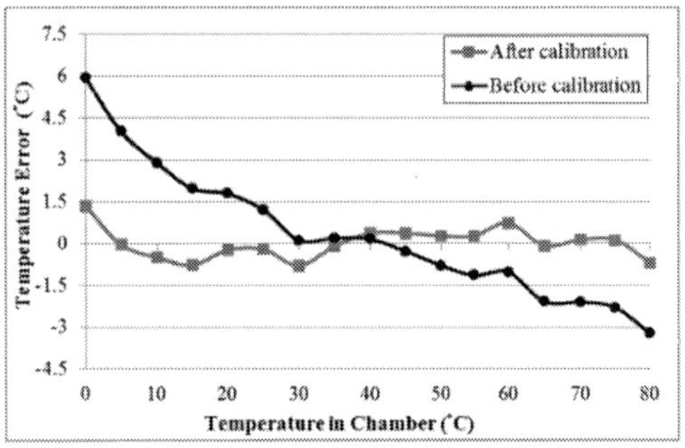

Figure 11 Temperature errors in different target temperature values

The relationship between the temperature in the sensing unit and the temperature in the chamber reading is shown in Figure 10. The vertical axis indicates the target temperature set in the chamber, while the horizontal axis represents the corresponding temperature obtained from the sensing module in our platform. The temperature of each temperature sensor system can be modeled as a function of the temperature obtained in the chamber. The transfer function can be expressed by the following equation, $y = -0.0011x^2 + 1.1915x - 5.6884$, where y indicates the chamber readings (°C), and x represents the sensor readings (°C). The App can thus use the equation to quickly obtain a calibrated and accurate temperature. Figure 11 shows the temperature errors before and after the calibration in different target temperature values. Before the calibration, large errors mostly fall on the low and high ends of the temperature, i.e., 0°C and 80 °C, and the error can be up to 6°C. After the calibration, the temperature error is balanced in different target temperature values and the temperature error can be thus lower than 1.5 °C.

Until now, we have developed several kinds of sensor systems, such as the ultraviolet (UV) sensor system, alcohol sensor system, atmospheric pressure sensor system, carbon monoxide (CO) sensor system, and so on. For each developed sensor system, the sensor calibration is performed and the corresponding transfer function according to the calibration result is embedded in the delivered Apps.

In this section, an ambient temperature detection application is adopted to show this sensor platform with a sensor auto identification scheme can work correctly. The calibration method for this temperature sensor system is also presented. In addition, we also compare 3 kinds of sensor systems in terms of their extensibilities, flexibility, identification methods, and cost. As shown in Table 2, our presented sensor platform owns better extensibility and flexibility benefited from the modular design. Besides, our platform also has lower cost feature while implementing a sensor identification scheme since a low-cost EEPROM only needs to be setup in the non-I^2C sensing modules.

TABLE II. COMPARISONS OF 3 KINDS OF SENSOR SYSTEMS

	[4]	[5]	This Work
Extensibility	Fair	Fair	Good
Flexibility	Fair	Fair	Good
Identification Method	N/A	TED	EEPROM
Cost	Low	Fair	Low

V. CONCLUSION AND FUTURE WORK

In this paper, we present a novel architecture of flexible sensor platform. The most significant features of the proposed architectures are high flexibility and reusability. By stacking different modules together, users can create their own sensor system. In addition, a low-cost sensor identification scheme is also proposed to detect which sensor is mounted on the platform automatically. A temperature sensor system is demonstrated to show that our presented platform works correctly. The comparisons of 3 kinds of sensor systems are also given in this paper regarding cost, extensibility and flexibility. Currently, this platform has been licensed to an industrial company and has become a commercial product. Users' feedback shows that the platform is very useful especially for the purposes of academic researches and industrial prototype verification. In the future, we will focus on providing more modules per users' requirement.

REFERENCES

[1] C. Savaglio, G. Fortino, and Mengchu Zhou, "Towards interoperable, cognitive and autonomic IoT systems: An agent-based approach," in *Proc. IEEE Conf. World Forum on Internet of Things (WF-IoT)*, pp. 58-63, Dec. 2016.

[2] N. Matthys, et al., "μPnP-Mesh: The plug-and-play mesh network for the Internet of Things," in *Proc. IEEE Conf. World Forum on Internet of Things (WF-IoT)*, pp. 311-315, Dec. 2015.

[3] A. Spanbauer, A. Wehab, B. Hemond, I. Hunter, and L. Jones, "Measurement, instrumentation, control and analysis (MICA): A modular system of wireless sensor," in *IEEE International Conference on Body Sensor Networks*, pp. 1-5, 2013.

[4] Y.-M. Yusof, A.-M Islam, and S. Baharum, "An experimental study of WSN transmission power optimisation using MICAz motes," in *IEEE International Conference on Advances in Electrical Engineering*, pp. 182-185, 2015.

[5] R. Morello, "Use of TEDS to Improve Performances of Smart Biomedical Sensors and Instrumentation," *Sensors Journal IEEE*, vol. 15, pp. 2497-2504, 2015

[6] A. Fatecha, J. Guevara, and E. Vargas, "Reconfigurable architecture for smart sensor node based on IEEE 1451 standard," *IEEE Sensors*, pp. 1-4, 2013.

[7] K. Mikhaylov and M. Huttunen, "Modular wireless sensor and Actuator Network Nodes with Plug-and-Play module connection," *IEEE Sensors*, pp. 1-4, Nov. 2014.

[8] K. Mikhaylov and A. Paatelma, "Enabling modular plug&play wireless sensor and actuator network nodes: Software architecture," *IEEE Sensors*, pp. 1-4, 2015.

[9] The temperatue forcing system: Thermonics T-2500SE datasheet.Availabe:https://www.atecorp.com/ATECorp/media/pdfs/data-sheets/Thermonics-T-2500SE_Datasheet.pdf

SAFESENS – Smart Sensors for Fire Safety

First Responders Occupancy, Activity and Vital Signs Monitoring

Brendan O'Flynn, Michael Walsh,
Tyndall National Institute
University College Cork,
Cork, Ireland
email: brendan.oflynn@tyndall.ie
michael.walsh@tyndall.ie

Eduardo M. Pereira, Piyush Agrawal
UTRC: United Technologies Research Center
4th Floor, Penrose Wharf Business Centre
Penrose Quay, Cork, Ireland
email: pereirem@utrc.utc.com
AgrawaP@utrc.utc.com

Tino Fuchs
Robert Bosch GmbH
Renningen, 70465 Stuttgart, Germany
email: Tino.Fuchs2@de.bosch.com

Jos Oudenhoven
Holst Centre-imec
High Tech Campus 31
Eindhoven, The Netherlands
email: jos.oudenhoven@imec-nl.nl

Axel Nackaerts
NXP Semiconductors Belgium
Interleuvenlaan 80
Leuven, Belgium
email: axel.nackaerts@nxp.com

Tanja Braun, Klaus-Dieter Lang
Technical University Berlin
Gustav-Meyer-Allee 25
Berlin, Germany
email: tanja.braun@tu-berlin.de
klausdieter.lang@izm.fraunhofer.de

Christian Dils
Fraunhofer IZM
Gustav-Meyer-Allee 25
Berlin, Germany
email:
christian.dils@izm.fraunhofer.de

Abstract - **This paper describes the development and implementation of the SAFESENS (Sensor technologies for enhanced safety and security of buildings and its occupants) location tracking and first responder monitoring demonstrator. An international research collaboration has developed a state-of-the-art wireless indoor location tracking systems for first responders focused initially on fire fighter monitoring. Integrating multiple gas sensors and presence detection technologies into building safety sensors and personal monitors has resulted in more accurate and reliable fire and occupancy detection information which is invaluable to firefighters in carrying out their duties in hostile environments. This demonstration system is capable of tracking occupancy levels in an indoor environment, as well as the specific location of fire fighters within those buildings, using a multi-sensor hybrid tracking system. This ultra-wideband indoor tracking system is one of the first of its kind to provide indoor localisation capability to sub meter accuracies with combined Bluetooth low energy capability for low power communications and additional inertial, temperature and pressure sensors. This facilitates increased precision in accuracy detection through data fusion, as well as the capability to communicate directly with smartphones and the cloud, without the need for additional gateway support. Glove based, wearable technology has been developed to monitor the vital signs of the first responder and provide this data in real time. The helmet mounted, wearable technology will also incorporate novel electrochemical sensors which have been developed to be able to monitor the presence of dangerous gasses in the vicinity of the firefighter and again to provide this information in real time to the fire fighter controller. A SAFESENS demonstrator is currently deployed in Tyndall and is providing real time occupancy levels of the different areas in the building as well as the capability to track the location of the first responders, their health and the presence of explosive gasses in their vicinity.**

Keywords - Gas Sensors; Body Area Networks; Activity Tracking; Vital Signs Monitoring; Occupancy Detection.

I. INTRODUCTION

The SAFESENS indoor first responder localisation and activity monitoring system [1] is designed based on latest available gas and activity tracking sensor technologies. It incorporates several solutions to an emergency situation including people counting for an efficient rescue operation and first responder location finding. To meet the most demanding application needs, we have designed a sensor board along with the wireless network infrastructure which is capable of delivering the next generation of safety devices. The aim of this document is to describe the indoor localisation platform of the SAFESENS project, the interconnection of the different parts of the system (SAFESENS boards, AXIS Cameras, Raspberry Pi and Server) and location calculation part of the server software. The objectives of the Tyndall National Institute (TNI) in this project, is to develop a wearable [2] indoor localization and activity monitoring system for first responders during emergency situations. In parallel, novel explosive gas sensor technologies and physiological health monitoring systems are being integrated into the fire fighters apparel to monitor their health and well-being as they are tracked through the system as presented in Figure 1.

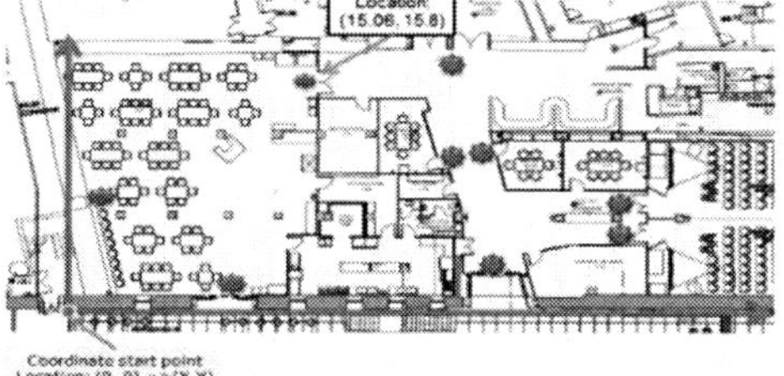

Figure 1. Deployment Area – Tyndall National Institute UCC.

This paper describes the development and validation of the SAFESENS system technologies. Section II describes the chosen architecture of the overall system. Section III describes the localization and activity tracking system development. Section IV describes the Vital signs monitoring technologies used to monitor the first responders health status. Section V describes the development of the explosive gas sensor. Section VI describes the Occupancy sensing developed in the project and the validation results are described in Section VII. Finally, conclusions and summary are contained in Section VIII

II. SYSTEM ARCHITECTURE

There are 8 separate system building blocks comprising the SAFESENS system: the server, mobile gateway (fire fighter's smartphone), Ultra Wide Band (UWB) localisation [3] Access Points, Raspberry Pi, Occupancy detection camera, Fire fighter tracking Node, the Physiological monitoring system and the explosive gas detector. With the implemented sensor platform, we are able to collect real time, real world data for research and analysis. The system architecture is shown in Figure 2.

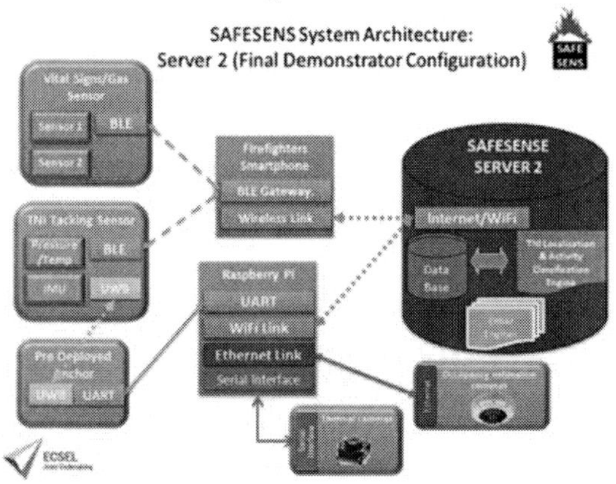

Figure 2. SAFESENS Demonstrator System Architecture.

The Smartphone carried by the firefighter acts as the integration system harvesting the sensory data sets from the firefighters apparel and sending it to the server for processing, running python based analytic/localisation engines and to facilitate visualisation of the data streams.

III. LOCATION AND ACTIVITY TRACKING

A. Introduction to First Responder Activity Monitoring

A significant number of firefighters are injured every year in the line of duty [4]. Tracking firefighters while deployed in dangerous environments is critical to mitigate risk to the personnel. In large buildings, there is often a requirement to enter and deal with fires from multiple directions in order to prevent the fire from spreading. Line of sight is often obscured with smoke and debris [5] and there is also the possibility that parts of the structure may be unstable and subject to collapse. Information relating to the position and activity status of the firefighter is therefore critical in helping the subject to navigate the environment and to enable safe extraction in the Non Line of Sight (NLOS) case [6]. This information is also valuable in search and rescue situations, to enable more optimal and efficient use of personnel on the ground.

B. SAFESENS Localisation Technologies

The SAFESENS project has developed a Personnel Safety Monitor, the purpose of which is to become a tool for first responders and their commanders to help with indoor navigation in obscured conditions in a fire situation, and to give an assessment of the safety of the first responder. For *indoor localisation*, a system is required that is independent of the existing building infrastructure, since this infrastructure may become unreliable or damaged in a fire situation. SAFESENS has integrated into the platform a hybrid inertial, positional and navigation module illustrated in Figure 3. The modules' onboard sensors are capable of providing information to enable activity to be classified and position to be determined in deployment scenarios where there is little supporting existing wireless infrastructure in place.

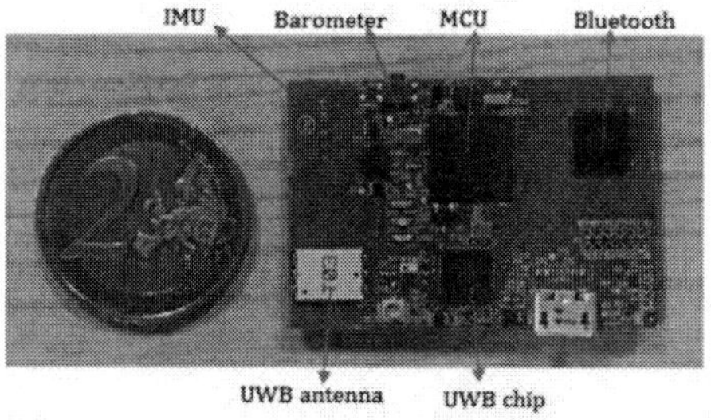

Figure 3. Hybrid Inertial, Positional and Navigation Module

The hybrid inertial, positional and navigation module is designed to be worn by each first responder attached to the straps of their Self-Contained Breathing Apparatus (SCBA). The hardware comprises inertial and magnetic sensors (accelerometer, gyro, and magnetometer), a barometer, a temperature and humidity sensor, an Ultra-Wide Band (UWB) ranging transceiver and a Bluetooth Low-Energy (BLE) transceiver. The module communicates sensor data to a smartphone carried by the firefighter employing BLE which in turn transmits data to a central server for processing. Ranging data is given by the UWB transceiver which measures the range between the worn module and the nearby anchors to track the firefighter [7]. Anchors can be stationary units deployed as part of the exercise or alternatively, other modules worn by accompanying firefighters. The firefighter's position and current activity is calculated on the central server as illustrated in the system architecture diagram in Figure 2.

IV. VITAL SIGNS MONITORING

A. SAFESENS Vital Signs Monitoring

The integration of vital physiological measurements could help commanders to better predict the firefighter's or other first responder's health condition while performing critical tasks or in harsh environments. An important vital parameter is the heart rate which can be calculated and monitored from either Electrocardiography (ECG) or Photo Plethysmography (PPG) signals. Fabric-based, dry electrodes have been intensively investigated for wearable ECG measurements but still need complex algorithms to eliminate motion [8]. In the SAFESENS project, we are focusing on reflective PPG measurements based on optical sensors which are more precise in mobile conditions when the sensor is attached to the skin in an appropriate way [9]. The skin volume changes due to blood pressure variations and thus correlates to the heart rate. An algorithm first removes the impact of ambient light leakage and motion artefacts, and determines the pulse period. By measuring the PPG at multiple wavelengths, it is possible to detect changes in blood composition. For instance, the change from hæmoglobin (Hb) to oxygenated hæmoglobin (HbO_2) can be detected by a relative change in red and infrared absorption [10].

B. *Integrating electronics into a firefighter glove*

The SAFESENS firefighter glove demonstrator consists of a selected multi-chip package featuring 3 emitters (green, red, infrared) and one detector in a small package (4.7mm x 2.5mm x 0.9mm) enabling the measurement of the heart rate and pulse oximetry. The chip is integrated into an EN 659:2003 + A1:2008 certified, professional leather glove for the fire brigade and features the highest industrial cut resistance and fire blocking levels. The sensor position is designed to be placed in an unobtrusive body area: the base of the left hands' index finger (assuming right-handed fireman) allowing the user to touch objects without feeling the electronics. In order to contact the sensor and skin, a small hole was pierced into the glove. The controller unit is placed in a little pocket at the edge of the cuff at a distance of 250mm to the sensor.

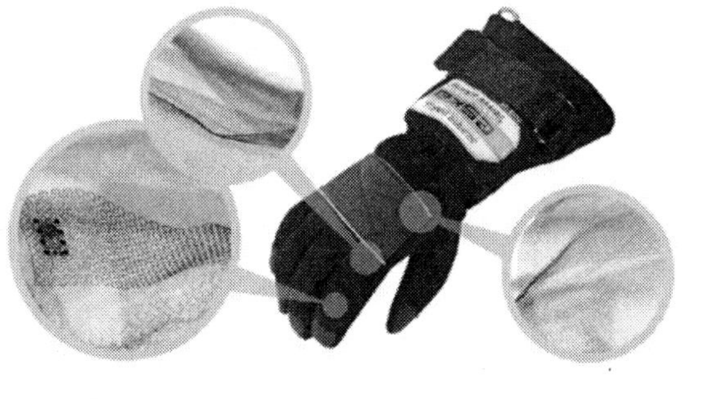

Figure 4. SAFESENS Firefighter Glove Demonstrator: X-ray images of the Textile-integrated Stretchable Electronic System

A soft and expandable circuit board was developed to integrate the components into the glove. The Stretchable Circuit Board (SCB) consists of thermoplastic elastomers and copper conductor tracks in a meandering shape as 2-D spring elements. Thus, the SCB withstands bending and stretching making it a suitable technology for the integration of electronics into textiles. The components were assembled on the SCB by low-temperature soldering (SnBi) and under filled with an epoxy material for improved reliability against mechanical stress. The system was applied to a fire retardant nonwoven and finally laminated onto the inner textile layer of the glove [11][12][13], as shown in Figure 4.

C. *Signal acquisition and processing*

The sensor front-end is a single integrated circuit containing all necessary analog circuits to drive the LEDs and to determine the photocurrent from the photodiode, and a full-featured ARM M0+ microcontroller core to run the algorithms for the heart rate and the blood oxygenation calculations. A second IC contains the wireless transceiver to connect the sensor to a Personal Area Network. In the demonstrator, the sensor communicates over a Bluetooth Low Energy link, with a protocol fully compatible with the indoor localization module. The PPG sensor can either transmit continuous measurements or act on user-selectable alarm thresholds.

V. FLAMMABLE GAS SENSING

A. *Introduction to Flammable Gas detection*

In the process of a burning building, a flashover is a much feared stage. A flashover occurs at the moment when temperatures are so high that present flammable materials and gasses will spontaneously combust. Flammable gasses pose a particular risk during flashovers. Before a flashover, the high temperature results in partial decomposition and release of flammable gasses. When sufficient oxygen is present, or is introduced due to opening or breaking of doors and windows, spontaneous combustion will occur that will accelerate the propagation of fire and pose a severe safety threat to the fire fighters. To be aware of the flashover risks, it is advantageous to be able to detect the presence of flammable gasses.

B. *SAFESENS technology developed for gas detection*

In the SAFESENS project, it is envisioned that the first responders bring gas sensors to the scene that are integrated in their current equipment. The helmet was chosen as the most suitable location for the gas sensor, since it is a rigid structure that is in close contact with the surrounding atmosphere.

Hydrogen may be detected using a Pd-Ni alloy as a thin film deposited onto a silicon wafer substrate, which changes its electrical resistance in the presence of H_2, which can be electrically transduced.

Methane may be detected using an amperometric electrochemical sensor. In this type of electrochemical sensor, a chemical reaction takes place that involves electron transfer in the chemical reaction pathway. By leading these electrons through an external circuit an accurate current measurement can be performed, that is directly related to the amount of gas that is reacting. The amount of reacting gas is in its turn linearly related to the amount of gas in the surrounding atmosphere. In the SAFESENS project, a thin film methane sensor was developed, that uses an ionic liquid as the electrolyte. Previously, it was reported that such sensors can detect ethylene [14], and ammonia [15].

The hydrogen sensor is based on an alloy system described in [16]. Instead of using a van der Paw structure, a Wheatstone half-bridge was realized, which gives first order temperature compensation. The Pd-Ni film was deposited using a co-sputter process from pure Pd and Ni sputter targets. Film thickness was in the range of 100nm.

The methane sensor is based on the ammonia sensor that was previously described in [15]. In brief, a system of interdigitated platinum micro electrodes is made on a silicon substrate. The third electrode is a gold electrode that meanders between these interdigitated electrode, and serves as a pseudo reference electrode. On top of these electrodes, a thin film of an ionic liquid is deposited, to obtain an electrochemical cell sensitive to methane. The chosen ionic liquid is $[C_4mpy][NTf_2]$, as this system results in an electrochemical cell that is sensitive to methane [17].

VI. Occupancy Monitoring

A. *Introduction to Occupancy Monitoring Systems*

Occupancy estimation uses the readings from a sensor network to extract more contextual information of the building usage. It can enable the idea of smart building in different ways by: i) improving the comfort of the occupants by controlling lights, temperature, and humidity based on occupancy; ii) reducing energy costs by controlling lights and Heating, ventilation, and air conditioning (HVAC) equipment based on occupancy; iii) improving the convenience; iv) providing real-time occupancy in fire events. It can also offer technical advantages in a two-fold way: i) cost-benefit trade-off analysis for the selection of sensors and their placement; ii) complementary sensor measurements based on models of building usage.

B. *SAFESENS Technologies for Occupancy Detection*

The challenge of real-time occupancy estimation is to determine the number of people in different areas of a building over time. Under such operational settings, an estimation variance, along with a confidence level, should be provided within a short delay and fast update rate.

Due to the high deployment cost and large errors that people counting sensors suffer from, measuring occupancy throughout a building from sensors alone is not sufficiently accurate. Indeed, data collection from sensors is not perfect, and it is assumed that each sensor is subject to noise and environment clutter. Also, if sparsely deployed, the ability of sensors to detect occupancy change is limited by their coverage. In this way, occupancy estimation largely depends on the existing sensor technologies.

Occupancy estimation aims to adaptively correct noise and lack of observability errors by subdividing the approach into two sub-problems [18]:

i) *modelling*, investigates how to build a model to utilize prior knowledge and to simulate the occupants' movement behaviors in the building;

ii) *estimation*, defined as the process to obtain the hidden state of a system given a model and incomplete observational data.

In SAFESENS, the modelling follows the spatial topology of the floor, as in [19], where each graph node is considered a state. It can assume either an *occupancy state*, related to any zone of the building, or a *flow state*, which reflects the uncertainty in how people move from zone to zone. This modelling permits to divide the building into non-overlapping zones, defined by a hierarchy of different spatial scales, namely floor-level, zone-level and room-level.

For the estimation, a Kalman filter (KF) framework is adopted. Due to the non-linearity of the underlying data (pedestrian behavior) and the adopted linear modelling approach, we study the performance of linear and non-linear kalman estimators, such as Ensemble KF (EnKF), bank-of-filters-based (IMM, MMAE), among others.

VII. Results

A. *Data Visualisation on the Smart App*

To validate our system, and to do more real life experiments, we have installed a demo of the SAFESENS localisation platform at Tyndall near the canteen area. Under heavy NLOS and with limited available anchor nodes, the system can achieve 0.5m accuracy. Figure 5 shows the visualization front end for the SAFESENS system.

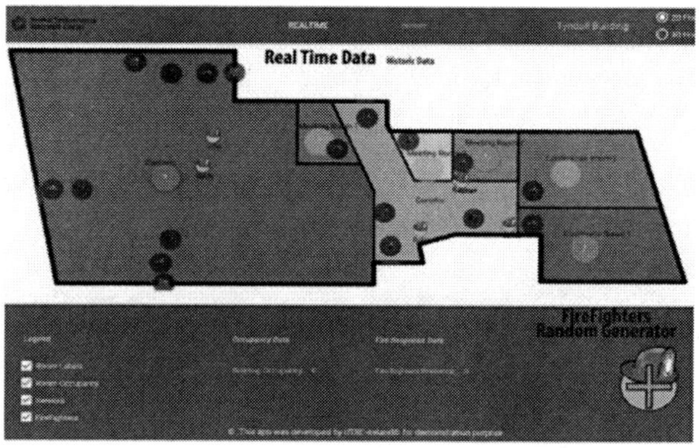

Figure 5. Occupancy and Firefighter Data Visualisation.

B. *Location Tracking and Activity Monitoring*

The positioning and tracking performance of the module has been evaluated. An additional calibration step was added to account for antenna delay and to improve ranging performance. The experiments comprise of an evaluation of the mobile performance employing a Least Square Estimation (LSE) algorithm. Results before and after calibration are illustrated in Figures 6 and 7, respectively. For each experiment, a reference path (shown in the figures below in blue) was determined for the mobile subject and communicated via markers on the floor. The tag was instrumented on the arm of the subject, who subsequently simulated the emergency responder walking along the reference path. The green path illustrates the calculated trajectory of the subject employing the module. The results indicate that the tolerances are acceptable for the prescribed application. Results for the activity classification machine learning algorithms are presented in [20].

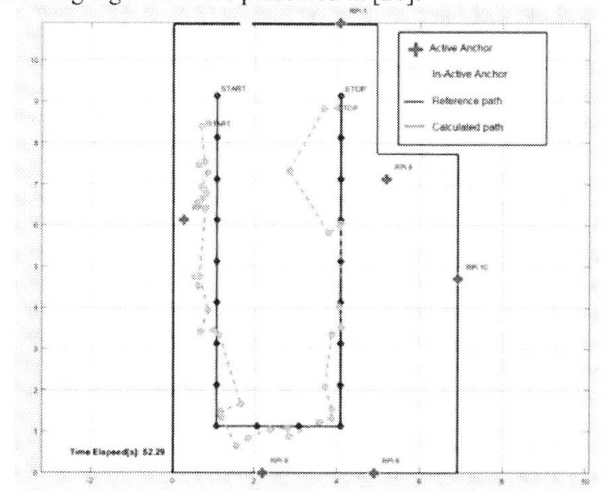

Figure 6. SAFESENS hybrid inertial, positional and navigation module mobile tracking performance prior to calibration

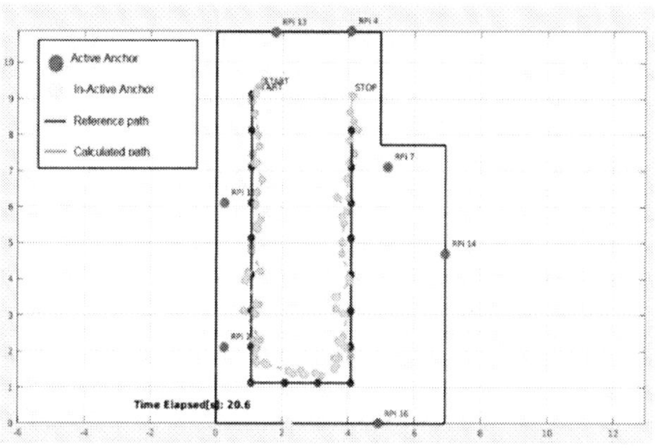

Figure 7. SAFESENS hybrid inertial, positional and navigation module mobile tracking performance following calibration

1) Vital Signs

The vital signs monitor is implemented as a finger ring embedded in the firefighter glove. It can operate in two different modes: high-resolution heart-rate, or combined heart-rate and blood oxygenation. The heart rate does not require multiple wavelengths, and thus a more optimal LED firing pattern can be selected to either lower the total power consumption or increase the sampling rate.

Estimation of the blood oxygenation requires alternate firing of red and infra-red (IR) Light Emitting Diodes (LEDs), and a more complex algorithm. An example of the captured data is shown in Figure 8.

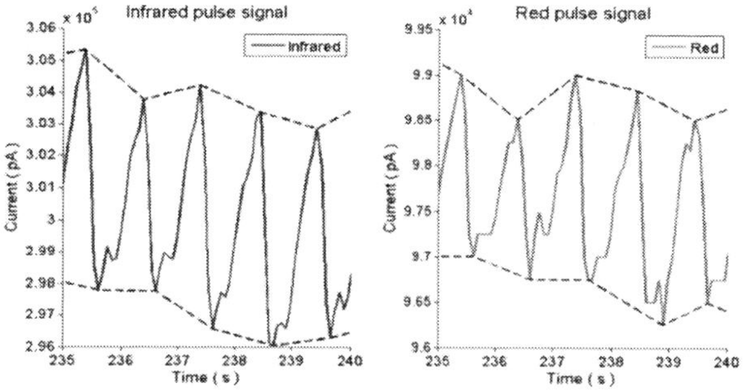

Figure 8. Captured infrared and red PPG signals.

The PEFAC algorithm [21] was selected for the heart rate detection. This method estimates the heart rate from the frequency spectrum. By expressing the frequency in the log-domain, the distance between the fundamental frequency and its harmonics doesn't depend on the absolute value of the fundamental frequency. By convolving the spectrum with a matched filter, the spectra of the harmonics are accumulated and noise is rejected. The oxygen saturation (SpO_2) is then derived from the ratio of ratios R, which is defined by equation 1:

$$R = \frac{(AC/DC)_1}{(AC/DC)_2} \quad (1)$$

Where AC and DC are the peak-to-peak amplitude and the baseline of the PPG pulse, respectively. These values are found by applying a min/max envelope tracker on the cleaned PPG signal. The following relationship between the ratio R and the SpO_2 is then used as in equation 2:

$$SpO_2 = \frac{\varepsilon_{d1} - R(l_2/l_1)\varepsilon_{d2}}{R\left(\frac{l_2}{l_1}\right)(\varepsilon_{o2} - \varepsilon_{d2}) + (\varepsilon_{d1} - \varepsilon_{o1})} \quad (2)$$

Where ε_o and ε_d are the extinction coefficients for HbO_2 and Hb. The constants l_1 and l_2 are the path-lengths for the two wavelengths and depend strongly on the scattering coefficient. For the two wavelengths, in the red and infrared regions which are used in the glove ring sensor (IR 950nm and red 660nm), l_1 and l_2 are expected to differ and they are unknown. SpO_2 can be derived from R through the calibration process by assuming that l_2/l_1 is a constant that is independent of inter-subject variability in the circulatory system. In this case, the coefficients are constants and can be determined through calibration. If the parameter l_2/l_1 changes between different subjects, in particular between the healthy subjects on whose fingers the calibration was performed and the fireman wearing the glove, inaccuracy in the SpO_2 measurement is to be expected. Relative changes for a single subject are accurate.

C. Flammable Gas Sensing

The hydrogen sensor was evaluated using humidified synthetic air with different amounts of H_2 added, in the range from 0.02% to 2% volume concentration. The gas was fed to the sensor with a nozzle with a flow of 1slm (standard liter per minute). The sensor chip was externally heated to temperatures of up to 140°C. It was found that 0.02% concentration already results in a detectable sensor signal. For concentrations above 0.5%, saturation of the signal began to be observed. Response time t_{90} was found to be in the range of 100s. Further reduction of response time is to be achieved by using Pulsed Laser Deposition (PLD) in order to generate a porous Pd-Ni layer, facilitating the H_2 transport into the layer.

The methane sensor was evaluated in a gas mixing chamber, where gas flows of methane were mixed with compressed dry air. Initial experiments consisted of cyclic voltammetry, where the voltage of the sensor is scanned to observe at which voltage the largest effect of methane exposure is observed. In Figure 9, the cyclic voltammogram of the sensor with and without 5% methane exposure is plotted. The difference between the current levels is plotted with the dotted line, and should be evaluated on the right Y-axis. The difference between the observed currents is small compared to the background current. To make the difference more visible, the currents with and without methane exposure were subtracted, and plotted. From these plots, it becomes clear that the largest current difference is observed between -0.5 and -1.5 V. The extreme voltages near -2 and +2 V are excluded, because water electrolysis will occur at these voltages when measurements are performed in humid air, which will interfere with the detection of methane.

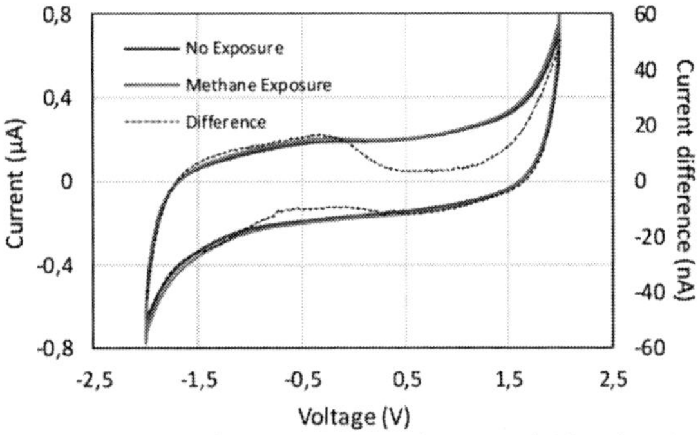

Figure 9. Cyclic voltammetry to determine most suitable voltage level for methane detection.

To determine the response of the sensor, the voltage was fixed, and the current was used as an indicator of the methane exposure. In Figure 10, the current that is resulting of 5% methane is given.

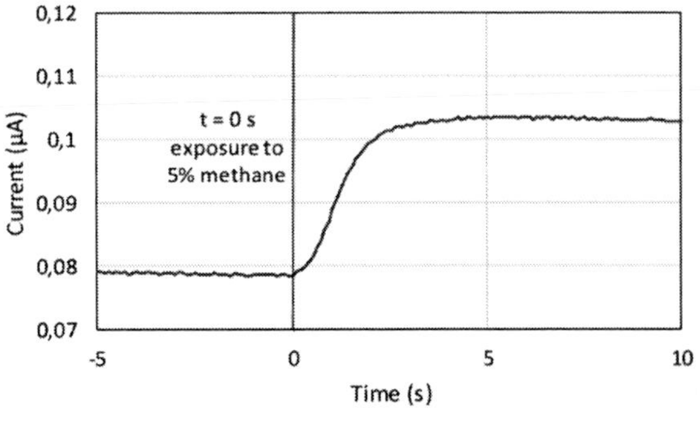

Figure 10. Current response to an exposure of 5% methane

This figure shows that the sensor has a fast response time, and that the gas level can already be detected within a few seconds, which is crucial for first responders.

D. Occupancy Detection

The deployment scenario is very particular since it depends on the physical venue, the sensor network characteristics and the application domain. Therefore, the solutions will perform very differently from scenario to scenario. For these reasons, the conducted experiments consider the combination of three characteristics: i) physical layout; ii) sensor topology; iii) data modelling (e.g., synthetic-random, synthetic- pedestrian; real sensors).

Due to lack of space, we here only present the results for some estimators and for one tested scenario, which consists of 6 rooms, with two different sensor topologies: TA) two camera sensors with oblique view towards ground-floor, situated in two rooms, and a camera sensor with top-down view, positioned between two rooms; TB) camera sensor in each room and the same top-down view camera between two rooms. The data was simulated using the Helbing social force model [22], rules for interactions between occupants and obstacle avoidance awareness. The simulation considers a total occupancy up to 6 people during 9000 samples (approximately lasting 7.5 minutes).

As expected, having a sensor in every zone dramatically improves the overall estimation. Considering all the experiments, we verified that the linear estimators are preferred for local measurements but they show degradation of performance through time, as well as for global estimation. An interesting conclusion is that a bank of linear filters solutions show competitive results, which might open further investigation issues regarding their extension to the combination of linear and non-linear estimators to balance local with global estimation. For more details, please refer to [23].

TABLE I. EVALUATION METRICS FOR EACH ESTIMATOR FOR T = 90000 SAMPLES

Estimator	Topology	MSE	Precision	Recall	F-measure
KF	TA	1.445	99.81	53.85	69.96
	TB	0.665	99.88	68.42	81.21
EnKF	TA	1.734	93.74	51.51	66.49
	TB	1.003	97.42	56.47	71.50
HF	TA	1.553	99.88	49.67	66.61
	TB	1.554	99.88	49.94	66.59
IF	TA	2.826	99.56	49.36	66.01
	TB	1.482	99.60	50.95	67.41
UKF	TA	1.373	99.37	54.76	70.61
	TB	0.657	99.88	68.44	81.22
IMM	TA	1.384	99.86	53.76	69.90
	TB	0.781	97.60	63.81	77.17
MMAE	TA	1.423	99.81	53.92	70.01
	TB	0.664	99.88	68.42	81.22

VIII. Conclusions and Future Work

The SAFESENS system is currently deployed in the Tyndall National Institute in Cork, Ireland where the integration activity focuses on the occupancy detection and firefighter activity tracking. The deployment activity continues to progress so as to integrate datasets from the other sensors integrated in the system, to improve accuracy of the sensor readings and develop robust communications mechanisms to augment the infrastructure based communications currently used in the demonstration activity which is Wi-Fi based. This will focus on UWB based Media Access Control (MAC), routing and scheduling protocols to maximize energy efficiency and minimize system latencies. The smart phone application is currently under development to integrate data sets from all sensors for upload to the data server for analytics and final demonstration.

Acknowledgment

This work is supported by ENIAC-JU-2013-1(621272), via the SAFESENS project (Sensor Technologies for Enhanced Safety and Security of Buildings and its Occupants).

The authors would like to acknowledge the support of National funding agencies including Enterprise Ireland. This publication has emanated from research supported in part by a research grant from Science Foundation Ireland (SFI) and is co-funded under the European Regional Development Fund under Grant Number 13/RC/2077. The authors would also like to thank VDI/VDE Innovation, Technik GmbH and BMBF.

References

[1] S. Tedesco, J. Khodjaev, and B. O'Flynn, "A novel first responders location tracking system: Architecture and functional requirements". Microwave Symposium (MMS), 2015 IEEE 15th Mediterranean, pp. 1-4. IEEE, 2015.

[2] M. Walsh, S. Tedesco, T. Ye, and B. O'Flynn. "A wearable hybrid IEEE 802.15. 4-2011 ultra-wideband/inertial sensor platform for ambulatory tracking, " In Proceedings of the 9th International Conference on Body Area Networks, pp. 352-357. ICST (Institute for Computer Sciences, Social-Informatics and Telecommunications Engineering), 2014.

[3] T. Ye, M. Walsh, P. Haigh, J. Barton, and B. O'Flynn. "Experimental impulse radio IEEE 802.15. 4a UWB based wireless sensor localization technology: Characterization, reliability and ranging" In ISSC 2011, 22nd IET Irish Signals and Systems Conference, Dublin, Ireland. 23-24 Jun 2011.

[4] N. N. Brushlinsky, M. Ahrens, S. V. Sokolov, and P. Wagner, "World Fire Statistics. Technical report 21", Center of Fire Statistics, International Association of Fire and Rescue Services, 2016.

[5] J. Khodjaev, P. Yongwan, and A. S. Malik, "Survey of NLOS identification and error mitigation problems in UWB-based positioning algorithms for dense environments" annals of telecommunications-annales des télécommunications 65, no. 5-6 (2010), pp. 301-311.

[6] J. Khodjaev, S. Tedesco, and B. O'Flynn. "Improved NLOS Error Mitigation Based on LTS Algorithm, " Progress In Electromagnetics Research Letters 58 (2016), pp. 133-139.

[7] J. Khodjaev, A. Narzullaev, Y. Park, W. Jung, J. Lee, and S. Kim. "Performance Improvement of Asynchronous UWB Position Location Algorithm Using Multiple Pulse Transmission, "In Positioning, Navigation and Communication, 2007. WPNC'07. 4th Workshop on, pp. 167-170. IEEE, 2007.

[8] Y. M. Chi, T. P. Jung, and G. Cauwenberghs, "Dry-Contact and Noncontact Biopotential Electrodes: Methodological Review," in IEEE Reviews in Biomedical Engineering, vol. 3, no. ,pp. 106-119, 2010.

[9] S. Sudin et al., "Wearable heart rate monitor using photoplethysmography for motion," 2014 IEEE Conference on Biomedical Engineering and Sciences (IECBES), Kuala Lumpur, 2014, pp. 1015-1018.

[10] D. Damianou, "The Wavelength Dependence of the Photoplethysmogram and its Implication to Pulse Oximetry", PhD Thesis, University of Nottingham, October, 1995

[11] T. Loher et al., "Stretchable electronic systems," 2006 8th Electronics Packaging Technology Conference, Singapore, 2006, pp. 271-276.

[12] M. Seckel, "Umsetzung einer elektronischen Schaltung auf Basis eines dehnbaren Schaltungsträgers" Diploma thesis, University of Applied Sciences, Berlin, 2008.

[13] R. Vieroth, T. Loeher, M. Seckel, C. Dils, C. Kallmayer, A. Ostmann, and H. Reichl. "Stretchable Circuit Board Technology and Application," 2009 International Symposium on Wearable Computers, Linz, 2009, pp. 33-36.

[14] M. A. G. Zevenbergen, D. Wouters, V.-A. T. Dam, S. H. Brongersma, and M. Crego-Calama "Electrochemical Sensing of Ethylene Employing a Thin Ionic-Liquid Layer" Analytical Chemistry 83 (2011), pp. 6300-6307.

[15] J.F.M. Oudenhoven, W. Knoben, and R. van Schaijk, "Electrochemical Detection of Ammonia Using a Thin Ionic Liquid Film as the Electrolyte" Procedia Engineering 120 (2015), pp. 983-986.

[16] R. C. Hughes and W. K. Schubert, Thin films of Pd/Ni alloys for detection of high hydrogen concentrations. 1992. J. Appl. Phys. 71(1), pp. 542-544.

[17] Z. Wang, M. Guo, G. A. Baker, J. R. Stetter, L. Lin, A. J. Mason and X. Zeng, Methane–oxygen electrochemical coupling in an ionic liquid: a robust sensor for simultaneous quantification. Analyst, 139(20), pp. 5140-5147.

[18] H. T. Wang, Q. S. Jia, C. Song, R. Yuan, and X Guan, 2010, December. Estimation of occupancy level in indoor environment based on heterogeneous information fusion. In Decision and Control (CDC), 2010 49th IEEE Conference on (pp. 5086-5091). IEEE.

[19] R. Tomastik, S. Narayanan, A. Banaszuk, and S. Meyn, 2010. Model-based real-time estimation of building occupancy during emergency egress. In Pedestrian and Evacuation Dynamics 2008 (pp. 215-224). Springer Berlin Heidelberg.

[20] S. Scheurer, S. Tedesco, K. N. Brown, and B. O'Flynn "Human Activity Recognition for Emergency First Responders via Body-Worn Inertial Sensors", BSN'17, 14th International Conference on Wearable and Implantable Body Sensor Networks, Eindhoven, The Netherlands, May 9-12, 2017, pp. 5-8.

[21] S. Gonzalez and M. Brookes, "PEFAC-a pitch estimation algorithm robust to high levels of noise" IEEE/ACM Transactions on Audio, Speech, and Language Processing, pp. 518-530, 2014.

[22] D. Helbing, and P. Molnar, 1995. Social force model for pedestrian dynamics. Physical review E, 51(5), pp.4282.

[23] E. M, Pereira, and P Agrawal, 2017, March. Linear vs Non-linear Estimators Comparison for Estimation of Building Occupancy in Normal Pedestrian Behavior. In 56th IEEE Conference on Decision and Control (CDC), 2017 (submitted).

Electrochemical Sensors for the Measurement of Relative Humidity and Their Signal Processing

Ivan Krejci, Michal Hedl
Dept. of Technical Studies
College of Polytechnics Jihlava, VSPJ,
Jihlava, Czech Republic
e-mail: krejci19@vspj.cz hedl@student.vspj.cz

***Abstract*— Highly sensitive and accurate determination of relative humidity of technical gases is required in many branches of human activities (health care, food packing, etc.). In this paper, we introduce a new series of sensors manufactured by BVT Technologies taking advantage of the hygroscopic material conductivity change with the water vapor content. The main topics of the contribution focus on sensor signal processing and electronic equipment architecture and its design.**

Keywords-relative humidity; hygroscopic material; synchronous detection; microcontroller.

I. INTRODUCTION

The amount of water vapor in a gas mixture is at any time less than that required to saturate the gas at a given temperature. The actual-to-saturated water vapor content ratio is called the relative humidity. It is usually expressed in % as

$$RH = (m/M).100, \quad (1)$$

where m is the actual vapor mass in the unit volume of the gas and M is the water vapor mass of the same volume of the saturated gas.

There are several methods to measure the relative humidity. For precise measurements, where high accuracy and resolution are required, the methods taking advantage of the impedance or resistance change of materials that absorb the tested gas humidity are used. These water absorbing materials are called hygroscopic.

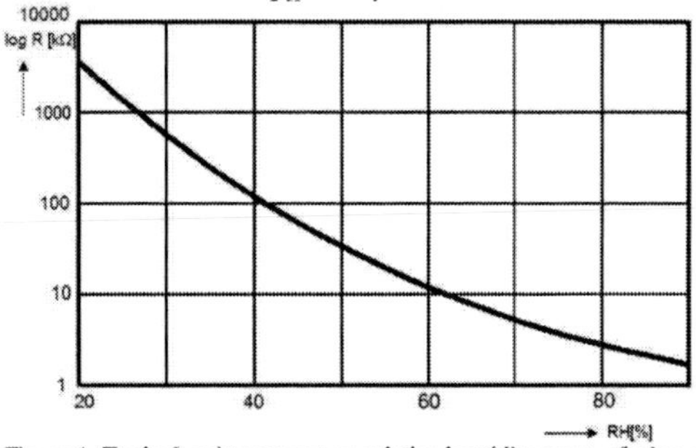

Figure 1. Typical resistance versus relative humidity curve of a hygroscopic material [1].

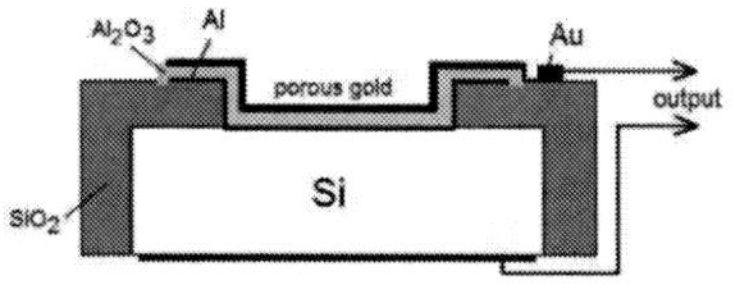

Figure 2. The resistive relative humidity sensor placed on the silicon substrate.

Figure 1 shows a typical plot of the electrical resistance change of a hygroscopic material as a function of increasing relative humidity. As can be seen, the measuring apparatus should be able to measure the resistance within the range of 1 kΩ to 10 MΩ.

This measuring method has been selected because it enables the use of electrochemical sensors that have been specifically developed for this purpose by the local company BVT Technologies (www.bvt.cz) [3]. As BVT Technologies has no electronic development department, VSPJ (Vysoka Skola Polytechnicka Jihlava, www.vspj.cz) was approached to propose an electronic design of the sensor signal processing unit.

II. SENSOR PERFORMANCE

Usually, the sensor taking advantage of the hygroscopic material resistance measurement is placed on a silicon substrate, on which the electrode system composed of the substrate itself and the porous gold electrode is placed. It is capable of directing the measured gas to the active hygroscopic layer. This layer consists of an aluminum base on which the active hygroscopic layer of alumina is applied, as shown in Figure 2 [2].

In our case, a different sensor arrangement has been used. The sensor, provided by the local manufacturer of the electrochemical sensors, BVT Technologies, uses a corundum ceramic base on which the electrode system is applied. The electrodes are made of platinum – gold alloy and are shaped as two combs, inserted into each other (Figure 3) [3]. The electrodes are connected with a sensor connector by silver paths, covered by an insulating protective layer.

The electrodes are covered by a hygroscopic alumina layer. The sensor dimensions are 25.4 x 7.62 mm and the active electrode system takes up a space of 2 x 2 mm.

Figure 3. The BVT Technologies CC1 conductometric sensor.

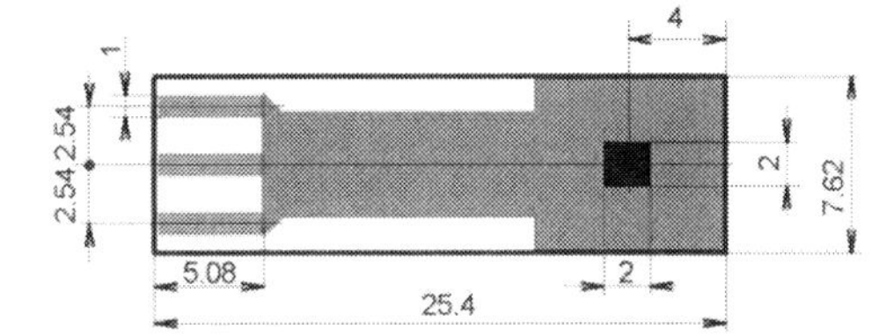

Figure 4. Real electrochemical sensor, including its dimensions.

A more detailed drawing of the sensor is given in Figure 4. It provides information about sensor dimensions and electrode and protective cover arrangements.

The main advantages of the resistive humidity sensors are the short response time 30 – 50 s as declared by the sensor producer [5] and high resolution which can be improved by using signal amplification.

III. Signal Processing Unit

The electronic design and construction of the signal evaluating unit were the main goals of our work. The design rules have been determined by assigned parameters.

A. *Required system parameters*

The essential parameter is the range of measured resistances which is from 100 Ω to 10 MΩ. Further, if the hygroscopic material absorbs water, the polarization of electrodes occurs. To prevent it, the sensor must be supplied by AC (alternating current), the frequency of which is above Warburg frequencies [4], i.e., above 5 kHz. For our purposes, the frequency of the supplying signal was 10 kHz. To achieve both high precision and high resolution of the measured resistance, the use of highly precise analog to digital converters (AD converter) was necessary. The requirement of the resistance measurement over five decades with the precision at least 1%, asks for the use of the 24 bit AD converter (the required resolution is 10^{-5} x 10^{-2}, it is 10^{-7}, the 24 bit AD converter resolution is 5.9 x 10^{-8}). As the effective number of bits is less than the AD converter's resolution, an additional digital filtering has to be done.

As for the mechanical arrangement, minimized electronic unit dimensions have been required, comparable to a common plug-in flash disc unit.

For the resistance measurement, the Ohm's method has been selected [6], based on the measurements of the voltage drop on the sensor, and current flowing in it.

Another problem of the applied method of measurement is the strain capacity of the sensor. To avoid this problem, the synchronous detection must be applied, to separate the real resistance from the imaginary reactance.

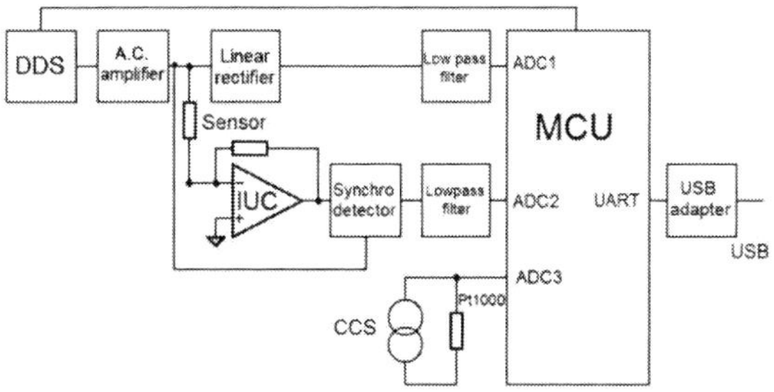

Figure 5. Hygrometer block diagram. DDS – direct digital synthesizer, IUC – current/voltage converter, CCS / constant current source, MCU – microcontroller.

The relative humidity magnitude depends on the temperature. This means, the system must be equipped with a precise thermometer capable of the measuring of the nearest 0.1 °C.

The transport of measured results to a host computer is provided by a USB 2.0 standard interface (Universal Serial Bus).

The equipment is designed so that it will create a small plug - in unit, which can be directly plugged into a computer USB connector (Figure 5).

B. *Electronic design – analog signal processing*

The analog part of the system involves three basic building blocks, the Direct Digital Synthesizer (DDS) with an amplifier of the AC signal supplying the sensor, and two signal traces measuring the voltage drop on the sensor and the current flowing through it. The voltage trace consists of a linear full-wave rectifier and a low pass filter that rejects residual AC signal components.

The current trace arrangement begins with the current to voltage converter (IUC), the output signal of which is detected in the full-wave synchronous detector. The sense of this detection type is to gain the real part of the measured current. After the detection, the output detector signal contains a useful DC (Direct Current) component and a residual AC component, which is filtered out in the low pass filter. The cut-off frequency of the second order low pass filters in both traces is 10 Hz. This frequency ensures sufficient 126 dB rejection of the residual 20 kHz components of the full/wave detected signals. Besides, the filters serve as anti-aliasing filters for AD converters (AD converter sampling frequency is 250 Hz – see the next paragraph).

The resistance thermometer using a platinum Pt1000 sensor is the last analog element of the circuit. The sensor is supplied from a constant current source (CCS).

From the technological point of view, high precision operational amplifiers have been used for the analog signal processing at the operating frequency, and the chopper stabilized amplifiers for the detected signal filtering and for the constant current source for supplying the Pt1000 thermometer.

C. *Digital signal processing*

The digital part of the equipment is controlled by the TI microcontroller unit (MCU) MSP430AFE253, which has small power consumption and contains three independent 24 bit analog to digital converters needed for the system realization. The AD converters of the microcontroller can be synchronized, and thus they offer their results simultanously. As the built-in converters are very fast Σ–Δ converters having a low effective number of bits, it was necessary to correct it using oversampling and additional digital filtering. The conversion results are obtained by an averaging filter taking advantage of the sum of 256 AD converter samples, shifted 8 bits right. The AD converter sampling period is 4 ms, thus the measurement itself takes about 1 s.

The microcontroller also controls the direct digital synthesizer producing the AC signal 10 kHz used for the sensor supplying. Further on, the microcontroller evaluates the measured resistance and calculates the relative humidity taking advantage of the polynomial approximation of the diagram in Figure 1. The calculated data is sent to a host computer via the standard USB link.

D. *Metrological aspects*

The accuracy of the measurement is determined by both the sensor calibration and the signal processing. As the signal processing has been discussed in the previous paragraphs, the calibration of the sensor represents the last obstacle in achieving the required parameters. To get the best results, the Agilent 34410A – the 6.5 digit multimeter - has been used to prepare the resistance standards. The basic measurement procedure measures the sensor conductivity, so that the calibration curve is linear, G =I/V (the conductance G is given by the current I, divided by the voltage V), if the voltage is kept constant. In this case, it is necessary to get two points of the line. These points were determined by the zero and maximum required conductivities of 10.0012 mS (nominal resistance value 100 Ω).

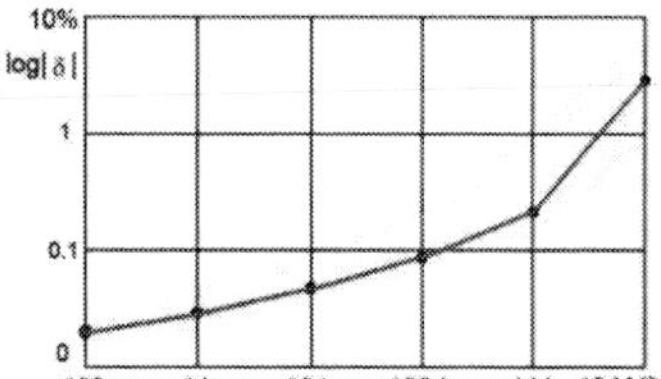

Figure 6. The absolute value of relative error as a function of the measured resistance.

The calibration was checked using the standards, the conventional true values of them were given by the Agilent multimeter measurements, and covered all decades of the required conductivity range (10 mS – 0.1μS). The results of the series of twenty measurements are given in Figure 6. The errors in the graph represent the worst results of the series. The obtained results show the error dramatically increases when high resistances are measured. It is caused by lower value of AD converter data, which is influenced by the digital noise of the AD converter. A possible improvement can be achieved by using an internal programmable gain amplifier built in the AD converter. This adaptation does not require any changes of the system hardware.

IV. CONCLUSIONS

The electronic system has been designed and its firmware created. The firmware also includes the system calibration procedure, described above, together with the calibration constants store in the microcontroller internal electrically erasable programmable read only memory (EEPROM). The system performance, the assembled printed circuit board (PCB), is shown in Figure 7a and Figure 7b. The PCB dimensions are 59 x 25 mm. If the achieved results are compared with the required parameters, the results are a little worse than it is required and the design needs some improvements, namely as for the calibration stability. At present, to get introduced results, it is necessary to do the re-calibration of the instrument whenever it is switched on. Although this procedure is simple and does not require much time, it is a complication of the measuring procedure. One possibility of the system accuracy improvement is the software adaptation of the sensitivity mentioned in the previous paragraph. For further improvement, it is necessary to re-design the hardware, which would involve the use of a better voltage reference and a possibility to divide the current range into several subranges.

V. ACKNOWLEDGMENT

The system described has been realized within the granted project of the College of Polytechnics Jihlava, Czech Republic, Nr.1170/4/1710, "The use of electrochemical sensors for the relative humidity measurement".

REFERENCES

[1] A. Brodgesell and B. Liptak, "Instrument Engineers' Handbook: Process Measurement and Analysis", 4th edition. J. Wiley & Sons, N.Y. 2003, pp. 1426.
[2] J. Fraden, "Handbook of modern sensors: physics, designs and applications". Springer science + business media, Inc., 2004, pp. 400.
[3] Electronic publication http://www.bvt.cz/ftp/Senzory/CC1.pdf : "Conductometric Sensor Substrates – CC1", Sensor Data Sheet, BVT Technologies, 2016, pp. 1, last access April 2017.
[4] I. Krejci, M. Musil, and P. Smetana, "Impedance Spectrometer for Application in Biology and Food Quality Control", Proceedings of XXI IMEKO World Congress, Prague 2015, pp. 2222.
[5] Electronic mail information - BVT Technologies proposals.

[6] V. Krejci and J. Stupka, "Electrical Measurements" (in Czech), Statni Nakladatelstvi Technicke literatury (SNTL), Prague 1973, pp.232.

Figure 7a. Upper view on the PCB of the electronic unit, the digital signal processing part.

Figure 7b. Bottom view on the PCB, the analog signal processing part.

A New Localization Scheme Using Gyro Sensor for Underwater Mobile Communication Systems

Sung-Joon Park
Dept. of Electronic Engineering
Gangneung-Wonju National University
Gangneung, Republic of Korea
e-mail: psj@ieee.org

***Abstract*—Efficient underwater localization is a challenging issue as the need for underwater convergence systems increases. In this paper, we present a method of position recognition for underwater mobile devices equipped with pressure and gyro sensors. In the proposed scheme, at least two cooperating surface nodes (or one surface node having two separate transducers) and two discrete-time data are required to recognize position. The main idea and procedure are addressed here and its prototype and experimental results will be provided in a following research paper.**

Keywords-underwater mobile communication systems; underwater acoustic communication; localization; position recognition; gyro sensor.

I. Introduction

Recently, there has been increased interest in underwater convergence systems, e.g., smart fish farm, mission-critical underwater robot, immersive marine leisure activities, water quality monitoring and maintenance. For these applications, the use of moving objects, such as underwater device, vehicle, drone, or mobile sensor node, would be very helpful if deployed together. Meanwhile, one of the major problems related to the underwater systems supporting mobility is location awareness because radio frequency (RF) based global positioning system (GPS) that is commonly used in terrestrial networks does not work in underwater.

Some studies focused on the localization of underwater wireless acoustic sensor network (UWASN) can be found in the literature [1]–[4]. Typically, in range-based schemes, three dimensional localization is simplified to a problem estimating the coordinates in two dimensions owing to Time of Arrival (ToA) measurement and a pressure sensor. In this work, we propose an efficient localization scheme utilizing a gyroscope in which the degree of freedom for an estimate of location is reduced.

The rest of this paper is organized as follows. Section II addresses the general system model of underwater localization. Section III describes the main principle and procedure of the proposed location awareness scheme. In Section IV, concluding remarks on the direction for further work close the article.

II. System Model

A conceptual diagram of range-based underwater localization is shown in Figure 1, where three anchor nodes, A_1, A_2, and A_3, are located at water surface and an object is launched underwater. It is assumed that ToA is measured at each anchor and a pressure sensor is mounted at the object. Then, an anchor node, e.g., A_1, easily knows the projected radius r_1 from the distance information d_1 and the water depth information D_1. Since other anchor nodes can calculate their projected radii in a similar way, the location of the object is finally determined as the intersection of three circles.

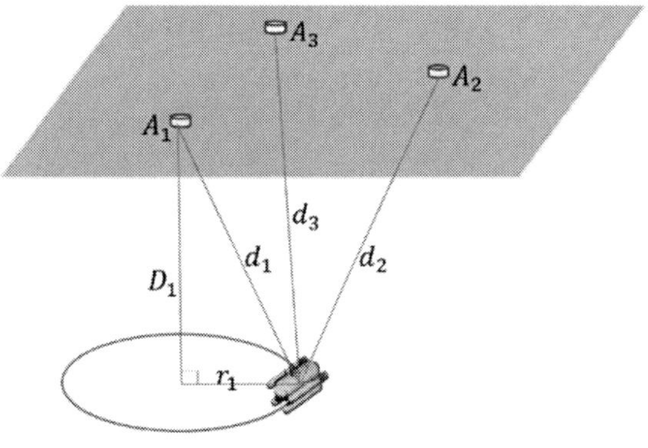

Figure 1. Range-based underwater localization.

III. Proposed Localization Scheme

A. Gyroscope-Assisted Localization

The basic assumption of the proposed range-based localization scheme is that two anchor nodes are placed at water surface and a mobile object equipped with a gyroscope exists underwater. Then, the main idea is as follows. At an arbitrary time, each anchor node extracts its projected radius from distance and depth information. The red-colored solid circles in Figure 2 represent the trajectories with the radii of r_1 and r_2, which informs us that the object is located at either X or X'. After a predetermined time, the entities taking part in the localization process repeat the same task, i.e., the object provides distance and depth information again and two anchor nodes acquire the blue-colored dotted trajectories as shown in Figure 2, which means that the current possible locations of the object are Y or Y'. Consequently, there remain four candidates on the movement of the object: 1) X to Y, 2) X to Y', 3) X' to Y, 4) X' to Y'. Further, since the object reports the direction of its movement acquired from a gyroscope to anchor nodes, an estimate among four candidates is finally chosen and the localization process is terminated.

It is noted that the accuracy of the proposed scheme will be improved if the number of time samples or anchor nodes increases. Also, a single anchor node having two transducers apart from each other could replace the two anchor nodes shown in Figure 2.

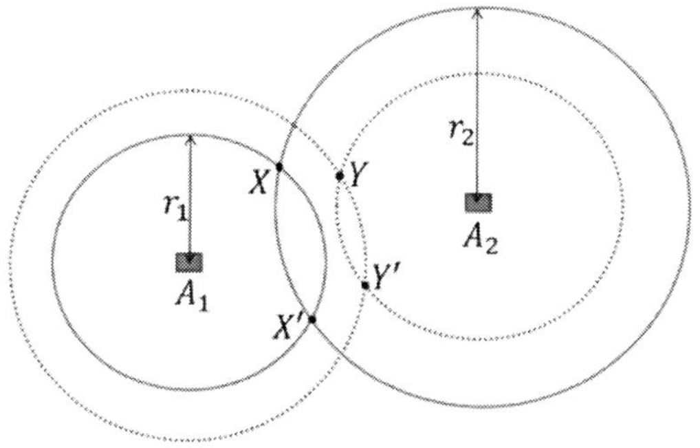

Figure 2. Top view of proposed localization with two anchor nodes and two time samples.

B. Localization Procedure

The specific procedure of the proposed localization scheme is given as follows.

- A master anchor node (or an onshore station or an anchor node having two transducers) initiates a localization process.
- The master anchor node sends a broadcasting message underwater.
- The moving object responds to it with depth information and two anchor nodes calculate each projected radius from the acquired depth information and the estimated distance information.
- After a predetermined time, the master anchor node sends the broadcasting message again.
- The moving object responds to it with the direction of movement as well as depth information, and then the two anchor nodes calculate each projected radius again.
- The master anchor node calculates the location of the moving object based on the trajectories provided at two time instants and the direction information and this terminates the localization process.

IV. Concluding Remarks

In this article, an idea of gyroscope-assisted localization for underwater mobile communication systems has been proposed. The direction of movement as well as range and depth information is utilized in the algorithm to help find location. The proposed scheme reduces the number of anchors required for the position recognition of an underwater moving object at the expense of complexity increase for the use of a gyro sensor.

As subsequent work, it is worth investigating other simple and efficient schemes for underwater localization using multiple sensors, specifically focused on acceleration sensor and magnetometer sensor. The implementation and verification of the proposed schemes are also challenging problems to be addressed.

Acknowledgment

This work was supported by Mid-career Researcher Program through NRF grant funded by the MSIP (2017R1A2A2A05001457).

References

[1] M. Erol-Kantarci, H. T. Mouftah, and S. Oktug, "A survey of architectures and localization techniques for underwater acoustic sensor networks," *IEEE Commun. Surveys & Tutorials*, vol. 13, no. 3, pp. 487–502, 2011.

[2] M. Moradi, J. Rezazadeh, and S. Ismail, "A reverse localization scheme for underwater acoustic sensor networks," *SENSORS*, vol. 12, no. 4, pp. 4352–4380, 2012.

[3] V. Chandrasekhar, W. K. G. Seah, Y. S. Choo, and H. V. Ee, "Localization in underwater sensor networks–survey and challenges," in *Proc. ACM WUWNet*, Los Angeles, CA, USA, Sep. 2006.

[4] H.-P. Tan, R. Diamant, W. K. G. Seah, and M. Waldmeyer, "A survey of techniques and challenges in underwater localization," *Ocean Engineering*, vol. 38, pp. 1663–1676, Oct. 2011.

Immersion Discriminated from Browsed Information in Writing Document Referring Web Pages

Takahisa Oe
Graduate School of Information Science and Engineering
Ritsumeikan University
Shiga, Japan
Email: oe2002@de.is.ritsumei.ac.jp

Shinya Yonekura
Graduate School of Information Science and Engineering
Ritsumeikan University
Shiga, Japan
Email: shinya@de.is.ritsumei.ac.jp

Hiromitsu Shimakawa
College of Information Science and Engineering
Ritsumeikan University
Shiga, Japan
Email: simakawa@de.is.ritsumei.ac.jp

Abstract—**This study proposes a method to distinguish student immersion in writing on computers without physical sensors. To improve the work efficiency of writing, students need support, such as warning when they have been distracted a long time from writing. A model using the Random Forest algorithm discriminates the immersion, examining windows of their operation target on the top of the display. In our experiment, the model discriminates the immersion of 5 subjects with the accuracy of 0.65 or higher in the F-measure, where placement of a specific window on the top of the screen turns out to be the most important feature. Various kinds of information is presented on the screen of the PCs of students. It includes not only information necessary for writing, but also entertainment information such as movies and games. The experiment result indicates that students tend to exclude entertainment information from their vision when they are under immersion in writing. It suggests that the student distraction from writing can be warned without extra effort from students, if we examine the top of the screen.**

Keywords–Sensorless detection; Immersion; Distraction; Machine learning.

I. Introduction

The popularization of the Internet has brought us the power of easy access to a wide variety of desired information. At the same time, we can also access information related to entertainment, which disturbs our concentration on works or activities. Students often write documents, such as technical reports and presentation materials using computers. They usually collect information necessary for the writing, using Web browsers. At the same time, their concentration is disturbed by Web-based information related to entertainment. A method to distinguish their immersion in the writing task from distraction is required to help students keep their concentration. For example, when a student has been distracted from writing for a long time, a self-management tool should send a warning to the student. Physical sensors are indispensable in existing methods to distinguish student immersion in their writing tasks [1]–[4]. However, it is not practical to use physical sensors for every writing task.

This study proposes a method to distinguish student immersion in writing, using only data which can be acquired without physical sensors. To achieve it, the method pays attention to the type of digital documents opened on the computers where the students engage in writing. Based on the bag-of-words algorithm, the proposed method figures out a document vector for each one of the documents used in the writing. They involve not only the target document, but also the ones accessed by Web browsers. We refer to the latter as browsed documents.

The association degree of browsed documents with the target one is calculated using the vectors. Browsed documents are categorized into 2 groups based on the degree of association. One group contains reference information, which is related to the target document. Students write a target document using information a from reference document. The other group contains supplemental information, which facilitates the writing of the target document, and entertainment information, which is unrelated to the writing. The contents of supplemental information are not directly related to the contents of the target document. However, they promote the writing, because they explain the knowledge to write comprehensive documents, such as how to organize technical documents in a general way, and how to write mathematical expressions in digital documents.

The proposed method distinguishes immersion of a student in writing by features of interactions the student is taking. The first feature is whether the student provides the computer with inputs, such as moving mouse cursor, clicking the mouse, or typing on the keyboard. In this feature, it is also important to know whether the inputs are used for the target document, the first group of browsed documents, or the second group. The second feature is related to windows handling documents. On the top of the display, the student places a window for either the target document, the first group of browsed documents, or the second group. The feature gives importance to what window is placed on the top of the display.

This study assumes students keep a specific behavior during their immersion. For example, they are typing characters in the target documents to write down their ideas. Others may stop the typing to consider their plans on target documents, or continue to search relevant information. This study examines if students engaging in writing keep one kind of behavior in terms of the above features of interaction during their immersion in writing.

To distinguish between their immersion in the writing and their distraction from the writing with the method, we conducted an experiment where five students worked on a task to summarize a specific technology. The method discriminated student immersion with an accuracy exceeding 0.65. The method trained the discriminator taking student interaction with computers and the continuity of the specific behavior as their explanation variables. The method discriminates the immersion of students, using a machine learning method. The method trains a discriminator with data sampled from students. The data consists of student interaction with computers and the continuity of the specific behavior in the interaction. This paper discusses which explanation variables are effective for the discrimination from the viewpoints of machine learning.

In Section 2, we describe the necessity to determine the concentration in writing and existing methods to determine concentration. In Section 3, we describe how to determine concentration in writing without a physical sensor. In Section 4, we describe the procedure of the experiment and the experimental result. In Section 5, we discuss experimental results. In Section 5, we describe the conclusion and future research tasks.

II. THE JUDGEMENT OF CONCENTRATION OF STUDENTS ATTENTION ON WRITING

Here, we present the necessity to determine the concentration in writing and existing methods to evaluate concentration.

A. Problem of writing on PC

Nowadays, we can easily obtain the information we want using the Internet. At the same time, we can also access information related to entertainment, which disturbs our concentration on the work or activity. The survey of the Ministry of Internal Affairs and Communications in Japan says about 40% of college students are netaholic [5]. They are caught by Web-based videos, social media, or net games for an excessively long time. Coker's study proved that extreme Web-surfing during work time degrades the progress of the work [6]. The use of the Internet prevents them from concentrating on their tasks. Focusing their attention on specific target tasks, people would enter into a state where they can show the best performance on their tasks. In this study, we refer to this state as immersion [7][8]. On the contrary, we refer to states where people cannot concentrate on their target tasks as distraction.

Using computers, students make documents, such as technical reports and presentation materials. During the writing, their concentration is disturbed by Web-based information related to entertainment. Focus of student attention on tasks other than writing degrades the efficiency to finalize documents, because the students run into distraction from the writing. It is not desirable for students to run into the distraction from writing. Students struggle with entertainment information on the Internet, trying to concentrate their attention on the writing. If we can detect the distraction from the writing, we can avoid the inefficiency problem students suffer from. The distraction from writing corresponds to the immersion in information related to entertainment. It is difficult to distinguish which information the students focus their attention on. This paper addresses a method to distinguish student immersion in writing from the distraction.

B. Necessity to evaluate concentration

Students engage in writing when they make technical reports, presentation materials, and so on. This study assumes the following tasks as writing. Students edit documents on a computer, using text editors, authoring tools for presentation materials, and so on. Students collect information necessary for the writing, using Web browsers on a computer. In the following, we refer to students engaging in the writing as users. The users gather necessary information for the writing from the Web. The Internet is full of Web pages related to entertainment. Since they are attractive to the users, the users are likely to be prevented from concentrating on the writing. When the users are prevented from concentrating, the work efficiency decreases. They might use up the time for other tasks, such as extra-curricular activities.

Users should be supported so that they can immerse into writing. For example, when a user has been distracted from writing for a long time, a self-management tool should send a warning to the user. It is necessary to determine whether the users concentrate their attention on the writing or they are distracted from it. This study aims to increase the learning efficiency of students, having them concentrate on writing. Writing is a really common task for students. To get high practicability, it is preferable to minimize efforts and costs in the method to evaluate concentration. We should avoid any method which imposes extra effort and costs on students, such as wearing physical sensors, to determine the concentration of their attention on writing.

C. Existing methods

Sarrafzadeh et al. measured emotional states from bio-signals like facial expressions [9]. Jang et al. identified human intention by eyeball movement patterns and pupil size variation [10]. Kapoor et al. predicted students' quit puzzle by facial expressions, dermal activity, posture, and mouse pressure [11]. Jraidi et al. proposed a method to presume human immersion in a task using the skin conductance, the heart rate and the electroencephalography [1]. Nacke and Lindley also used physical sensors measuring from orbicularis oculi and zygomaticus major to know human immersion [2]. Leelasawassuk et al. tried to identify the target of attention using a Google Glass and an Eye Tracke [3]. Lee et al. measured emotional state from bio-signals like EGG signals [12]. They also measured the degree of human immersion from pupil movement and eye blinks using a webcam and an Eye Tracker. All of these methods need to use physical sensors [4]. Mello detected students who were bored, disengaged or zoning out by an eye tracker [13]. However, the necessity of physical sensors for every writing imposes extra efforts and costs on users. These methods should be avoided for the evaluation of immersion in writing. A method free from physical sensors is required to easily evaluate immersion into writing.

III. CONCENTRATION JUDGMENT USING BEHAVIOR LOGS

Here, we present how to evaluate concentration on writing without physical sensors.

A. Method overview

This study proposes a method to distinguish user immersion in writing without physical sensors. Figure 1 illustrates a use case of the method. The system gets a behavior log, which consists of applications and Web pages displayed on the screen, as well as inputs from the mouse and the keyboard along with their targets.

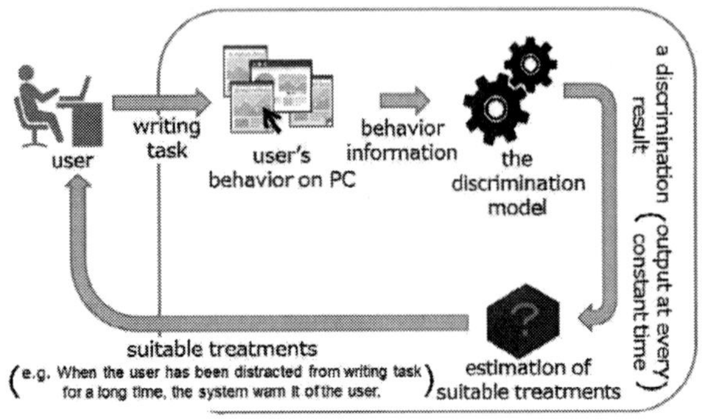

Figure 1. A use case of the method.

The discrimination model takes behavior logs of users to examine whether they get immersed at every constant period. Users may take a long time for writing. However, it is useless to provide discrimination results for them in a long period. It is desirable for the users to get immersed during the writing task as much as possible. To achieve it, the study proposes a method to provide a discrimination result at every short constant time. It enables provision for users while writing task to get discrimination results at every constant time. For example, when users have been distracted from writing tasks for the time being, the method warns it of them.

The data flow in the discrimination model is shown in Figure 2.

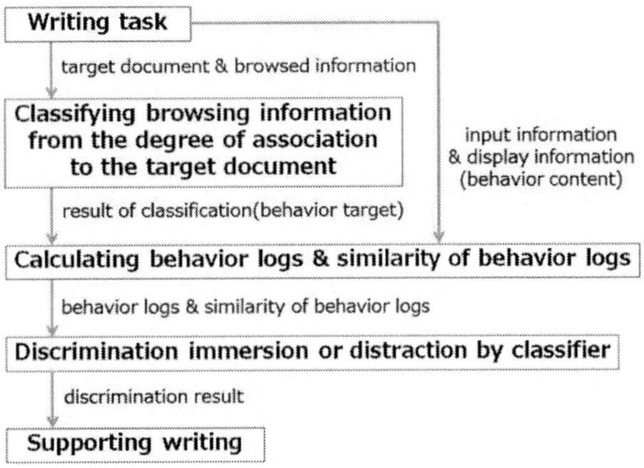

Figure 2. Discrimination Model.

A user usually makes a target document, referring to various kinds of information, such as Web pages. The discrimination model first clusters browsed information with its association degree with the target document. A behavior log is composed of results of the clustering, inputs with the mouse and the keyboard. It also contains what applications and Web pages are placed on the top of the screen, which indicates information the user is referring at the time point.

This study assumes users keep the same behavior during their immersion. For example, some users may go on typing characters in target documents to embody specific ideas in their minds. Others may stop the typing to consider their plans on target documents, or continue to search relevant information. Even if they are immersed into tasks other than writing, such as enjoying movies, they keep the same behavior. Based on this assumption, the discrimination model evaluates if users get immersed when they keep the same behavior. To distinguish immersion in the writing from that in other tasks, the discrimination model examines the information they refer to. Through the process above, it can detect distraction from writing without physical sensors.

B. Classification of browsed information

The study regards a target document as an electronic document being edited. It assumes only one document is addressed in a writing task. Browsed information means the information browsed by the Web browser. In this study, it is categorized into 3 types: reference information, supplemental information, and entertainment information, Reference information means any information, which contributes to the contents of a target document. In the study, it is assumed to be written in the same language as the target document. Taking a report assignment to explain the multiple regression analysis as an example, Web pages explaining the multiple regression in the same language as the target document, are examples of reference information. Supplemental information corresponds to information which is helpful to form the target writing, but not related to its contents. Back to the example of the report assignment on the regression analysis, supplemental information are Web pages explaining how to write a reference list, how to denote mathematical expression with TEX, and so on. Entertainment information involves unnecessary information for the writing. It is usually browsed by users' preference. In the report assignment example, Web pages on news article unrelated to the multiple regression, videos for users' entertainment and so on are categorized into entertainment information. For the writing task, reference information and supplemental information are necessary information, while entertainment information is unnecessary information. If we examine words, the association of reference information with the target document seems to be high, because reference information seems to have words similar to the target document. The association of supplemental information or entertainment information with the target document would be low, because supplemental information and entertainment information seem to have few words related to the target document. Measuring the degree of the association based on words, browsed information can be classified into the two groups: the group of reference information and the group of supplement information and entertainment information. This study classifies supplemental information and entertainment information into one group, because it is difficult to distinguish supplemental information from entertainment information by the word-based degree of association.

At a regular interval, the proposed method analyzes morphologically the target document at a specific time point and all documents browsed in the interval. It categorizes the browsed documents in the following way.

1) With the bag-of-words method, it generates the document vectors of the target document and each of the browsed ones using nouns other than pronouns, non-autonomous words, suffixes, and numerals.
2) It calculates the degree of the association with the cosine similarity between the document vector of the target document and that of the browsed ones.

3) It clusters browsed documents into 2 clusters based on the degree of the association with the k-means method [14]. It regards the cluster of high degree of the association as the group of reference information, while the one of low degree of the association as the group of supplemental information and entertainment information.

Pronouns, non-autonomous words, suffixes, and numerals are removed from elements of document vectors, because these nouns do not seem to represent the peculiarity of the target document and browsed ones. The bag-of-words considers the peculiarity of sentences from only the occurrence of specific words in the sentence [15][16]. In this study, each element of a document vector corresponds to a specific noun. It takes 1 if the noun appears in the document, otherwise 0 [See Figure 3].

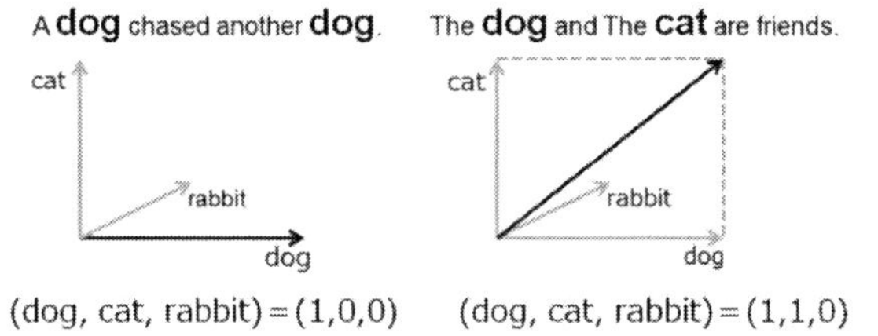

Figure 3. The bag-of-words.

The cosine similarity is calculated with (1), where the document vector of the target document is $\vec{m}$, while that of the browsed one is $\vec{r}$.

$$cos(\vec{r}; \vec{m}) = \frac{\vec{r} \cdot \vec{m}}{|\vec{r}||\vec{m}|} \quad (1)$$

The proposed method classifies browsed documents into 2 clusters based on the degree of the association in the following k-means method.

a). It assigns each browsed document into 2 clusters randomly.
b). It calculates the centroid in each cluster.
c). It reclassifies each browsed document into the new cluster whose centroid is nearest to the browsed document.
d). It repeats b) and c) until the result of reclassification are the same.

C. Behavior log

The proposed method detects users' immersion in writing using the behavior log. At a regular interval, it examines the target document, documents in the group of reference information, and the ones in the group of supplemental information and entertainment information. It tests whether the user provides something for what is examined as its input, as well as whether the user places what is examined on the top of the screen. A behavior log contains binary values, which indicate the test results, as depicted in Figure 4.

To discriminate the user immersion in a short period, the duration to figure out the behavior log is far shorter than that to classify browsed information. The method regards the target document or the browsed information takes something as its input, if the user gives it typing with the keyboard, moving the mouse cursor or clicking the mouse. The method regards the target document or the browsed information is placed on the top of the screen, if any part of the window tool presenting it appears on the top of the screen. The target document or the browsed information is regarded not to be placed on the top, when the whole part of the tool has been hidden with other windows, or when the tool has been closed throughout the duration.

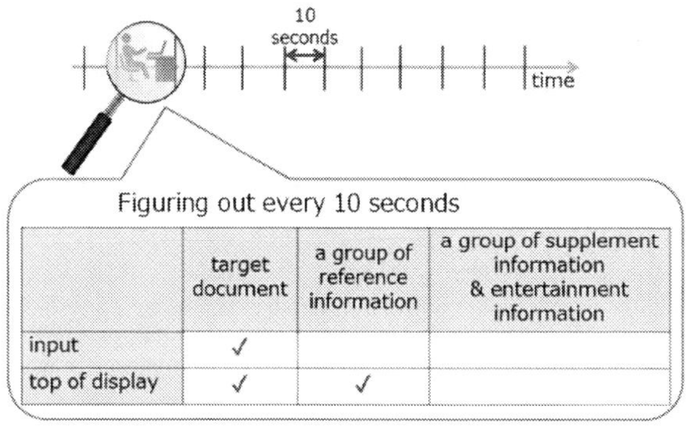

Figure 4. Behavior log.

D. Similarity of behavior logs

The method addresses the 3 kinds of documents: the target document, a group of reference information, and a group of supplemental information and entertainment information. To make behavior logs, it examines 2 characteristics in each of them: their input and their appearance on the top of the screen. The behavior logs consist of 6 kinds of binary data items.

The method distinguishes users' immersion in writing using each of the similarity of behavior logs under the assumption that users keep the same behavior during their immersion. To figure out the similarity of behavior logs, the 2 characteristics of the 3 groups of the information is examined, which means the proposed method consider 6 kinds of binary data items for the similarity. The similarity of each binary data item is the number of matching behavior logs within a time window of a fixed length. The similarity for the k-th binary data item is figured out with (2).

$$similarity_k = \sum_{i=1}^{m-1} \sum_{j=i+1}^{m} (a_{i;k}, a_{j;k}) \quad (2)$$

where a_i denotes the i-th behavior log, and $a_{i;k}$ denotes the k-th binary data item inside a_i. Function is defined as (3).

$$(a_{i;k}; a_{j;k}) = \begin{cases} 1 & (a_{i;k} = a_{j;k}) \\ 0 & (otherwise) \end{cases} \quad (3)$$

Apparently, this value gets large when the user keeps the same behavior.

IV. EXPERIMENT TO EVALUATE THE PROPOSED METHOD

Here, we present the procedure of the experiment and the experimental results.

A. Purpose and procedure of experiment

The experiment was conducted to verify whether it is possible to distinguish users' concentration for the writing from the similarity of behavior logs. Five students in a university worked on the task where they summarized investigation results on the will power [17] in a report for 150 minutes. They worked under a dual display environment in order to bring it closer to their usual working environment. Every 10 seconds, their computers recorded both of the windows, which become the input target and the windows, which are placed on the top of the screen even a moment during the period. The intermediate state of the target document is also recorded every 1 hour. The working of the subjects was recorded with a video camera during the experiment. After the experiment, the subjects answered the questionnaire, which asked the period during which they were immersed in the writing, watching the video.

B. Results of the experiment

The length of time window to calculate the similarity of behavior logs was set to 120 seconds. The discrimination models are constructed by the random forest, support vector machine and gradient boosting to distinguish whether the subjects get immersed in the writing. Figure 5 illustrates the explanatory variables in these models.

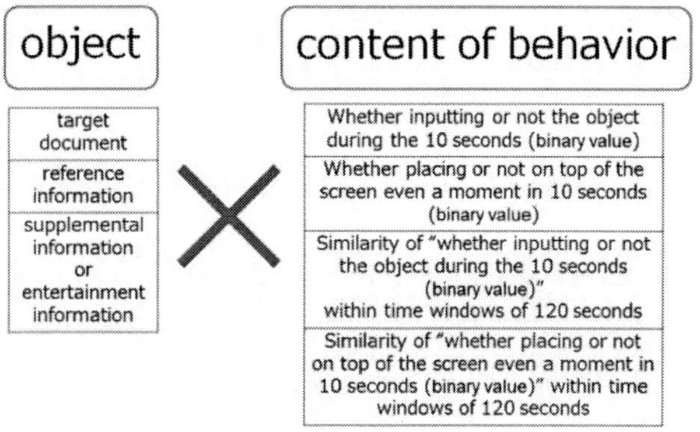

Figure 5. The explanatory variables.

5-fold cross validation was used for the evaluation. The precision, the recall, and the F-measure of the evaluation result for the 5 subjects are shown in Tables I, II, and III.

TABLE I. THE DISCRIMINATION RESULT BY THE RANDOM FOREST

	distraction from writing task	immersion in writing task
precision	0.63	0.71
recall	0.80	0.51
F-measure	0.70	0.59

Note that the F-measure value the distraction from the writing is 0.70 in all of these discrimination. The study to presume human immersion from the skin conductance, the heart rate and the electroencephalography using physical sensors [1] reported the accuracy of the discrimination of the distraction was 0.76, though the experimental environments and the situations are different. The result suggests that it is possible

TABLE II. THE DISCRIMINATION RESULT BY THE SUPPORT VECTOR MACHINE

	distraction from writing task	immersion in writing task
precision	0.65	0.74
recall	0.82	0.53
F-measure	0.72	0.62

TABLE III. THE DISCRIMINATION RESULT BY THE GRADIENT BOOSTING

	distraction from writing task	immersion in writing task
precision	0.70	0.66
recall	0.73	0.60
F-measure	0.72	0.63

to distinguish the distraction from the writing using the above explanatory variables instead of physical sensors, although the accuracy decreases slightly. We can detect users who do not concentrate on the writing for a long time.

C. Important factors in discrimination

It is necessary to investigate whether the discrimination is caused by the similarity of behavior logs. The variable importance of the Random Forest algorithm indicates which explanatory variable is important in the discrimination. It says that the most important explanatory variable is not the similarity of behavior logs, but the binary variable representing whether supplemental information or entertainment information is placed on the top of the screen during the period of 10 second. To confirm the importance of the variable, let us regard the user runs into distraction from the writing when supplemental information or entertainment information is placed on the top of the screen, while he stays in the immersion in the writing when the information is not placed on the top of the screen. The data set collected in the experiment was discriminated again based on the simple criterion. The precision, the recall, and the F-measure of the discrimination are shown in Table IV.

TABLE IV. THE DISCRIMINATION RESULT BY SUPPLEMENTAL INFORMATION AND ENTERTAINMENT INFORMATION

	distraction from writing task	immersion in writing task
precision	0.67	0.72
recall	0.76	0.63
F-measure	0.71	0.67

Both of the F-measure values of the immersion and the distraction are higher than those of Section 4.*B*. Whether supplemental information or entertainment information is placed on the top of the screen is quite important among the explanatory variables in the experiment. On the contrary, the similarity of behavior logs is not as important as the placement of supplemental information or entertainment information.

V. DISCUSSION

The experimental result suggests the placement of supplemental information or entertainment information on the top of the screen is important to distinguish whether concentration of users leads to their immersion in writing. Users who want to concentrate on the writing seem to exclude entertainment information from their vision under their immersion. On the contrary, they place entertainment information on the top of the screen when they are distracted. The following tendency was manually confirmed from the videos during the experiment. The subjects displayed entertainment information when they got distracted when they cannot concentrate on the writing any more. Meanwhile, they hid the entertainment information, switching the tabs on their browsers, or placing other windows covering the entertainment information when their mode changes from distraction to immersion.

Since supplementary information is not related to the distraction, the simple criterion assumed in Section 4.*C* may lead to erroneous discrimination. After the experience, the subjects manually classified browsed information into 3 categories: reference information, supplemental information, and entertainment information. The total number of entertainment information browsed by each subject in the experiment is 299, while that of supplemental information is 99. Accordingly, the entertainment information is approximately 3 times larger than the supplemental information. Since the supplemental information is far less than the entertainment information on this experiment, the accuracy of the discrimination is high, although the supplemental information is treated in the same group of the entertainment information. It is expected the accuracy is improved, distinguishing supplemental information from entertainment information.

The significance of the experiment results should be proved by increasing the number of the subjects. Also, the accuracy of the discrimination should be improved more for the practical usage. It would be improved, adding explanatory variables, such as the frequency of typing and clicking, the contents of the typed information, and so on. Additionally, it is necessary to confirm the validity of the questionnaire to form training data. They were determined through the answers of the subjects for questions asking the period where they were immersed into the writing. It is necessary to improve the validity of the questionnaire and the method of evaluation by using existing research to measure human immersion.

VI. CONCLUSION

In this paper, we have proposed a method to distinguish user immersion in writing without physical sensors. The method has been suggested to distinguish users' immersion in writing using each of the similarity of behavior logs under the assumption that users keep the same behavior during their immersion. It has turned out the most important explanatory variable is the binary variable representing whether supplemental information or entertainment information is placed on the top of the screen during the period of 10 seconds. From the videos during the experiment, it has been manually confirmed the subjects would display entertainment information when they have run into a distraction from writing. It implies they are likely to place entertainment information on the top of the display, when they cannot concentrate on the writing any more. Meanwhile, they would hide the entertainment information, switching the tabs on their browsers, or placing other windows covering the entertainment information, when their mode changes from distraction to immersion.

In the future, the significance of the experimental results should be proved by increasing the number of the subjects. Additionally, in actual environments, it may be possible for users to engage in multiple tasks at the same time. For example, while they are engaging in writing, they also have to handle interrupts of their work, such as responding to incoming calls. The range of adaptation of the method should be expanded to deal with such multitasking.

ACKNOWLEDGMENT

We gratefully appreciate the help of Prof. Yusuke Kajiwara who gave us a lot of advice and suggestions for conducting this research and writing this paper. We also express our gratitude to all members and colleagues of Data Engineering Laboratory from Ritsumeikan University who supported us and cooperated with the experiment.

REFERENCES

[1] I. Jraidi, M. Chaouachi, and C. Frasson, "A Dynamic Multimodal Approach for Assessing Learners' Interaction Experience," ICMI '13 Proceedings of the 15th ACM on International conference on multi-modal interaction, 2013, pp. 271–278.

[2] L. Nacke and C. A. Lindley, "Flow and Immersion in First-Person Shooters: Measuring the player's gameplay experience," Future Play '08 Proceedings of the 2008 Conference on Future Play: Research, Play, Share, 2008, pp. 81–88.

[3] T. Leelasawassuk, D. Damen, and W. Mayol-Cuevas, "Estimating Visual Attention from a Head Mounted IMU," ISWC '15 Proceedings of the 2015 ACM International Symposium on Wearable Computers, 2015, pp. 147–150.

[4] G. Lee, A. Ojha, and M. Lee, "Concentration Monitoring for Intelligent Tutoring System Based on Pupil and Eye-blink," HAI '15 Proceedings of the 3rd International Conference on Human-Agent Interaction, 2015, pp. 291–294.

[5] Ministry of Internal Affairs and Communications Institute for Information and Communications Policy, "Survey findings report on Internet use and dependency trend among young people," 2013, URL: http://www.soumu.go.jp/iicp/chousakenkyu/data/research/survey/telecom/2013/internet-addiction.pdf [accessed: 2016-12-21].

[6] B. L. S. Coker, "Workplace Internet Leisure Browsing," Human Performance, vol. 26, 2013, pp. 114–125.

[7] M. Csikszentmihalyi, Finding Flow: The Psychology of Engagement with Everyday Life. Basic Books, 2008.

[8] J. Saiki and E. Inoue, "Relationship between Concentration and Tempo-ral Duration Estimation: Implications for Flow Experience," Psycholo-gia, vol. 54, 2011, pp. 206–221.

[9] A. Sarrafzadeh, S. Alexander, F. Dadgostar, C. Fan, and A. Bigdeli, ""How do you know that I don't understand?" A look at the future of intelligent tutoring systems," Computers in Human Behavior, vol. 24, no. 4, 2008, pp. 1342–1363.

[10] Y.-M. Jang, R. Mallipeddi, S. Lee, H.-W. Kwak, and M. Lee, "Human intention recognition based on eyeball movement pattern and pupil size variation," Neurocomputing, vol. 128, 2013, pp. 421–432.

[11] A. Kapoor, W. Burleson, and P. Rosalind W, "Automatic prediction of frustration," International Journal of Human-Computer Studies, vol. 65, 2007, pp. 724–736.

[12] G. Lee, M. Kwon, S. K. Sri, and M. Lee, "Emotion recognition based on 3D fuzzy visual and EEG features in movie clips," Neurocomputing, vol. 144, 2014, pp. 560–568.

[13] S. D 'Mello, A. Olney, C. Williams, and P. Hays, "Gaze tutor: A gaze-reactive intelligent tutoring system," International Journal of Human-Computer Studies, vol. 70, 2012, pp. 377–398.

[14] J. MacQueen, "Some Methods For Classification and Analysis of Multivariate Observations," Proc. Fifth Berkeley Symp. on Math. Statist. and Prob, vol. 1, 1967, pp. 281–297.

[15] S. Dumais, J. Platt, D. Heckerman, and M. Sahami, "Inductive Learning Algorithms and Representations for Text Categorization," CIKM '98 Proceedings of the seventh international conference on Information and knowledge management, 1998, pp. 148–155.

[16] S. M. Weiss, C. A. andFred J. Damerau, D. E. Johnson, F. J. Oles, T. Goetz, and T. Hampp, "Maximizing Text-Mining Performance," IEEE Intelligent Systems archive, vol. 14, 1999, pp. 63–69.

[17] K. McGonigal, The Willpower Instinct: How Self-Control Works, Why It Matters, and What You Can Do To Get More of IT. Avery, 2011.

Issues in Designing 6TiSCH Wireless Networks

Sunghee Myung†

Cho Chun Shik Graduate School of Green Transportation†
Korea Advanced Institute of Science and Technology
Daejeon, Republic of Korea
1992happy@kaist.ac.kr†

Chaewoo Lee* and Dongsoo Har†

Graduate School of Information and Communication*
Ajou University
Suwon, Republic of Korea
cwlee@ajou.ac.kr*, dshar@kaist.ac.kr†

Abstract—**Industrial Internet of Things (IoT) communication systems are becoming critical for the efficient operation of industrial wireless sensor networks. The IPv6 over IEEE 802.15.4e Time Slotted Channel Hopping (TSCH) (6TiSCH) group enables system to fill in the blank between IP-enabled protocol stack and IEEE 802.15.4e link layer. In this paper, we identify and investigate three issues related to 6TiSCH networks and suggest potential solutions.**

Keywords-Industrial IoT; Wireless sensor networks; 6TiSCH.

I. INTRODUCTION

Sustainable operation is critical for Wireless Sensor Networks (WSNs), such as the recently developed industrial IoT. Particularly, to offer the desired level of service, wireless computer networks, characterized by Information Technology (IT) and Operational Technology (OT), are expected to operate over long duration. IT deals only with data and OT deals only with the physical world; therefore, the convergence of IT and OT is necessary. Nowadays, a lot of studies have been reported related to the convergence of IT and OT [1][2].

Of these Industry 4.0 related research areas, the IoT is expected to play the main role of data acquisition system, which is fundamentally important for Industry 4.0. The IoT stack consists of the IEEE 802.15.4 simple physical layer, IEEE 802.15.4e (TSCH) MAC layer, Internet Engineering Task Force (IETF) 6TiSCH, IETF IPv6 over Low-power Wireless Personal Area Networks (6LoWPAN), the User Datagram Protocol (UDP), and the Constrained Application Protocol (CoAP) [3]. Especially, IETF 6TiSCH is related to the scheduling of the resources and is thus important for efficient resource allocation and traffic management.

To implement efficient resource allocation of the IoT, many scheduling approaches have appeared in the literature. Scheduling in wireless networks can be divided into two groups: centralized scheduling methods and decentralized (distributed) scheduling methods. The centralized scheduling strategy for 6TiSCH wireless networks is introduced in [4]. This strategy deals with a Traffic Aware Scheduling Algorithm (TASA), which allocates cells and resources to all the nodes deployed in the service area. On the other hand, the Decentralized Traffic Aware Scheduling (DeTAS) algorithm was investigated to solve four critical problems, which can be enumerated as small end-to-end latency, small queue but still capable of traffic, collision-free networking, and distributed scheduling [5].

In this paper, we address three issues in industrial IoT and suggest potential solutions for each. The first issue is the problem of multiple sensor nodes running out of power or malfunctioning. The second issue is data processing of information sensed by two or more sensors. Out of these multiple sensor nodes, selection of a sensor node in charge of data transmission to the root (sink) node depends on various criteria. The third issue is to detect malfunctioning sensor nodes. To this end, choosing the right sensing results, obtained from two or more sensor nodes, should be implemented.

Compared to the other works presented above, our contributions are to manage the network balance efficiently so that end-to-end delay can be dramatically reduced, and to bring up practical issues that have not been raised in the literature up to now, thus improving our knowledge of the 6TiSCH network.

The rest of this paper is organized as follows. In Section II, the 6TiSCH IoT network is presented. Section III deals with three issues of network operation; Section IV concludes this paper.

II. SYSTEM MODEL

The baseline 6TiSCH configuration is presented in Table 1.

TABLE I. 6TISCH CONFIGURATION [7]

Property	Value
Number of timeslots per Slotframe	Variable (default 11)
Number of available frequencies	16
Number of scheduled cells (active)	1
Number of unscheduled cells (off)	The remainder of the slotframe
Number of MAC retransmissions (max)	3 (4 transmission attempts)
Default timeslot timing	10ms
Enhanced Beacon Default Period	10s
Default Channel Hopping sequence for the 2.4GHz OQPSK PHY	[5, 6, 12, 7, 15, 4, 14, 11, 8, 0, 1, 2, 13, 3, 9, 10]

We adopt the topology of wireless sensor networks described in [6]. The balanced binary tree from [6] enables us to characterize the network width. Also, this topology is suitable for adopting nearly realistic dense networks. The Destination-Oriented Directed Acyclic Graph (DODAG) root has rank 1, which is denoted as 0 in Figure 1. This root can be represented as: $S_{1,1}$, $S_{a,b}$ where a and b represent the rank and the ID of the node numbered from the leftmost one in the rank. For instance, the node with ID=1 in the 2nd rank is represented as $S_{2,1}$ and the node with ID=2 in the 2nd rank is labeled as $S_{2,2}$.

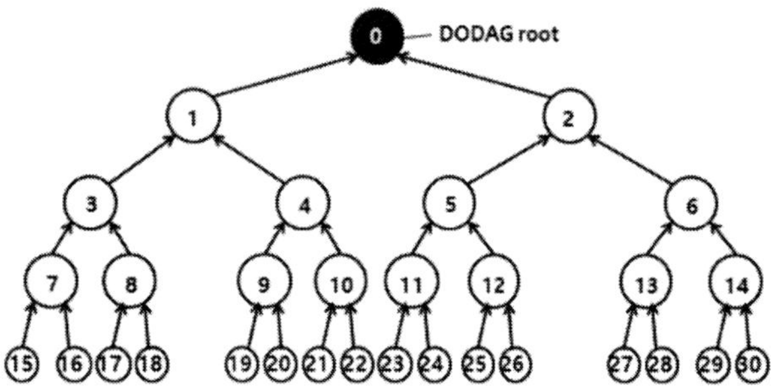

Figure 1. Topology of balanced binary tree.

This wireless sensor network is assumed to be randomly distributed in the service area. The density of the sensor nodes can be visualized according to the corresponding population in the binary tree topology. In Figure 1, circles with numbers represent sensor nodes, which are individual entities of nodes in the wireless sensor network. Arrows represent the directions of data flow.

III. Issues in Network Operation

A. *Solution to eliminate the problem of sensor nodes running out of energy and/or malfunctioning*

Time Slots

Frequency Offsets						
0						...
1						...
2						...
3						...
4	18	19	25	24	18	...
5	0	1	2	4	0	...
6	7	5	3	6	7	...
7	11	15	20	12	11	...
8	30				30	...
9						...
10						...
11	26	28	29		26	...
12	9	14	10	8	9	...
13						...
14	22	21	27		22	...
15	13	17	23	16	13	...

Figure 2. 6TiSCH cell coloring mechanism.

In Figure 2, we propose a coloring method that is characterized by 'two-hop skipping'. This method enables nodes of the same color to use the resources as efficiently as possible, while avoiding collision. The process of 'two-hop skipping' is carried out by placing nodes of the same color in the two hops higher position. These nodes of the same color are activated after a certain timeslot period; in this case, after four time slots, as shown in Figure 2.

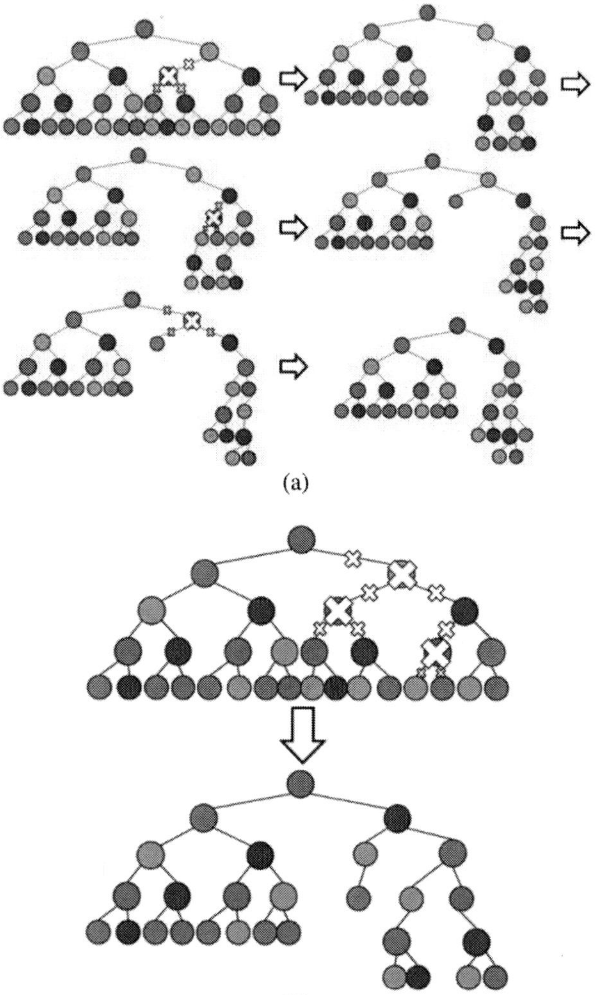

(a)

(b)

Figure 3. Scenarios for dropping sensor nodes out of wireless sensor network squentially and simultaneously: (a) sequential drop out, (b) simultaneous drop out.

Figure 3 shows network topology changes after introduction of least amount of degradation by the 'two-hop skipping' method.

B. *Solution for the problem of choosing a sensor node to send information to DODAGroot when two or more sensor nodes simultaneously sense the object*

For example, when sensor nodes $S_{5,15}$ and $S_{5,16}$ detect the same object, sending all the sensed information is not a good idea from the point of view of network sustainability, because using more sensor nodes in communications will incur more energy consumption. Therefore, we have to set a criterion to ameliorate this issue. Suppose that node $S_{5,15}$ has only 100mJ of energy, while node $S_{5,16}$ has 500mJ of energy. Then, node $S_{5,16}$ sends the information to the DODAGroot.

C. *Solution for the problem of choosing sense results obtained from two or more sensor nodes that demonstrate dissimilarity*

When sensor nodes $S_{5,15}$ and $S_{5,16}$ detect the same object, but with different sensed information, it is likely that one or both of them are providing erroneously sensed information. Therefore, for the sustainability of the 6TiSCH network, erroneously working sensor nodes must be removed. This issue can be solved by comparing the Signal to Noise Ratio (SNR) of the sensed signals of the sensor node to the other. For example, when node $S_{5,15}$ sensed a signal with an SNR value ten times larger than that of sensor node $S_{5,16}$, the sensed results of $S_{5,15}$ can be selected.

IV. Conclusion and Future Work

Sustainable operation of 6TiSCH networks is a critical issue in the realization of industrial IoT. To attain such sustainability, we have to deal with practical issues in 6TiSCH networks. This paper has identified three issues that can occur in 6TiSCH networks. Each issue has been addressed with practical solutions. For future work, by considering various network performance metrics, solutions to these issues will be derived.

References

[1] M. R. Palattella, P. Thubert, X. Vilajosana, T. Watteyne, Q. Wang, and T. Engel, "6tisch wireless industrial networks: Determinism meets ipv6," In *Internet of Things*, Springer International Publishing, pp. 111-141, 2014.

[2] M. Domingo-Prieto, T. Chang, X. Vilajosana, and T. Watteyne, "Distributed pid-based scheduling for 6tisch networks," *IEEE Communications Letters*, vol. *20*, no.5, pp. 1006-1009, 2016.

[3] B. Martinez et al., "I3Mote: An Open Development Platform for the Intelligent Industrial Internet," *Sensors*, vol. *17*, 2017.

[4] M. R. Palattella, N. Accettura, M. Dohler, L. A. Grieco, and G. Boggia, "Traffic Aware Scheduling Algorithm for reliable low-power multi-hop IEEE 802.15. 4e networks," In *Personal Indoor and Mobile Radio Communications (PIMRC), 2012 IEEE 23rd International Symposium on*, pp. 327-332, September 2012.

[5] N. Accettura, M. R. Palattella, G. Boggia, L. A. Grieco, and M. Dohler, "Decentralized traffic aware scheduling for multi-hop low power lossy networks in the internet of things," In *World of Wireless, Mobile and Multimedia Networks (WoWMoM), 2013 IEEE 14th International Symposium and Workshops on a*, pp. 1-6, June 2013.

[6] N. Accettura et. al., "Decentralized traffic aware scheduling in 6TiSCH networks: Design and experimental evaluation," *IEEE Internet of Things Journal*, vol. 2, pp. 455-470, 2015.

[7] X. Vilajosana, and K. Pister. Minimal 6TiSCH Configuration. [Online]. Retrieved: August, 2017. Available from: https://tools.ietf.org/html/draft-ietf-6tisch-minimal-16

Optimal Energy Management in Nanogrids

Sangkeum Lee, Dongsoo Har
Cho Chun Shik Graduate School of Green Transportation
Korea Advanced Institute of Science and Technology
Daejeon, Republic of Korea
E-mail: sd974201@kaist.ac.kr, dshar@kaist.ac.kr

***Abstract*—Home energy management is not efficient for a number of reasons. In this paper, we discuss a home energy management scheme which uses a nanogrid that introduces peak load shifting for energy control using the location patterns of the user. Sensors in the home can monitor the locations of residents and adjust the power consumption of the home in real time. This allows the system to estimate the behaviors of occupants in various situations to reduce the amount of power used. Major ideas and experimental systems are expected to be applied not only to green buildings but also to a large number of existing buildings to reduce the level of power consumption without sacrificing human comfort or convenience.**

Keywords—energy management; joint control; nanogrid; peak load shifting; person location pattern; multi-objective optimization

I. INTRODUCTION

The existing power infrastructure in homes and buildings faces a number of challenges that are difficult to solve. The conventional power distribution method causes large power losses and reduces the efficiency of the power grid. Moreover, grids are susceptible to costly outages due to environmental events (e.g., heavy rain or wind) as well as non-environmental events (e.g., age-related equipment failures). A nanogrid can be used for one building, while a microgrid can serve an island of 15000 consumers. Typically, a nanogrid is technically smaller than a microgrid [1] [2].

Control strategies for buildings to operate heating and cooling, lighting, and ventilation are important to the living standards and health of the residents. Heating, ventilation and cooling (HVAC) is the single largest contributor to a home energy component and accounts for 33% of residential power consumption in the US [3]. Thermal comfort, visible comfort and the indoor air quality are considered to be the three main factors that affect the quality of life of residents in a building environment [4] [5]. Occupant presence and behavior in building have been shown to have large impacts on space heating, ventilation and cooling demand, power consumption by lighting and space appliances, and building control strategies [6].

With regard to energy management, minimizing the energy cost, maximizing the overall efficiency, and the efficient control of peak demand loads are important factors [7] [8]. In addition, maximizing the lifetimes of the energy storage system (ESS) and the generator as well as reliability and security of the power provision are of great importance. To minimize the peak load, the emphasis has been on allocating appliance operation over time scales where there will be a leveling of the peak demand load over the given range of time [9]. The proposed demand-side management strategy achieves substantial savings while reducing the peak load demand on the smart grid using heuristic optimization [10]. These efforts range from improving the energy efficiency by using better materials to smart energy tariffs with incentives for certain consumption patterns and to sophisticated real-time control of distributed energy resources [11]. The development and application of load-shifting control strategies have been discussed in the literature [12].

In this study, an experimental system which optimizes power consumption and human convenience using the positions of people in a nanogrid is presented [13]. In the experiments done to test the system, user location patterns serve to realize optimal control of user locations through a hidden Markov model (HMM) which is calibrated using time-use data collected from the Korea Power Exchange (KPX) Institute. Multi-objective optimization methods are implemented in the system to find Pareto-optimal solutions. The total power consumption and the overall comfort level are considered as the two contrasting goals of building energy management and comfort management [14] [15].

This paper is organized as follows. In Section 2, the HMM for the occupant patterns is explained. The operational characteristics of the house energy management scheme are expressed in terms of the relationships between power consumption and human location patterns. Section 3 provides details of the optimal energy management scheme. Section 4 presents the experimental results. Section 5 concludes this paper with a summary.

II. OCCUPANT BEHAVIOR MODELING

A. *Korea Time Use Survey (KTUS)*

Korea Time Use Survey (KTUS) creates a resident behavior model for the average individual in Korea.

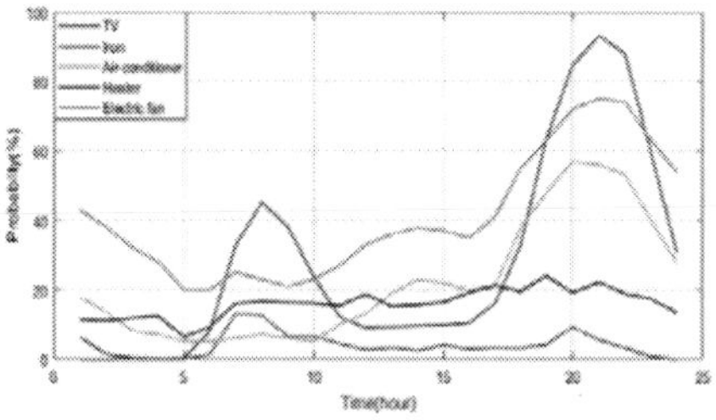

Fig. 1. Profile of merged activity types people are at home: patterns for the TV, iron, air-conditioner, heater, and electric fan

KPX measures the amount of time people spend engaged in various activities, such as washing, watching TV, or cooking. The information collected by KPX includes the start and end times (hours) of each activity. The KTUS data collected in 2013 were used here to create a statistically driven occupant behavior model. An analysis of the KTUS data provides an outline of pattern information related to the respondents' activities. This is shown in Figure 1. We use a sample size of 500 houses, a sample time interval of 1 hour, and a power consumption interval of 60kWh ~ 1000kWh.

B. Hidden Markov Model (HMM)

An HMM was used to model the behavior of home residents [16]. The HMM is used to model the likelihood of transitioning to the next state from the current state. This transition probability is entirely dependent on the current state and does not depend on the state sequence preceding the previous state [17]. A visual representation of the HMM is shown in Figure 2. Resident behavior can be modeled by a hidden state that represents complex behavior that affects the observation and the observed behavior [18] [19]. The HMM is a probabilistic model consisting of the transition and emission probabilities. The emission probability refers to symbols that can be emitted by models related to actions performed by occupants, such as a shutdown of the air conditioning system or a change of the thermostat level.

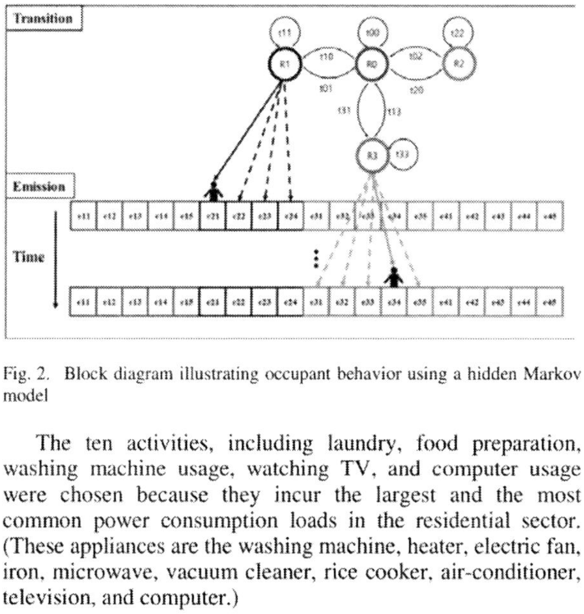

Fig. 2. Block diagram illustrating occupant behavior using a hidden Markov model

The ten activities, including laundry, food preparation, washing machine usage, watching TV, and computer usage were chosen because they incur the largest and the most common power consumption loads in the residential sector. (These appliances are the washing machine, heater, electric fan, iron, microwave, vacuum cleaner, rice cooker, air-conditioner, television, and computer.)

III. OCCUPANT-LOCATION-DEPENDENT OPTIMAL CONTROL SCHEME

Multi-objective optimization involves selectively minimizing or maximizing multiple objective functions that are dependent on a set of constraints. The goal is to solve complex optimization problems by simultaneously considering potential conflicting goals.

With this scheme, we consider a system with n modules and set the power of the *i*th module to $P_i\ (t)$ watts when it operates in the usual manner prior to energy management. The switching on/off status of the *i*th module in the proposed energy management scheme can be represented by the following switching function,

$$\min_{u_i(t)} \sum_{i=1}^{N} P_i(t)u_i(t) \tag{1}$$

$$\max_{u_i(t)} \sum_{i=1}^{N} \frac{u_i(t)}{D_i(t)} \tag{2}$$

subject to

$$CO_{2,inner}(u_i(t)) - CO_{2,inner,\max} \leq 0 \tag{3}$$

$$T_{inner}(u_i(t)) - T_{inner,\max} \leq 0 \tag{4}$$

where $u_i(t)$ is the switching on/off status of the *i*th module, $D_i(t)$ is the appliance distance relative to the position of the human, $CO_{2,inner}(u_i(t))$ is the inner CO_2 concentration, $CO_{2,inner,\max}$ is the maximum allowed inner CO_2 concentration, $T_{inner}(u_i(t))$ is the inner temperature, and $T_{inner,\max}$ is the maximum allowed inner temperature.

IV. EXPERIMENTAL RESULTS

A. Experimental setup

In the experiment, the outdoor temperature is determined using temperature information from the meteorological office and the outdoor CO_2 concentration is set to 490 ppm. The $CO_{2,inner,\max}$ level is 470 ppm and $T_{inner,\max}$ is 23°C.

TABLE I. INDEXES OF ELECTRIC APPLIANCES FOR THE APPLIANCE SET

Index	Type	Power	Index	Type	Power
1	Air conditioner	2.07kW	6	Washing machine	242W
2	Fan	60W	7	Vacuum cleaner	1.07kW
3	Heater	1.16kW	8	Computer	255W
4	Iron	1.23kW	9	Microwave	1.04kW
5	TV	130W	10	Rice cooker	1.03kW

Table 1 shows the amounts of power used by household appliances. In this experiment, ten appliances and four rooms are considered.

B. Experiment

The experiment compares power consumption patterns with respect to the location, which is based on the user's location with priority distances of 5m and 10m. Figure 3 shows that optimizing the use of a device depends on the person's location, leading to less power use. The blue line represents the optimizations of independent user locations. In every room, an air conditioner and an electronic fan are used to maintain the target temperature and CO_2 level. It can be confirmed that the priority distance of 5m, as optimized according to the location of a person in the building, is useful in terms of power consumption.

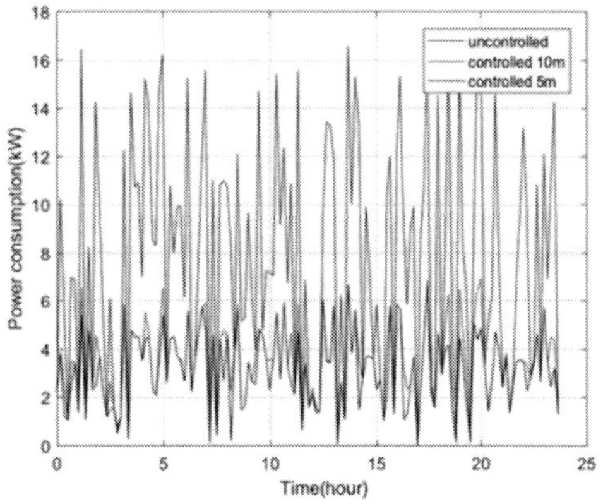

Fig. 3. Experimental results of multi-objective optimization depending on the user location and not depending on the user location (priority: depending on the user location - 5m and 10m, and then independent of the user location)

As a result, when considering this distance, the peak power can be reduced. The capital and operating costs can be reduced.

V. Conclusion

This paper discusses home energy management of a nanogrid with shifting of the peak load according to the location patterns of residents. Sensors in the building can monitor residential location patterns. This allows residents with diverse roles to participate in energy efficiency efforts using a HMM to determine the occupant pattern. Major ideas and experimental systems are expected to be applied not only to green buildings but also to a range of existing buildings in order to reduce power usage without sacrificing human comfort or convenience. Human comfort is linked to the maximum number of devices without scheduling. The operational characteristics of the house energy management scheme here are expressed according to the relationships between power consumption and human location patterns. Experimental results indicate that the reduction of power consumption based on the resident location optimization scheme is superior to that independent of resident locations. End users of this system can save electricity and continue to feel comfortable.

References

[1] A. Werth, N. Kitamura, and K. Tanaka, "Conceptual Study for Open Energy Systems: Distributed Energy Network Using Interconnected DC Nanogrids," IEEE Transactions on Smart Grid, vol. 6, no. 4, pp. 1621-1630, Jul 2015.

[2] D. Burmester, R. Rayudu, W. Seah, and D. Akinyele, "A review of nanogrid topologies and technologies," Renewable & Sustainable Energy Reviews, vol. 67, pp. 760-775, Jan 2017.

[3] T. A. Nguyen and M. Aiello, "Energy intelligent buildings based on user activity: A survey," Energy and Buildings, vol. 56, pp. 244-257, Jan 2013.

[4] J. Page, D. Robinson, N. Morel, and J. L. Scartezzini, "A generalised stochastic model for the simulation of occupant presence," Energy and Buildings, vol. 40, no. 2, pp. 83-98, 2008.

[5] D. Kolokotsa, A. Pouliezos, G. Stavrakakis, and C. Lazos, "Predictive control techniques for energy and indoor environmental quality management in buildings," Building and Environment, vol. 44, no. 9, pp. 1850-1863, Sep 2009.

[6] R. Yang and L. F. Wang, "Multi-objective optimization for decision-making of energy and comfort management in building automation and control," Sustainable Cities and Society, vol. 2, no. 1, pp. 1-7, Feb 2012.

[7] F. A. Qayyum et al., "Appliance Scheduling Optimization in Smart Home Networks," (in English), IEEE Access, Article vol. 3, pp. 2176-2190, 2015.

[8] S. Lee, B. Kwon, and S. Lee, "Joint Energy Management System of Electric Supply and Demand in Houses and Buildings," IEEE Transactions on Power Systems, vol. 29, no. 6, pp. 2804-2812, Nov 2014.

[9] A. Middelberg, J. F. Zhang, and X. H. Xia, "An optimal control model for load shifting - With application in the energy management of a colliery," Applied Energy, vol. 86, no. 7-8, pp. 1266-1273, Jul-Aug 2009.

[10] T. Logenthiran, D. Srinivasan, and T. Z. Shun, "Demand Side Management in Smart Grid Using Heuristic Optimization," (in English), IEEE Transactions on Smart Grid, Article vol. 3, no. 3, pp. 1244-1252, Sep 2012.

[11] P. Palensky and D. Dietrich, "Demand Side Management: Demand Response, Intelligent Energy Systems, and Smart Loads," (in English), IEEE Transactions on Industrial Informatics, Article vol. 7, no. 3, pp. 381-388, Aug 2011.

[12] Y. J. Sun, S. W. Wang, F. Xiao, and D. C. Gao, "Peak load shifting control using different cold thermal energy storage facilities in commercial buildings: A review," (in English), Energy Conversion and Management, Article vol. 71, pp. 101-114, Jul 2013.

[13] S. H. Baek, E. C. Choi, J. D. Huh, and K. R. Park, "Sensor information management mechanism for context-aware service in ubiquitous home," IEEE Transactions on Consumer Electronics, vol. 53, no. 4, pp. 1393-1400, Nov 2007.

[14] Y. Lium et al., "Peak-to-Average Ratio Constrained Demand-Side Management with Consumer's Preference in Residential Smart Grid," IEEE Journal of Selected Topics in Signal Processing, vol. 8, no. 6, pp. 1084-1097, Dec 2014.

[15] W. M. Wang, R. Zmeureanu, and H. Rivard, "Applying multi-objective genetic algorithms in green building design optimization," Building and Environment, vol. 40, no. 11, pp. 1512-1525, Nov 2005.

[16] J. Virote and R. Neves-Silva, "Stochastic models for building energy prediction based on occupant behavior assessment," Energy and Buildings, vol. 53, pp. 183-193, Oct 2012.

[17] J. Widen and E. Wackelgard, "A high-resolution stochastic model of domestic activity patterns and electricity demand," Applied Energy, vol. 87, no. 6, pp. 1880-1892, Jun 2010.

[18] M. Muratori, M. C. Roberts, R. Sioshansi, V. Marano, and G. Rizzoni, "A highly resolved modeling technique to simulate residential power demand," Applied Energy, vol. 107, pp. 465-473, Jul 2013.

[19] I. Richardson, M. Thomson, and D. Infield, "A high-resolution domestic building occupancy model for energy demand simulations," Energy and Buildings, vol. 40, no. 8, pp. 1560-1566, 2008.

Automatic Identification Monitoring System for Fishing Gear Based on Narrowband Internet-of-Things Communication Systems

Sangmin Lee, Dongsoo Har
The Cho Chun Shik Graduate School of Green Transportation
KAIST
Daejeon, Korea
E-mail: dwarang@kaist.ac.kr, dshar@kaist.ac.kr

***Abstract*—Lost and derelict fishing gear is devastating for the marine environment, causing marine accidents and decreasing the catch of fish. Therefore, South Korea is attempting to reduce this lost and derelict fishing gear by developing a new monitoring system that can track the location of fishing gear and manage this type of debris. This monitoring system will use what is known as the Narrowband Internet of Things (NB-IoT) for marine communication. Marine communication encounters a signal strength problem when a wave invades the first Fresnel zone. This article suggests relaying by drones to solve this problem and extend the coverage of communication modules.**

Keywords—Marine communication; Fishing gear; Narrowband Internet of Things; First Fresnel zone; Drone; Relaying

I. INTRODUCTION

Various types of fishing gear are used in the fishery and aquaculture industries both in nearshore and offshore locations. In particular, 131,000 tons of fishing gear are used each year in South Korea, which is surrounded by seas on three sides [1]. Lost and derelict fishing gear is causing great damage to marine environments, and marine accidents caused by derelict fishing gear are threatening the safety of fishermen. This devastation of the marine environment due to these debris decreased the catch of fish by an estimated 10% in 2016 in South Korea. Derelict fishing gear sometimes causes marine accidents in South Korea. Currently, fishing boats have become larger and use advanced fishing methods. However, the productivity of fisheries in nearshore and offshore locations has decreased. It is assumed that this decrease is caused by overfishing, ghost fishing (a term referring to lost and derelict fishing gear), and illegal fishing. Therefore, fishing gear management laws, monitoring systems, closed seasons, and resource management efforts have been considered. The FAO (Food and Agriculture Organization) of the United Nations has promoted the development of a management plan to maintain marine resources and to guarantee their efficient use. However, some feel that the efforts of the FAO will decrease productivity of fisheries. The Code of Conduct for Responsible Fisheries of the FAO recommends the marking of fishing gear during the operation of a fishery, emphasizing the importance of developing new technologies or new fishing methods to minimize ghost fishing [2].

South Korea revised the rule to permit fisheries and to register them, also introducing a real-name fishing gear system to prevent the overuse of fishing gear in nearshore and offshore areas. However, these regulations, despite much sympathizing with them, were not followed closely due to perceived inconvenience and unfairness. Therefore, South Korea suggested the necessity of developing a new real-name fishing gear system, a monitoring system to manage fishing gear, new technology to handle derelict fishing gear, and technology by which derelict fishing gear can be collected. In certain more advanced countries, such as Norway, Canada, and France, technology to check the condition of fishing gear on fishing boats and to monitor fish catches is being developed based on marine communication and navigating technology. However, no country can monitor all fishing gear around the world. South Korea, which has implemented a real-name fishing gear system, is attempting to adopt a new automatic identification monitoring system using NB-IoT [3], one of the latest IoT technologies, in cooperation with a mobile communication company to reduce the amount of lost and derelict fishing gear.

Section 2 outlines the current knowledge on automatic identification monitoring systems. Section 3 discusses several issues, including the decline of signal strength levels caused by the invasion of first Fresnel zone area related to antenna buoys and wave heights. Drones for relaying are then suggested as a solution for the signal strength and coverage issues of NB-IoT modules. Section 4 concludes this article.

II. AUTOMATIC IDENTIFICATION MONITORING SYSTEM FOR FISHING GEAR BASED ON NB-IOT

A. Narrowband Internet of Things

The IoT as the next generation of mobile communication has been developed rapidly by mobile communication companies and manufacturers. NB-IoT, a form of the IoT, uses low-power wide-area (LPWA) communication technology. Related to this, 3GPP approved NB-IoT based on narrowband LTE including OFDMA/SC-FDMA and it was included as a working item (WI) in Release 13 of Radio Access Network (RAN) #70 to cope with issues related to LPWA, LoRa, and Sigfox. NB-IoT can communicate via small amounts of data on a bandwidth of 180 kHz in the licensed LTE frequency domain. NB-IoT has three operation modes, the guard-band, in-band, and stand-alone modes, as described in

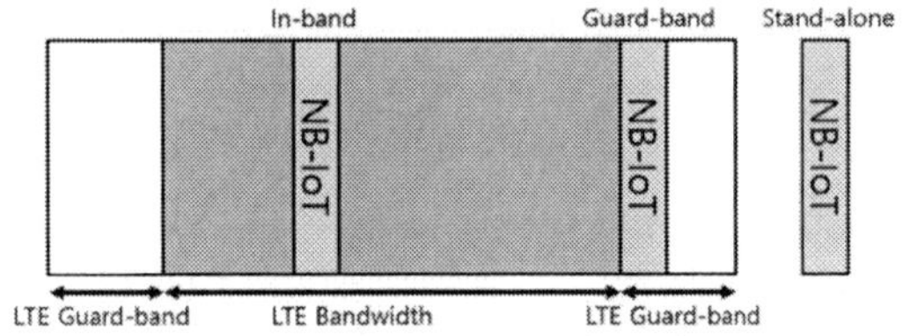

Figure 1. Operation modes of NB-IoT

TABLE I. SUMMARY OF NB-IOT

	NB-IoT
Deployment	In-band & guard-band LTE, stand-alone
Coverage	164dB for standalone, FFS others
Downlink	OFDMA, 15kHz tone spacing, 1 Rx
Uplink	Single tone, 15kHz and 3.75kHz spacing SC-FDMA, 15kHz tone spacing, Turbo code
Bandwidth	180kHz
Peak rate (DL/UL)	DL: ~200kbps UL: ~200kbps
Duplexing	HD, FDD
Coverage	~15km
Modulation	QPSK/16QAM
Power saving	PSM, ext. I-DRX, C-DRX
Power class	23dBm

Figure 1. Table 1 presents the specifications of NB-IoT. RAN #72 approved an enhanced NB-IoT (eNB-IoT) which requires additional improved technology as specified in the WI of Release 14 [3].

NB-IoT has several advantages. First, the NB-IoT modules are typically small and therefore inexpensive. Second, NB-IoT uses existing LTE base stations, which are already widespread in South Korea. Therefore, this technology allows communication everywhere in South Korea. Third, the batteries used in NB-IoT modules are expected to work for ten years because NB-IoT uses LPWA. Thus, maintenance is also inexpensive. NB-IoT is thus clearly suitable for small data communications.

B. *Concept of the automatic identification monitoring system*

The automatic identification monitoring system as a new system developed by the government attempts to prevent lost and derelict fishing gear from causing harm to marine environments while also maintaining a safe environment for fishermen by attempting to prevent marine accidents which are caused by the derelict fishing gear, among other tasks. The government wants to successfully manage fishing gear near the shore and in offshore areas. The monitoring system can always track the positons of fishing gear and judge whether or not these items are lost. Furthermore, the real-name fishing gear system serves to prohibit the overuse of fishing gear and to control fish catches. Above all, these measures motivate fishermen to maintain control over their fishing gear. The adoption of IoT technology for communication between fishing gear and the base station, between the base station and management ships, and between the base station and fishing boats is the key aspect of this monitoring system. The monitoring system utilizes NB-IoT communication technology, broadcasting on empty bandwidth segments of the licensed LTE frequency domain.

The automatic identification monitoring system for fishing gear based on NB-IoT consists of satellites, buoys, fishing gear, base stations, integrated base station on land, management ships, and fishing boats. Figure 2 shows the concept of this monitoring system. A satellite provides a global positioning system (GPS). Buoys, management ships, and fishing boats use GPS to determine current positions. Buoys form a connection to the fishing gear components and send information which includes the current position and data pertaining to the connections between buoys and these fishing gear components to the base station on land. These processes require very little data; therefore, NB-IoT, a type of LPWA, can handle these tasks. The integrated base station can receive data from all buoys in nearshore and offshore locations and track the positions of all of the fishing gear. The integrated base station sends all data to the management ships after accumulating data from the' buoys. However, communication between the integrated base station and the management ships uses existing LTE because the data from the integrated base stations are in the form of multimedia information including image data, such as positions of fishing gear, marine maps, and bathymetric charts. NB-IoT cannot handle this data, which is considered to be 'big' data.

Buoys have global navigation satellite system (GNSS) antennas for GPS, RF antennas for NB-IoT, communication modules for LPWA, and modules to identify fishing gear. The buoys float on the surface of the sea while maintaining a connection to the fishing gear. Fishing gear components, located underwater, typically have acoustic transmitters. When fishing gear becomes lost and/or detached, the fishing gear identification module detects the loss and sends information pertaining to the loss. At the same time, the acoustic transmitter in the fishing gear starts to work. The velocity of sound waves is 340 m/s in air and about 1500 m/s in water. Sound waves are elastic waves, which transfer energy more rapidly in a dense material. Therefore, they offer an advantage when used in water. The integrated base station sends the loss information to the fishing boat that originally installed the lost fishing gear after receiving information about the lost fishing gear. Fishing boats should have wireless nodes for NB-IoT communication. The fishing boats and management ships have acoustic receivers, allowing the fishing boats to move to the position of the lost fishing gear and receive the signal sent from the acoustic transmitter. Due to the use of an acoustic receiver, fishing boats can track the exact position of the fishing gear and collect it even when moved by sea currents.

III. ISSUES OF THE AUTOMATIC IDENTIFICATION MONITORING SYSTEM FOR FISHING GEAR

A. *First Fresnel zone and wave height*

The automatic identification monitoring system for fishing gear uses NB-IoT. Communication is mainly

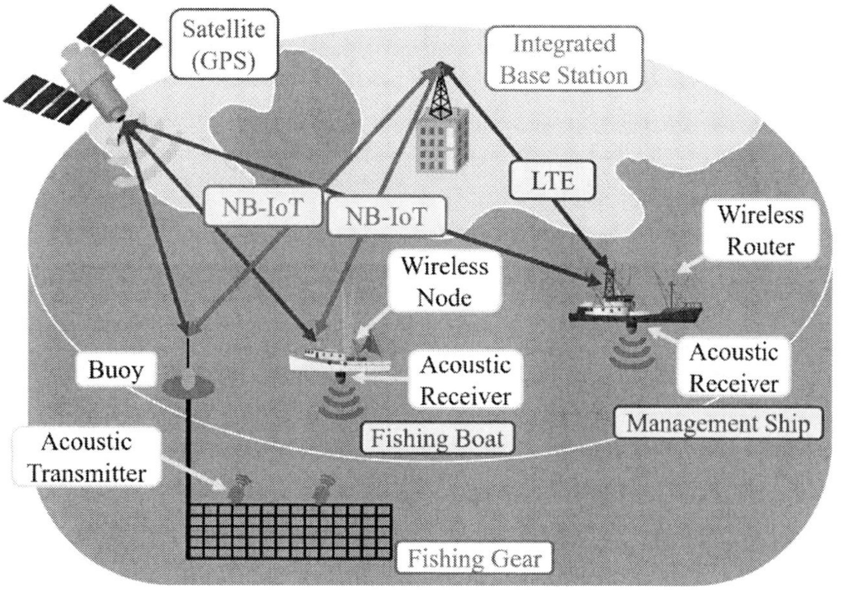

Figure 2. The automatic identification monitoring system for fishing gear based on NB-IoT

between buoys and the base station, which is on land. NB-IoT uses the licensed frequency domain. LTE is a type of wireless communication; therefore, it has the same characteristics as electromagnetic waves. A certain amount of empty air space is necessary for electromagnetic waves to propagate from the transmitter to the receiver without a decline of the signal strength.

Energy in space cannot arrive at a receiver in a straight line. Electromagnetic waves require an ellipsoid space following the minimum distance between the transmitter and the receiver. This space is called the Fresnel zone. In fact, it is possible to extend the space of the Fresnel zone infinitely. In principle, the first space, known as the first Fresnel zone, contributes to transfer the greatest amount of energy of a wave. The signal strength can decrease when obstacles exist in the first Fresnel zone. This weak signal strength increases the loss of transmitted data and the probability of errors. The first Fresnel zone is an ellipsoid space formed by the electromagnetic wave arriving at the receiver with following the shortest distance, which has a path difference of λ/2. Here, λ is the wavelength of the electromagnetic wave. The electromagnetic wave passing through the first Fresnel zone arrives at the receiving point after being superposed. Propagation loss in the first Fresnel zone becomes close to the theoretical value of the empty space. Therefore, good signal strength is guaranteed when no obstacles exist in 60% of the radius of the first Fresnel zone [4].

$$F_1 = \frac{1}{2}\sqrt{\lambda D} = \frac{1}{2}\sqrt{\frac{cD}{f}} \qquad (1)$$

Equation (1) is used to determine the radius of the first Fresnel zone. F_1 is the radius of the first Fresnel zone, D is the distance between the transmitter and the receiver, f is the frequency of the transmitted signal, and $c \simeq 2.997 \times 10^8$ m/s is the speed of light in air. According to (1), the radius of the first Fresnel zone is wide when the distance is long or the frequency is low. A small radius of the first Fresnel zone offers a low probability to lose the signal.

The automatic identification monitoring system for fishing gear based on NB-IoT requires a marine communication environment. The surface of the sea continually changes due to waves. For example, the radius of the first Fresnel zone of a buoy with a 1.8GHz electromagnetic wave with a distance of 1km is 6.452m. In this case, 60% of the radius is 3.871m, indicating that the buoy should have an antenna which is longer than 3.871m to ensure an empty first Fresnel zone. However, obstacles such as waves and other ships likely exist between the buoy and the base station. It is difficult to make the antenna longer when the size of the buoy is considered. Of course, the base station on land is located at a high altitude. The radius of the first Fresnel zone of the buoy with 850 MHz electromagnetic waves and with a 15 km distance is 36.362m, and 60% of the radius is 21.817m. This radius must encounter obstacles as those shown in Figure 3. Therefore, the communication between the buoy and the base station will not always be smooth.

B. Using drones for relaying

Using drones for relaying has been suggested to solve first Fresnel zone problem on the sea. The automatic

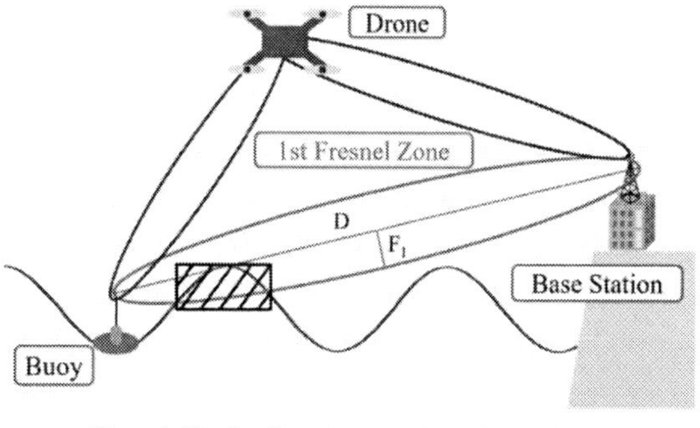

Figure 3. The first Fresnel zone and relaying by drones

identification monitoring system for fishing gear operates on management ships. These ships have drones that have NB-IoT communication modules and signal amplifiers for relaying. The management ship flies the drone through the air. The signal from the buoy is then transmitted to the base station via the drone, as shown in Figure 3. It is possible to remove obstacles and to communicate smoothly when the drone is in the air at an altitude in the tens of meters. Furthermore, relaying by drones is able to extend the communication coverage of NB-IoT between the buoy and the base station via the signal amplifier [5].

IV. CONCLUSION

This article briefly introduces a new automatic identification monitoring system for fishing gear based on NB-IoT communication that is being developed in South Korea. Some issues are discussed related to the realization of this monitoring system. The problem of the decreased signal strength arises when the wave height invades the first Fresnel zone. Therefore, relaying by drone was suggested to solve this signal strength problem and to extend the coverage of NB-IoT communication. The objectives of this monitoring system are to track the locations of lost and derelict fishing gear components with the real-name fishing gear system and to collect these items. Furthermore, the system can prevent lost and derelict fishing gear from devastating marine environments and can reduce ghost fishing and marine accidents caused by this fishing gear. In several years, this automatic identification monitoring system for fishing gear will be developed and will hopefully contribute to marine environment preservation efforts and to better fishery practices in many parts of the world.

REFERENCES

[1] SG. Kim, WI. Lee, and Y. Moon, "The estimation of derelict fishing gear in the coastal waters of South Korea: Trap and gill-net fisheries," Marine Policy, vol. 46, pp. 119-122, 2014.

[2] SM. Garcia, "The FAO definition of sustainable development and the Code of Conduct for Responsible Fisheries: an analysis of the related principles, criteria and indicators," Marine and Freshwater Research, vol. 51, no. 5, pp. 535-541, 2000.

[3] R. Ratasuk, B. Vejlgaard, N. Mangalvedhe, and A. Ghosh, "NB-IoT system for M2M communication," Wireless Communications and Networking Conference (WCNC), pp. 1-5, 2016.

[4] A. Sorrentino, G. Ferrara, and M. Migliaccio, "The reverberating chamber as a line-of-sight wireless channel emulator," IEEE Transactions on Antennas and Propagation, vol. 56, no. 6, pp. 1825-1830, 2008.

[5] A. Jaziri, R. Nasri, and T. Chahed, "Congestion mitigation in 5G networks using drone relays," International Wireless Communications and Mobile Computing Conference (IWCMC), pp. 233-238, 2016.

Multiple Stage Charging of Rechargeable Wireless Sensor Networks with a Directional Antenna

Celso Moraes and Dongsoo Har
Cho Chun Shik Graduate School of Green Transportation
KAIST
Daejeon, Republic of Korea
asura254@kaist.ac.kr, dshar@kaist.ac.kr

Abstract— **Wireless sensor networks are finding widespread use nowadays with the development of Internet of Things (IoT) technology. Due to their wireless nature, these devices use batteries as their main source of power. This creates the problem of continuity of operation, because batteries have a limited lifetime. Therefore, sensors capable of performing energy harvesting are preferred. The harvested energy can be acquired from ambient or dedicated sources consisting of mobile chargers. This paper deals with a charging scheme for randomly distributed sensor nodes using a mobile charger. The charging scheme consists of a multiple-stage charging procedure, in which in each stage an energy goal for the target sensor nodes is set up. For charging in the first stage, all the sensor nodes are classified into clusters. The theory of an inclusion circle is used in this process. By clustering based on the inclusion circle, a sensor node that is located around the center of grouped sensor nodes is highly likely to be selected as the cluster head. The mobile charger only concentrates about charging the cluster heads. The charging path of the moving charger is determined according to the locations of cluster heads. In the following stages, new clusters are formed based on the energy level of the sensor nodes in the system, and a new target energy goal is set up for them.**

Keywords-Charging Sensors; Clustering;Wireless Sensor Networks; IoT; Energy HarFin thisvesting.

I. INTRODUCTION

The currently rapid development of the IoT has seen a large increase in the usage of sensor networks, generating challenges for the performance of this technology [1]. The provision of operating energy for IoT devices is becoming a major bottleneck in the development of this technology. Due to advances in chip design and in the deep submicron fabrication process, sensors that feature characteristics of low-power and low-cost are being adopted for a variety of applications, including mission-critical ones. These mission-critical applications, such as seismic activity [2][3], volcano temperature [4], space monitoring [5], disaster relief situation [6], human activity [7], and oceanic monitoring [8] instruments are associated with hard-to-reach sensor locations. In these environments, it is extremely dangerous and sometimes impossible to replace the batteries of the sensor nodes. Depletion of energy by a sensor node is a very important matter, one that highlights the importance of power provisioning. From this perspective, wireless (re)charging is a viable solution for sensor nodes capable of energy harvesting [9].

The rest of this paper is structured as follows. In Section II, we present the state of the art. In Section III, the proposed scheme of the rechargeable wireless sensor node with directional antenna is presented. Section IV details the results of the simulation. Finally, Section V concludes the paper.

II. STATE OF THE ART

There are many different ways to provide energy to sensor nodes in a rechargeable wireless sensor network. Fu et al. [10] presented a charging scheme with a mobile charger. The goal of their charging scheme is to find optimal locations of the mobile charger that can facilitate minimum charging time for all the sensor nodes to reach a target energy level. Linear programming is used to find the optimal spots at which the charger should be stationed over individual sojourn times. Madhja et al. [11] proposed a charging scheme employing multiple chargers, with two different classes of mobile chargers being used. The chargers that belong to the mobile charger class are responsible only for charging the infrastructure sensor nodes; the charger in the super charger class has the duty of charging the other chargers in the mobile charger class as well as the sensor nodes. Wang [12] presented a charging scheme with two different types of energy sources. The sensor nodes are clustered and the cluster heads have the capability of harvesting solar energy, while the other nodes are charged by mobile chargers transferring RF energy.

A charging scheme comprising multiple stages is proposed in this paper. Initially, using the concept of an inclusion circle, described by Moraes and Har [13], clusters and cluster heads are formed amongst the sensor nodes. Afterwards, the mobile charger will proceed to charge these cluster heads until a target energy level E_l is reached. The mobile charger can have either a directional or an omnidirectional antenna. After all the cluster heads reach the target energy level, a second charging stage is initiated. The old clusters are disregarded and new clusters are formed, but these clusters now include the energy level of each sensor node as a criterion for being eligible for clustering. Only nodes under the target energy level E_l from the previous stage can participate in the new clustering procedure. A new charging stage is carried out by the mobile charger with the new cluster heads. The process of formation of new clusters and charging by the charger is repeated until all the sensor nodes in the system are charged to the final required level. This avoids favoring more centralized sensor nodes in the charging process, and the distributed nature of the charging procedure contributes to both decreasing the charging time and reducing energy expenditure

III. PROPOSED SCHEME

Consider that there are N_T sensor nodes randomly scattered in a square area. It is assumed that the sensor nodes in this case are fixed location nodes, for which the position of each node is known by the charger. Also, the charger has knowledge of each sensor node SoC (state of charge), which is a common assumption. The charger can move freely in the total service area.

The first step in the charging process is the initial formation of clusters in the system. Many clustering algorithms already exist in the literature, and for this work the clustering algorithm utilized was the one described in [13]. The number of clusters in this algorithm is determined by the distribution of the sensor nodes, and not predetermined before the clustering starts.

During the charging stages, the moving chargers only focus on supplying energy to the cluster heads, as was done in [13]. The time-varying change of charger location during the charging process can be modeled by concatenated discrete movements. The possible actions of the charger at each discrete time step are either to stay at the same location or to move to the next best location. The time interval Δt_c for the next movement is uniformly set at 2.5msec; distance r_m between the current location and the next optimal location is set at 0.05m during the simulations. If the next discrete movement to the next location circle occurs over a sizable time, and the location of the mobile charger is continuously shifted accordingly, the velocity of the mobile charger is (0.05m/2.5ms)=72km/hour. This circle is shown in Figure 1 (a). While the next location circle is concerned with the location of the mobile charger, the service sector with radius R_s, shown in Figure 1(b), is used to evaluate the amount of power received by the cluster heads, which influences the decision regarding the next optimal location on the next location circle.

The interior angle of each service sector is the beam width of the antenna, labeled as 2B; the bisector of the interior angle connects the charger and an undercharged cluster head. Therefore, the sector size increases as the antenna gain decreases. In the case of an omni-directional antenna, 2B is set to 360°.

Let $\theta_i(t)$, i=1,.., $N_{uch}(t)$, where $N_{uch}(t)$ is the total number of cluster heads at time t, be the θ of the i-th undercharged cluster head at time t. The $\theta_i(t)$ is formed by the horizontal line and the line connecting the charger and

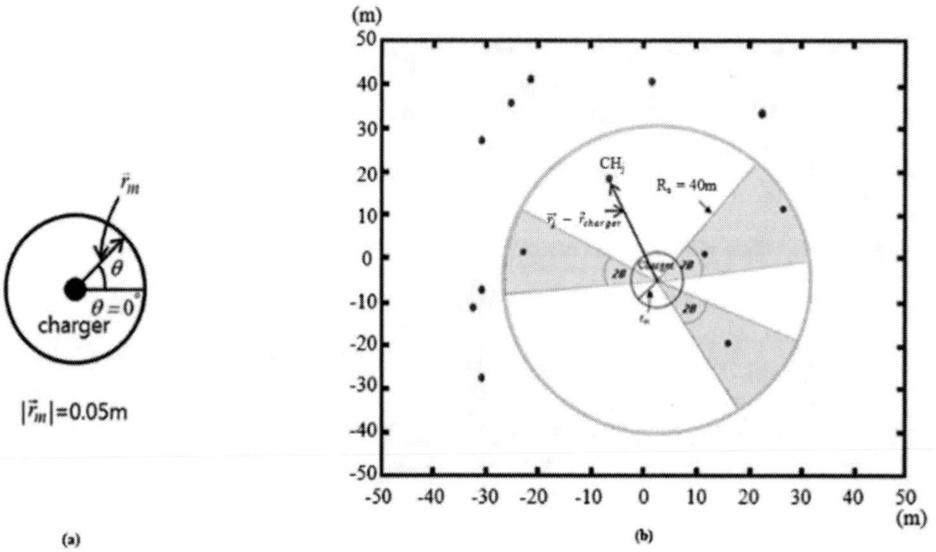

Figure 1. Next location circle and service sector for charging undercharged cluster heads: (a) next location circle; (b) sectors including undercharged cluster heads [13].

the i-th undercharged cluster head, as shown in Figure 1(b). For an angle $\theta_i(t)$ the number of undercharged cluster heads $N_{ss}(\theta_i(t))$ within the sector having a range of angle $(\theta_i(t)-B) \sim (\theta_i(t)+B)$ is considered to determine the movement of the charger. Then, the sum of the power $P_{ss}^A(\theta_i(t))$, received by the undercharged cluster heads within the i-th sector is given as [13]

$$P_{ss}^A(\theta_i(t)) = \sum_{s=1}^{N_{SS}(\theta_i(t))} P_r^A(\vec{r}_{is}(t), \vec{r}_{charger}(t) + \Delta\vec{r}_{\theta_i(t)}, \phi_{is}(t)) \quad (1)$$

with $i = 1,\ldots,N_{uch}(t)$ and $s = 1,\ldots,N_{ss}(\theta_i(t))$ and $N_{uch}(t) \geq N_{ss}(\theta_i(t))$. The $\vec{r}_{is}(t) = (x_{is}(t)\ y_{is}(t))$ is the location of the s-th undercharged cluster head within the i-th sector and the $\Delta\vec{r}_{\theta_i(t)} = (r_m \cos\theta_i(t)\ \ r_m \sin\theta_i(t))$ is the incremental vector from the location of the charger to a point on the next location circle at angle $\theta_i(t)$. Note that the locations of the undercharged cluster heads are functions of time t, because the undercharged cluster heads become overcharged over time one after another.

The next optimal location on the next location circle in terms of optimal $\theta_{opt}(t)$ can be mathematically expressed as [13]

$$\begin{aligned}\theta_{opt}(t) &= \arg\max_{\theta_i(t)} P_{ss}^A(\theta_i(t)) \\ &= \arg\max_{\theta_i(t)} \sum_{s=1}^{N_{SS}(\theta_i(t))} P_r^A(\vec{r}_{is}(t), \vec{r}_{charger}(t) + \Delta\vec{r}_{\theta_i(t)}, \phi_{is}(t)) \\ &= \arg\max_{\theta_i(t)} \sum_{s=1}^{N_{SS}(\theta_i(t))} g(\phi_{is}(t)) \frac{\alpha}{\left(d_{is}^{\theta}(t)+\beta\right)^2}\end{aligned} \quad (2)$$

IV. Simulation Results

For the simulation results, the number of sensor nodes to be considered were set to be 100 and 200. The total size of the area occupied by the sensor nodes was 100 x 100 meters.

Figure 2 shows the probability density function (PDF) for the number of sensor nodes charged in the first stage charging for 100 sensor nodes. The number of sensor nodes charged in the first stage for 0 dB gain is much larger than that number for 12 dB gain. This happens because the beam width with 12 dB is much narrower, and the number of sensor nodes that will also be charged during the charging of the cluster heads is small, so the amount of energy needed by the undercharged sensor nodes in the following stages will be larger. For 0 dB, the beam width is omnidirectional, so many sensor nodes will also be charged alongside the cluster heads. Therefore, the number of sensor nodes that need to be charged and the amount of energy necessary to charge them will be significantly lower.

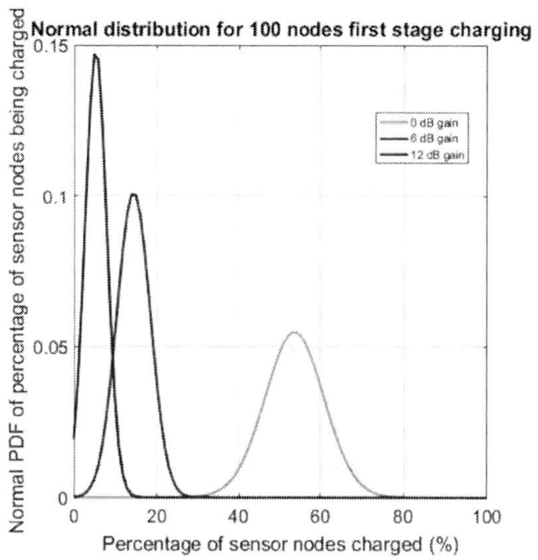

Figure 2. Probability density function of charged sensor nodes for 100 nodes in the first stage.

Figure 3 shows the PDF for the number of sensor nodes charged after the second stage charging. In this case, it is noticeable that there is a high probability that all sensor nodes will be charged with the 6 dB antenna. The 6 dB antenna appears to have the ideal tradeoff range value between 12 dB and 0 dB. At 6 dB the antenna presents a directional pattern, and so it will be able to focus on the cluster heads and speed up the charging process; however, because there is still a wide beam width angle for this antenna, many of the clustered nodes will also be charged during the charging of the cluster heads. To verify that this trend is maintained for larger numbers of sensor nodes, a sensor network with 200 nodes was simulated. Figure 4 shows that for 200 nodes the same trends continue, with the difference that for 0 dB and 6 dB the probability is more evenly spread out, providing the possibility of charging larger numbers of sensor nodes. Figure 5 shows the PDF for the second stage charging. For 200 nodes, it is shown in Figure 5 that the trend of 6 dB having the best trade-off value remains in place, with the only difference being that now the probability of all of them being charged is lower, which is understandable due to the higher number of sensor nodes in the system.

V. Conclusion

An alternative charging procedure for wireless sensor networks was proposed. The procedure consisted in splitting the charging time into stages so that a mobile charger could focus on cluster head sensor nodes instead of on the whole system, changing the assignments of cluster heads with increases of energy in the system. The procedure was shown to be able to charge sensors better by using a 6 dB gain antenna, due to the tradeoff between beam width and directional gain. The next steps will be to test the time and energy expenditure incurred with this charging process and compare those values with values of current models in the literature.

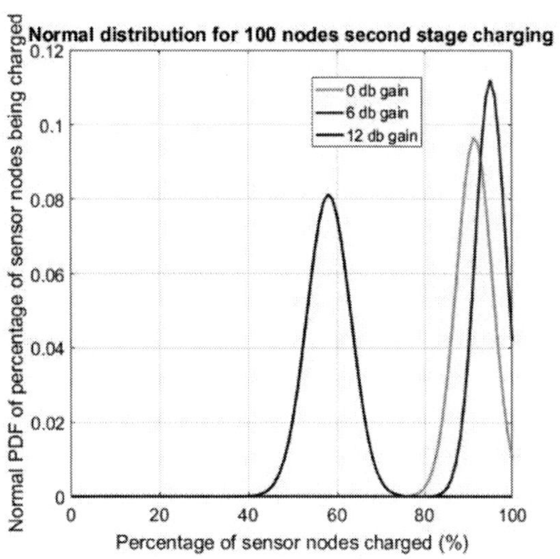

Figure 3. Probability density function of charged sensor nodes for 100 nodes in the second stage

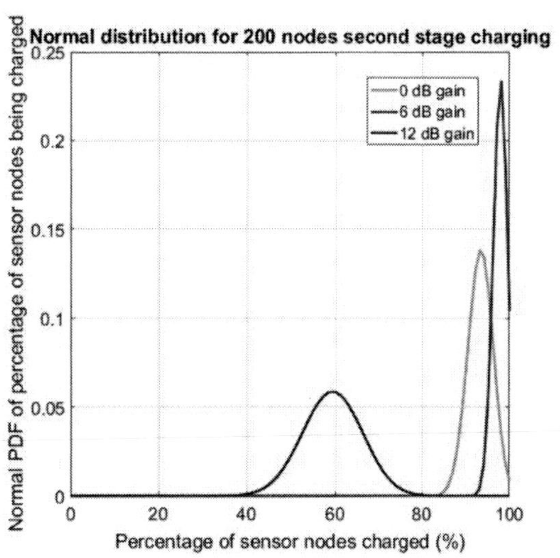

Figure 4. Probability density function of charged sensor nodes for 200 nodes in the first stage

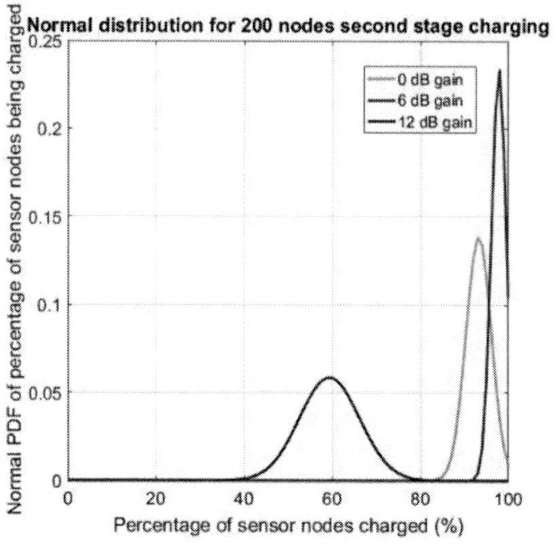

Figure 5. Probability density function of charged sensor nodes for 200 nodes in the first stage

REFERENCES

[1] F. Li and P. Xiong, "Practical Secure Communication for Integrating Wireless Sensor Networks Into the Internet of Things", IEEE Sensors Journal, Vol. 13, No. 10, Oct. 2013.

[2] A. Amditis, Y. Stratakos, D. Bairaktaris, M. Bimpas, S. Camarinopolos, and S. Frondistou-Yannas, "Wireless sensor network for seismic evaluation of concrete buildings," in Proc. 5th Eur. Workshop Struct. Health Monitor., Sorrento, Italy, July 2010.

[3] T. Torfs et al., "Low power wireless sensor network for building monitoring," IEEE Sensors J., Vol. 13, no. 3, pp. 909–915, Mar. 2013.

[4] G. Werner-Allen, K. Lorincz, M. Ruiz, O. Marcillo, J. Johnson, J. Lees, M. Welsh, "Deploying a Wireless Sensor Network on an Active Volcano," IEEE Internet Computing, Vol. 10, no. 2, pp. 18-25, 2006.

[5] H. F. Rashvand, A. Abedi, J.M. Alcaraz-Calero, P.D. Mitchell, and S. C. Mukhopadhyay, "Wireless sensor systems for space and extreme environments: A review," IEEE Sensors Journal, Vol. 14, no.11, pp.3955–3970, Sept. 2014.

[6] N. Aziz and K. Aziz, "Managing disaster with wireless sensor networks," IEEE Proceedings of 13th International Conference on Advanced Communication Technology (ICACT) , 2011, pp. 202–207, 2011.

[7] S. C. Mukhopadhyay, "Wearable Sensors for Human Activity Monitoring: A Review." IEEE Sensors Journal, Vol. 15, no. 3, pp. 1321-1330, 2015.

[8] C. Albaladejo et al., Torres, R. "Wireless Sensor Networks for Oceanographic Monitoring: A Systematic Review". *Sensors*, pp. 6948-6968, 2010.

[9] H. G. Lee and N. Chang, "Powering the IoT: Storage-less and converter-less energy harvesting," inProc. 20th Asia South Pacific Design Autom.Conf. (ASP-DAC), Jan. 2015, pp. 124–129.

[10] L. Fu, P. Cheng, Y. Gu, J. Chen and T. He, "Optimal Charging in Wireless Rechargeable Sensor Networks", *IEEE Trans. Veh. Technol.*, Vol. 65, no. 1, pp. 278-291, Jan. 2016.

[11] A. Madhja, S. Nikoletseas and T. P. Raptis, "Hierarchical collaborative wireless charging in sensor networks", *IEEE WCNC*, pp.1285-1290, 2015.

[12] C. Wang, J. Li, Y. Yang and F. Ye, "A hybrid framework combining solar energy harvesting and wireless charging for wireless sensor networks".

[13] C. Moraes and D. Har "Charging Distributed Sensor Nodes Exploiting Clustering and Energy Trading," *IEEE Sensors Journal*, Vol. 17, no. 2, pp. 546-555, 2016.

Exhaustive Study on Medical Sensors

Nadine Boudargham*, Jacques Bou Abdo†, Jacques Demerjian‡, and Christophe Guyeux§
*Faculty of Engineering
Notre Dame University, Deir El Kamar, Lebanon
Email: nboudargham@ndu.edu.lb
†Faculty of Natural and Applied Sciences
Notre Dame University, Deir El Kamar, Lebanon
Email: jbouabdo@ndu.edu.lb
‡LARIFA-EDST, Faculty of Sciences
Lebanese University, Fanar, Lebanon
Email: jacques.demerjian@ul.edu.lb
§FEMTO-ST Institute, UMR 6174 CNRS
Univ. Bourgogne Franche-Comté, Belfort, France
Email: christophe.guyeux@univ-fcomte.fr

Abstract—**The advances in electronics allowed the development of smart miniature devices called medical sensors, that can collect physiological data from the human body and its surrounding and send it wirelessly to healthcare providers in order to help avoiding life threatening events. This article presents a general overview on the types of medical sensors, their properties, and the wireless technologies used to convey collected data. Also, this article is the first to provide a summary about the wearable sensors' brands available on the market, along with their interface and connection types [1, 2].**

***Keywords*—wearable sensors; body sensors; medical sensors.**

I. Introduction

The Wireless Sensor Networks (WSNs) are formed of small computing devices called sensor nodes that can be implanted in or placed around the human body. These intelligent sensors collect physiological data from the body and send them wirelessly to medical personnel through personal devices like PDA or smartphone, allowing continuous health monitoring of the current state of the person to make proper decisions [3, 4].

There are two applications for sensor nodes: medical and non-medical [5]. In medical applications, sensors collect physical attributes from human body like blood pressure, respiration, and temperature to detect any anomaly as early as possible and take appropriate action before it is too late. These sensors can be implanted in the human body (i.e. implanted sensors), either under the skin or in the blood stream, to detect abnormalities like cancer and cardiovascular diseases, or they can be placed on the human body (i.e. wearable sensors) to be used for disability assistance like fall detection and blinds' assistance in obstacles avoidance, and for performance assessment like soldiers' status evaluation in a battle and athletes' condition assessment during sports training, besides of anomaly detection like asthma and heart beat problems. As for non-medical applications, examples include emotion detection applications, secure authentication, entertainment applications, and non-medical emergencies through gathering data from the environment and warning people in case of disaster or danger like fire or possibility of flood.

There are numerous sensors used in medical applications. Table I summarizes the most used sensors along with their position [6]. Depending on their type, sensors are either placed on the human body (wearable), or in the surrounding, or implanted inside the human body. These sensors include the accelerometer that is used to perceive the expenditure of human energy, the artificial cochlea utilized for hearing aid, the artificial retina used for visual aid, the camera pill deployed to monitor the gastrointestinal track, the carbon dioxide sensor used to measure the content of carbon dioxide from various gas, the ECG utilized to detect heart diseases, the EEG used to detect brain anomalies, and the EMG deployed to perceive muscles and nerve cells problems. This is in addition to many other sensors measuring blood pressure, humidity, blood oxygen, pressure, respiration, and temperature.

These sensors face many challenges like self-calibration requirements to adjust the sensitivity of the sensors based on the environment where they are placed, low- maintenance requirements, compatibility and interference problems induced by integrating multiple sensors operating at different frequencies and need to communicate between each other, and limited energy resources [16].

The rest of the paper is organized as follows: The major properties of sensors are presented in Section II; sensor wireless communication technologies are listed in Section III, and a summary on the available sensors in the market is presented in Section IV, to conclude in Section V.

II. Major Properties of Sensors

Since sensor nodes are small wireless devices placed on, around and in the human body, and can capture various physiological parameters, they usually have the following properties [3]:

- The size of the sensor nodes is very small (not more than 1 cm^3), thus the battery size inside sensors is miniature and the energy available is often restricted. Also, sensors are requested to serve for a long period of time, and it is very hard to replace sensors' batteries specially when they are implanted inside the human body. Therefore finding ways to reduce energy consumption and to harvest additional energy is always needed in medical sensors.

- Sensor nodes are usually heterogeneous and require different data rates, bandwidth, and energy resources form the network depending on the type of data they are collecting. Table II illustrates sensors' heterogeneity based on the different data rate requirements [5, 6]. The table shows that the data rate can vary considerably from few Kbps to several Mbps.

- There are no redundant nodes. All nodes have the same level of importance and are added depending on their need in the application.

- Nodes have very limited transmit power in order to avoid interference and to address health concerns.

- Nodes should support self-organization and self-maintenance characteristics since they are usually operated by medical staff and not engineers. Once a node is added to the human body and turned on, it should be able to join the network and set up connections without any involvement.

III. Sensors' Wireless Communication Technologies

In general, there are three types of networks formed by the sensors wireless communication [7, 8]:

- In-body network communication: used for communication between wearable sensors, or between implanted sensors in the body and the receiver located outside the body.
- On-body network communication: used for communication between wearable sensors and the coordinator or sink device used to gather data and transfer sensing data to a local processing.
- External Network communication: Used for communication between the coordinator and a remote back-end server.

Table III presents the different technologies and standards used for both short range and long range communication between sensors, coordinator device and external back-end server. It shows that the radio standards used to implement in-body and on-body network communications are short-range communication standards including Industrial Scientific and Medical (ISM) band, Medical Implant Communication Service (MICS) band, Wireless Medical Telemetry Service (WMTS), Radio-Frequency Identification (RFID), Bluetooth, Zigbee, and WLAN (Wi- Fi) technologies; whereas the radio standards used to implement external network communication are medium and long-range communication standards including Cellular Networks, WiFi, GPRS, Zifbee, Wibro, and Satellite technologies.

IV. Available Sensors in the Market

There are many companies specialized in wearable medical sensors designed to collect data from the human body and the surrounding environment. Table IV presents the sensors provided by some of the well-known companies in the sensor business, along with the corresponding connection type [9–17].

Table IV shows that the parameters captured by these sensors include body temperature, ECG and activity sensor, EMG, respiration, heart rate estimate, weight, force, SpO2, humidity, body position, fall alert, invasive blood pressure, barometric air pressure, and ambient light acquisition. It also shows that most sensors send the collected data via Bluetooth Low Energy (BLE). Some sensors have micro-USB interface, and many sensors are equipped with microSD card for local storage of data. In addition, many sensors are provided with external connector to connect to an external dock used to program and charge the sensor and to access the microSD card, whereas few others have digital serial interfaces.

V. Conclusion

In this article, the different types of medical sensors were presented, along with their properties and the wireless communication technologies used to send collected data. Also, the wearable medical sensors available on the market were listed along with their communication interface. The main aim of this article is to provide a clear understanding on the medical sensors, and to make it easier for the end user to select the appropriate sensor brand available on the market based on the type of data collected by the sensor and its interface and connection type.

This work is partially funded by the Lebanese University Research Program and the Labex ACTION program (contract ANR-11-LABX-01-01).

References

[1] S. Patel, H. Park, P. Bonato, L. Chan, and M. Rodgers, "A review of wearable sensors and systems with application in rehabilitation," *Journal of NeuroEngineering and Rehabilitation*, vol. 9, no. 1, p. 21, Apr. 2012, ISSN: 1743-0003. DOI: 10.1186/1743-0003-9-21. [Online]. Available: https://doi.org/10.1186/1743-0003-9-21.

[2] D. J. Reinkensmeyer, P. Bonato, M. L. Boninger, L. Chan, R. E. Cowan, B. J. Fregly, and M. M. Rodgers, "Major trends in mobility technology research and development: Overview of the results of the nsf-wtec european study," *Journal of NeuroEngineering and Rehabilitation*, vol. 9, no. 1, p. 22, Apr. 2012, ISSN: 1743-0003. DOI: 10.1186/1743-0003-9-22. [Online]. Available: https://doi.org/10.1186/1743-0003-9-22.

[3] B. Latré, B. Braem, I. Moerman, C. Blondia, and P. Demeester, "A survey on wireless body area networks," *Wireless Networks*, vol. 17, no. 1, pp. 1–18, 2011.

[4] N. Boudargham, J. Abdo, J. Demerjian, C. Guyeux, and A. Makhoul, "Investigating low level protocols for wireless body sensor networks," in *3rd ACS/IEEE International Conference on Computer Systems and Applications*, IEEE, 2016.

[5] S. Movassaghi, M. Abolhasan, J. Lipman, D. Smith, and A. Jamalipour, "Wireless body area networks: A survey," *IEEE Communications Surveys & Tutorials*, vol. 16, no. 3, pp. 1658–1686, 2014.

[6] X. Lai, Q. Liu, X. Wei, W. Wang, G. Zhou, and G. Han, "A survey of body sensor networks," *Sensors*, vol. 13, no. 5, pp. 5406–5447, 2013.

[7] R. D. Caytiles and S. Park, "A study of the design of wireless medical sensor network based u-healthcare system," *International Journal of Bio-Science and Bio-Technology*, vol. 6, no. 3, pp. 91–96, 2014.

[8] S. T.-B. Hamida, E. B. Hamida, and B. Ahmed, "A new mhealth communication framework for use in wearable wbans and mobile technologies," *Sensors*, vol. 15, no. 2, pp. 3379–3408, 2015.

[9] Movisens Website, URL: www.movisens.com, 2017.

[10] Shimmer Sensing Website, URL: www.shimmersensing.com, 2017.

[11] TE Connectivity Website, URL: www.te.com, 2017.

[12] MC10 Website, URL: www.mc10inc.com, 2017.

[13] Withings Website, URL: www.withings.com, 2017.

[14] Equivital Website, URL: www.equivital.co.uk, 2017.

[15] Somaxis Website, URL: www.somaxis.com, 2017.

[16] Vital Connect Website, URL: https://vitalconnect.com/, 2017.

[17] ST Microelectronics Website, URL: www.st.com, 2017.

TABLE IV: SENSOR TYPES AND CONNECTION INTERFACE

Company	Sensor Name	Description	Interface
Movisens (Germany) [9] https://www.movisens.com	Move III Activity Sensor	Sensor for the acquisition of 3D acceleration, barometric air pressure and temperature	Micro-USB - Bluetooth Low Energy (BLE)
	LightMove 3 (Light and Activity Sensor)	Sensor for the acquisition of ambient light, 3D acceleration, barometric air pressure and temperature	Micro-USB - BLE
	EcgMove 3 (ECG and Activity Sensor)	Sensor for the acquisition of ECG, 3D acceleration, barometric air pressure and temperature	Micro-USB - BLE
	EdaMove 3 (EDA and Activity Sensor)	Sensor for the acquisition of EDA, 3D acceleration, barometric air pressure and temperature	Micro-USB - BLE
Shimmer (Ireland) [10] www.shimmersensing.com/	Shimmer3 IMU	9 DoF inertial sensing via accelerometer, gyroscope, and magnetometer, each with selectable range	Bluetooth or local storage via microSD card - Includes external connector to connect to Shimmer Dock (refer to Accessories)
	Shimmer3 ECG	Sensor for the acquisition of ECG, 3D acceleration, barometric air pressure and temperature	Micro-USB - BLE
	Shimmer3 EMG	EMG, ECG, Respiration, 9 Degree of Freedom (DoF) inertial sensing	Bluetooth Radio RN-42 - Integrated 8GB micro SD card - Includes external connector to connect to Shimmer Dock (refer to Accessories)
	Shimmer3 GSR+	GSR, PPG, heart rate (HR) estimate , 9 DoF inertial sensing	Bluetooth RN42 - Integrated 8GB microSD card slot - Includes external connector to connect to Shimmer Dock (refer to Accessories)
	Shimmer3 Bridge Amplifier	Load, Weight, Force, Torque, Pressure, 9 DoF inertial sensing	Class 2 Bluetooth Radio Roving Networks RN42 - microSD card supporting up to 32GB - Includes external connector to connect to Shimmer Dock (refer to Accessories)
	PROTO3 Deluxe Unit	Expansion boards for the Shimmer3 platform. Provides an interface between Shimmer3 and analogue output sensor, digital output sensor, serial UART or parallel bus interface. Allows application developers to add functionality to the Shimmer and to develop customized applications based on user requirement	Two 3.5mm 4-position jacks (TRRS Cables. Or through-hole connections
Accessories	Shimmer Dock	The Shimmer Dock is a multipurpose device which can provide three primary functions: charging the Shimmer, MicroSD card access, and programming the Shimmer	The Dock includes mini USB port and connects to a PC via a USB cable

Company	Sensor Name	Description	Interface
TE Connectivity Ltd. (USA) [11] www.te.com	TE Medical Sensors	Air Bubble, Force, Humidity, Liquid Level, Piezo Film, Position, Pressure, Pulse Oximetry, Temperature Vibration. Assemblies designed to withstand the harsh environments of diagnostic equipment including ECG, EEG, TENS, temperature, SpO2 and invasive blood pressure	I2C interface - Mini USB- MicroSD card storage
MC10 (USA) [12] https://www.mc10inc.com/	BioStampRC	Access to raw kinematic and electrophysiological data 6 degrees of freedom inertial sensing with 3-axis accelerometer and gyroscope Electric biopotential	BLE
	WiSP™	Cardiac monitoring and ECG recording	BLE
Withings (USA) [13] https://www.withings.com/	Pulse Ox	Advanced tracking, every step of the way. During the day it captures steps, distance walked, elevation climbed and calories burned. At night, it monitors sleep cycles. And when asked, it measures the heart rate and blood oxygen level	BLE
	Steel HR	Continuous HR monitoring when running and in workout mode. 10+ activities tracked via automatic and learned recognition. Automatic analysis of sleep cycles, wake-ups, and sleep duration, plus silent smart alarm	BLE
	Wireless Blood Pressure Monitor	Blood Pressure and heart rate monitoring	BLE
Equivital (UK) [14] www.equivital.co.uk/	EQ02 LifeMonitor Sensor Electronics Module (SEM)	The LifeMonitor can simultaneously provide the following data : ECG, Heart rate, R-R interval, Respiratory rate, Skin temperature, Accelerometer XYZ, Body position, Motion status, Fall alert, Device alarms, Subject alerts	Class 1 Bluetooth 2.1 (100m operating range) - Connectivity: USB (2.0 compatible) - 8GB memory for up to 50 days of continuous data logging
	Equivital's Orann system for pharma	Continuous physiological - Respiratory endpoints - Ambulatory BP - Activity and sleep - Glucose monitoring	Bluetooth
Accessories and Ancillary Sensors	VitalSense Core Temp Capsule	Ingestible temperature capsule captures body temperature and transmits real time readings	Wired or wireless (Bluetooth)
	VitalSense® Dermal Patch	Patch for dermal temperature measurements. It measures skin temperature and sends data in real time to the SEM	Wired or wireless (Bluetooth)
	Nonin iPod® Sp02	Probe to measure oxygen saturation with finger clip and SEM connector	Wired or wireless (Bluetooth)
	EQ-GSR (Galvanic Skin Response Sensor)	Sensor mounted on wrist to measure galvanic skin response	Wired or wireless (Bluetooth)

Company	Sensor Name	Description	Interface
	EQ02 M-Dock	Allows simultaneous charging and 2-way data transfer communication with up to six SEM's. Five M-Docks can be chained to support 30 simultaneous connections through USB	Wired or wireless (Bluetooth)
	EQ02 SEM Lead	Allows simultaneous charging and 2-way data transfer with a single SEM	Wired
	Equivital™ Bluetooth Dongle	Dongle with easy connection that enables fast communication of 2 SEMs in full disclosure and up to 6 SEMs in partial disclosure directly to a PC in real time. Up to 100m range	Bluetooth
	Equivital™ Hub	The Equivital™ Hub is a Bluetooth access point allowing to communicate in real time with up to 18 SEMs from a PC or LAN. Networkable via WiFi or Ethernet connection. Works with eqView professional software	Bluetooth
	Omron Blood Pressure 708BT(EU)	The Bluetooth blood pressure cuff measures subject blood pressure data, can be pre-paired with a single EQ02 SEM and can send data to store or be transmitted on from the SEM	Wired or wireless (Bluetooth)
	WristOx2 Bluetooth Oxygen Saturation (3150)	The Bluetooth, wrist worn oxygen saturation monitor measures saturation, can be pre-paired with a single EQ02 SEM and can send data to store or be transmitted on from the SEM	Wired or wireless (Bluetooth)
Somaxis (UK) [15] https://www.somaxis.com/	Cricket	EXG and IMU sensors that measure and train muscles (EMG), heart (EKG), brain (EEG), posture and movement	Bluetooth
Accessories	Chirp	iPad app controls and communicates with Cricket	Bluetooth
Vitalconnect (USA) [16] https://vitalconnect.com/	VitalPatch	Single-Lead ECG Heart Rate - Heart Rate Variability - Respiratory Rate - Skin Temperature Body - Fall Detection Activity	Bluetooth
STMicroelectronics (USA) [17] www.st.com	INEMO-M1	9 DoF inertial system: 3-axis accelerometer - 3-axis magnetometer - 3-axis gyroscope	Flexible interfaces: CAN, USART, SPI and I2C serial interfaces - full-speed USB 2.0 or BLE Module
	LPS331AP	High-resolution digital pressure sensor	SPI and I2C interfaces or BLE Module
	LIS3DH	Ultra-low-power accelerometer (motion sensor)	Digital I2C/SPI serial interface standard output or BLE Module
	HM301D	ECG acquisition system	SPI or BLE Module

TABLE I: DIFFERENT TYPES OF SENSORS

Sensors Type	Description	Position
Accelerometer	Collecting acceleration on the spatial axis of three-dimensional space.	Wearable
Artificial cochlea (hearing aid)	Transforming voice signal into electric pulse and sending them to electrodes implanted in ears, providing hearing sensation through simulating aural nerves.	Implanted
Artificial retina (visual aid)	Capturing pictures by external camera and converting them to electric pulse signals to be used to provide visual sensation through simulating optic nerves.	Implanted
Blood-pressure sensor	Finding the maximum systolic pressure and the minimum diastolic pressure.	Wearable
Gastrointestinal sensor (camera pill)	Identifying gastrointestinal tract via wireless capsule endoscope technique.	Implanted
Carbon dioxide sensor	Using infrared technique to measure the content of carbon dioxide from diverse gas	Wearable
ECG/EEG/EMG sensor	Placing two electrodes on the body skin and measuring the voltage difference between them.	Wearable
Humidity sensor	Using changes in capacitance and resistivity caused by humidity variations to measure humidity.	Wearable
Blood oxygen saturation sensor	Computing the ratio of absorption of infrared and red light passing through a thin part of human body to measure blood oxygen saturation.	Wearable
Pressure sensor	Using piezoelectric effect of dielectric medium to measure the value of pressure.	Wearable/ Surrounding
Respiration sensor	Perceiving the expansion and contraction of chest or abdomen to assess the respiration.	Wearable
Temperature sensor	Using the variations in the physical properties of materials to measure temperature.	Wearable
Visual sensor	Assessing different parameters like length, area, and location.	Wearable/ Surrounding

TABLE II: SENSORS DATA RATES REQUIREMENTS

Sensor Type	Data Rate
ECG (12 Leads)	288 Kbps
ECG (6 Leads)	71 Kbps
EMG	320 Kbps
EEG (12 Leads)	43.2 Kbps
Blood saturation	16 bps
Glucose level	1.6 Kbps
Temperature	120 bps
Motion	35 Kbps
Artificial retina	50-700 Kbps
Audio	1 Mbps
Voice	50-100 Kbps
Endoscope Capsule	2 Mbps

TABLE III: RADIO COMMUNICATION STANDARDS

Communication Type	In-Body	On-Body	External Network
Description	Between sensor nodes	Between sensor nodes and coordinator	Between coordinator and external server
Communication range	Short range	Short range	Medium to long range
Radio communication standard	Low- frequency inductive coupling, ISM, MICS	WMTS, RFID, Bluetooth, Zigbee, WLAN (Wi- Fi)	Cellular Networks (CDMA/ HSDPA/ GPRS/ EDGE/ (UMTS), WiFi, GPRS, Zifbee, Wibro, satellite
Data format	Raw signal	Raw signal	XML, CSV, JSON, etc.

On The Problem of Energy Efficient Mechanisms Based on Data Reduction in Wireless Body Sensor Networks

Carol Habib, Abdallah Makhoul, and Raphaël Couturier
Femto-st institute,
Univ. Bourgogne Franche-Comté,
19 av du Marchal Juin,
90000 Belfort, France,
firstname.lastname@univ-fcomte.fr

Rony Darazi
TICKET Lab,
Antonine University,
Hadat-Baabda,
Lebanon,
firstname.lastname@ua.edu.lb

***Abstract*—Wireless Body Sensor Networks have emerged as a low-cost solution for healthcare applications and telemedicine solutions replacing unnecessary hospitalization and ensuring continous health monitoring. Many challenges exist in such a network, especially because the sensor nodes have limited resources. In this paper, the energy consumption problem due to periodic transmission is targeted. We present a work in progress on energy-efficient mechanisms based on data reduction for body sensor networks. Many approaches have been proposed in the literature that aim to reduce the size and the amount of data collected and sent via the network. Our main idea in this paper is to confront Compressive Sensing (CS) and adaptive sampling techniques in order to come out with a problem formulation and a comprehensive comparison. The objective is to show if the adaptive sampling approach which is based on on-node processing ensure a better Performance/Energy trade-off than CS theory applied on biosignals.**

***Keywords*-Wireless Body Sensor Networks, Energy Consumption, Compressive Sensing, Adaptive Sampling**

I. Introduction

Wireless Body Sensor Networks (WBSNs), a subset of Wireless Sensor Networks (WSNs), have been gaining popularity in the last decade due to the potential they bring out in telemedicine solutions. They are mainly composed of sensor nodes deployed on the patient's body as wearables and a coordinator. The former sense and collect physiological measurements such as the heart rate, the blood pressure and the ECG etc. The latter receives the collected measurements and signals from the sensor nodes for fusion and manages the whole network.

The fusion process, depending on the monitoring scenario and application needs, includes: the detection of emergencies, the identification/detection of the patient's medical and/or physical status, the making of a diagnosis, the making of health decisions, the aggregation of the collected data before transmission to a higher level such as a sink or a server for storage and further processing.

Many challenges exist in such a network, especially because the sensor nodes have limited power, storage and processing resources. Energy consumption is one of the main issues given that WBSNs are characterized by periodic power consuming transmission of huge amounts of collected data namely signals and measurements. Many approaches concerning energy-efficient models and mechanisms have been proposed in the literature [1] [2] [3] [4] [5]. Data reduction is one of the means ensuring an efficient usage of the transmission unit of the sensor nodes and energy savings in the whole network. On the one hand, we have proposed in previous works [6] [7] an adaptive sampling rate model at the sensor node level. The approach aims at periodically specifying the amount of measurements to be collected by each sensor node depending on the variations presented by each vital sign in the last two periods. Furthermore, the amount of transmitted measurements is reduced by employing an early warning score system. Thus, only measurements indicating a change in the status of the vital sign are sent to the coordinator. On the other hand, many approaches [3] [4] [8] [5] [9] based on Compressive Sensing (CS) have been proposed in the literature due to its potential. CS guarantees the reconstruction of sparse signals such as the ECG while largely reducing the amount of sampled data. Thus, it reduces the amount of wirelessly transmitted data and consequently the energy consumption on the sensor node level.

In this paper, we present a work in progress on energy-efficient mechanisms based on data reduction for body sensor networks. Our objective is to confront adaptive sampling and CS as two different approaches ensuring energy-efficiency in WBSNs and come out with a problem formulation. Several CS approaches and data samling methods are compared in order to give open research issues in this domain.

The remainder of the paper is oragnized as follows. In Section II, the components of the sensor nodes are presented and their energy characteristic is dicussed. In Section III, a classification of the energy-efficient mechanisms from the literature is given. In Section IV, a previsouly proposed method which is based on adaptive sampling is briefly discussed. In Section V, compressive sensing is defined and different approaches from the literature are exlpained and compared. In SectionVI, further discussions are presented and the problem is formulated. Finally, Section VII concludes the paper.

II. Wireless Sensor Nodes: Components and Energy Characteristic

A wireless sensor node is constituted of three components: the sensing unit, the processing unit and the transmission unit. All three units need power to perform their tasks (see Figure 1) [10]. Yet, transmission is considered to be the most power-hungry task. The sensing unit is composed of the sensor and the ADC (Analogic-Digital Convertor) which converts the analog signal sensed with a given frequency (Nyquist-Shannon)[11] into a digital signal. The latter is fed to the processing unit, including a processor and a memory, where the digital signal processing algorithms are run. These include: compressive sensing, traditional compression techniques, feature extraction in the temporal and frequential domains, vital signs extraction (calculation) such as heart rate, classification, and other on-node processing algorithms. Furthermore, the processor controls the sensing and the transmission units and it activates and/or changes their status according to the application and the used protocol. Many energy-efficient mechanisms have been proposed in the literature, namely for WBSNs.

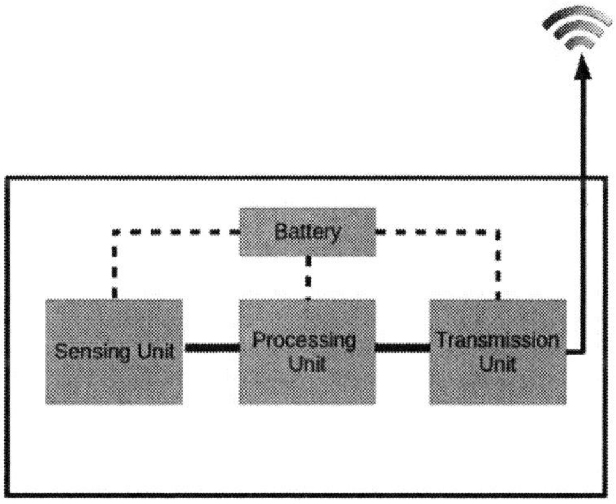

Figure 1. A wireless sensor node

III. Classification of Energy-Efficient mechanisms in WSNs

Energy-efficient mechanisms dedicated to wireless sensor networks are classified into five categories as follows [12]:

- Data reduction approaches: Aggregation, adaptive sampling, compression and network coding.
- Sleep/Wakeup schemes: Duty-cycling, passive wake-up radio, scheduled based MAC protocols and topology control.
- Radio optimization techniques:transmission power control, modulation optimization, cooperative communication, directional antennas and energy efficient cognitive radio.
- Energy-efficient routing methods: cluster architectures, energy as a routing metric, multipath routing, relay node placement and sink mobility.
- Battery repletion: energy harvesting and wireless charging.

These approaches can be split up into software and hardware strategies [1]. In addition, some of these mechanisms are suitable for large scale networks such as environmental monitoring, industry, public safety of military systems etc. applications. Thus, they cannot be applied in WBSNs where the network characteristics are different. For example, energy-efficient routing methods as well as transmission power control and topology control approaches cannot be directly used in WBSNs [2]. Many existing approaches have used context-awareness based on activity recognition to perform adaptive sampling or adaptive sensing. Some of them applied these approaches only on WBSNs composed of inertial detection sensor nodes such as accelerometers and gyroscopes [2]. Others used activity recognition to adapt the sensing rate of a vita sign of interest in the context of a give disease [13].

IV. Adaptive Sampling as an Energy-Efficient Mechanism

In order to increase the network lifetime and to reduce the huge amount of the collected data adaptive data collection models have been proposed in the litterature [14] [15] [6]. The main idea behind these models is to allow each sensor node to adapt its sampling rate to the physical changing dynamics of the monitored phenomenon. In this way, the oversampling can be minimized and the power efficiency of the overall network system can be further improved.

In [6], we proposed a distributed self-adaptive data collection approach in the context of WBSNs. Two contributions have been highlighted. First, a local detection system based on an early warning score system is proposed to be used on the biosensor node. The latter reduces the amount of transmitted data by only sending detected changes in the monitored vital sign measurements. Thus, reducing the amount of redundant information as well as the overall amount of transmitted measurements. Changes in vital signs are identified when the local detection system detects a change in the score of the measurement indicating a deterioration or improvement of the status of the vital sign. Second, an adaptive sampling rate schema, having a direct impact on the sensing task of the biosensor node, has been proposed. Using a Quadratic Bezier Curve as a BehaVior (BV) Function [14] [15], it takes into account two parameters: the evolution of the monitored vital sign over time and its monitoring importance, based on a medical judgment, regarding the patient's health condition. These parameters are, respectively, determined by the Fisher Test and One-way ANOVA model[15] which study the variances of the sensed measurements over time and by a risk level variable r^0 whose values range between 0 and 1. We have defined two risk levels, pointing out the importance of a given vital sign to be monitored knowing the patient's health condition:

- Low Risk: $0 \leq r^0 < 0.5$
- High Risk: $0.5 \leq r^0 \leq 1$

However, the overall health condition of a patient, being continuously and remotely monitored on a long-term basis, changes over time. It is subject to many health events which can be acute or even chronic. Thus, it can vary from day to day as well as from an improvement state into a deterioration state and vice versa. As a consequence, the monitoring importance given to each vital sign should be adapted with these changing conditions. This matter, has a direct influence on the sensing and processing tasks; therefore on the energy consumption of the WBSN and the early detection of critical events. In another work [7], we have proposed to dynamically adapt the risk level r^0 of a vital sign according to the health condition of the patient. Thus, the corresponding biosensor node will be given a higher risk level r^0 when the health condition of the patient is at a higher risk and it will be given a lower risk level r^0 when the health condition of the patient is at a lower risk. The proposed distributed and on-node approach is a software-based strategy and it belongs to the data reduction category.

V. Compressive Sensing

In the recent years, Compressive Sensing (CS) theory emerged as an energy-efficient approach for wireless communication. Capitalizing on signal sparsity, CS guarantees an accurate signal reconstruction by sampling signals at a much lower rate than the traditional Shannon-Nyquist theorem. Thus, it has the potential to dramatically reduce the power consumption since the amount of wirelessly transmitted data is considerably reduced. Furthermore, it reduces the amount of resources required for processing and storage and it promises significant compression rates while using computationally light linear encoders compared to traditional compression methods. CS theory has been applied in diverse domains including WSNs. Particularly, many contributions based on CS theory have been proposed in the literature so far for WBSNs due to the fact that biosignals such as the ECG are sparse [9], [5], [8], [4], [3].

Mamaghanian et al. [9] have proposed compressed sensing for real-time and energy-efficient ECG compression. They have demonstrated that CS extends the node's lifetime of about 37.1 % compared to the traditional compression method by DWT (Discrete Wavelet Transform). This is mainly due to the fact that the former requires less computation for the code execution than the latter. The have used Shimmer motes for the validation of their proposal. However, they have clearly stated that they have proposed "digital CS" which takes place after the ADC, thus raw samples are sensed at a Nyquist rate and only digital samples are sampled using CS theory. In accordance, the results showed that the node's lifetime extension is only 6 % compared to no compression at all. This is due to the amount of energy consumed to execute the code. Therefore, "analog CS" remains the ultimate goal, where the compression occurs in the analog sensor read-out prior to ADC. It would then reduce the energy consumption due to sampling and running the OS. Unfortunately, it still requires extensive work.

Faust et al. [5] have proposed to apply CS for heart rate(HR) monitoring. They have demonstrated that the ECG signal after the R-wave form extraction is a sparse signal in the time domain, thus the CS theory is applicable. The latter shows the spikes in the ECG signal which indicate a heart beat, thus the HR can be calculated from this signal. However, the density of the ECG signal changes from a disease to another thus, CS does not provide a good signal reconstruction for all types of ECG. They have concluded by proposing an implementation of their system on sensor nodes at the analog level.

Wang et al. [3] have proposed a configurable energy-efficient compressed sensing architecture for wireless body sensor networks. They have focused on the effect of the quantization in CS and studied the impact of the sampling rate M as well as the number of quantization bits b on the energy consumption. They have proposed an algorithm which finds the best configuration pair (M,b) meeting the performance-energy trade-off requirement. However, the authors only studied the energy consumption due to transmission and did not mention the power resources required for sensing and processing the data. The results showed very close energy consumption when comparing traditional CS and configurable CS, however, the latter showed much better reconstruction error rates. Figure 2 summarizes the three works chosen from the literature.

VI. Further Discussion and problem formulation

All the CS approaches that have been previously discussed as well as the proposed approach contribute on the digital signal processing level. All of them focus on reducing the energy consumption due to transmission by reducing the amount of wirelessly transmitted data. The CS approaches reduce the sampling rate used to sample the digital signal, thus reducing the amount of samples to be transmitted. The proposed adaptive sampling approach, as described in section IV, is twofold:

Approach	Objective	Contributions	Assumptions	Inputs	Outputs	Constraints	Context	Validation	Results	Drawbacks
Mamaghanian et al. (2011)	Comparison between CS theory and DWT	Several compression algorithms implementations and optimizations	ECG sparsity	Digital ECG samples	Compressed low-dimensional vector	Limited energy and resources	Real-time ECG monitoring using WBSNs	Real implementation on Shimmer motes, ECG data from the MIT-BIH Arrhythmia Database	MSP430 is not suited for digital signal processing operations Digital compression does not extend the lifetime of the node up to considerable amounts CS theory has a better trade-off between energy consumption and compression ratios than DWT	Default reconstruction algorithm with high computation resources
Faust et al. (2012)	Apply CS theory for heart rate monitoring	Apply CS theory on time domain sparse signal	Sparsity of R-wave form extraction of ECG	Digital R-wave extraction of ECG samples	Compressed low-dimensional vector	----------------	Heart rate monitoring	ECG data from the MIT-BIH Arrhythmia Database	HR signals are sparse in time domain thus CS can be used, CS reduces the data rate compared to standard sampling method, Practical realization of the proposed system is a must to validate it	No contribution at the compression and reconstruction algorithms, Limitations of resources are not taken into consideration, No solution is given in case of different ECG patterns corresponding to different diseases
Wang et al. (2016)	Configurable CS Architecture : Sampling rate and quantization	Impact of quantization and sampling rate on signal reconstruction and energy consumption, Proposal of an optimization algorithm RapQCS	Sparsity of biosignals	High-dimensional raw analog signal	Quantized random measurements	Limited energy and resources	Biosignals monitoring using WBSNs	ECG data from the MIT-BIH Arrhythmia Database	Energy consumption in traditional CS and configurable CS are close but there is a remarkable difference in the reconstruction error rate, RAPQCS has good results in terms of speed and performance	The energy required for sensing and processing the data is not taken into consideration (the sampling rate is much greater in configurable CS than in traditional CS), The energy setup is not clear

Figure 2. Compressive Sensing approaches in the context of wireless body sensor networks taken from the literature.

- Adaptation of the sampling rate: It adapts the sampling rate at which a vital sign is extracted(calculated measurement) from the digital signal.
- Local Detection: It transmits the calculated measurement of a vital sign only if its score indicates a change in the status of the vital sign.

The adaptation of the sampling rate is done based on vital signs, which are in most of the cases calculated based on raw sensed signals. For example the HR (bmp) is calculated from the R-wave extraction of the ECG signal. Thus, the adaptation of sampling rate indicates at what rate (time interval) the processor should process a new vital sign measurement, regardless the sensing frequency of the sensor node which is usually fixed by the type of the raw biosignal. However, the adaptation of the sampling rate can be extended to not only impact the processing of a new measurement but also to manage the sensing task of the sensing unit. In other words, it could allow the sensor node to control the sensing unit by activating/desactivating the sensor each time interval δ_t based on the adaptation of the sampling rate. However, this still needs extensive work in terms of delay and power consumption especially if it needs to be implemented on a real architecture where some hardware limitations might exist. Finally, none of the approaches contribute directly on the analog raw signal aquired by the sensor nor on the sensing frequency, thus none reduces the energy consumption due to sensing. Nevertheless, all of the approaches can be adapted in order to do so. However, the CS approaches face hardware limitations as for the proposed approach it can be extended to control the sensing tasks by activiting/desactivating the sensor.

Since, the chosen approaches from the literature and the proposed approach have one common goal: reduce the energy consumption due to transmission. Furthermore, for the following reasons:

- All of the techniques are software-based.
- All of them rely on data reduction mechanisms.
- All of them contribute on the same level: digital signal processing.

Then, the adaptive sampling approach is comparable to the chosen approaches from the literature. The only difference remains in that the CS theory is complemented by a reconstructionn algorithm at the base station in order to reconstruct the sensed biosignal for further processing.

The open question can be formalized as follows: *Does the adaptive sampling approach which is based on on-node processing (extraction of vital signs from biosignals and local detection) ensure a better Performance/Energy trade-off than CS theory applied on biosignals ?*

The performance metric englobes: the detection of critical events, the detection of improving/worsening conditions, the reduction of redundant data, execution time of the code, complexity. The energy metric includes: the energy consumption due to sensing (if our approach is extended), and especially the energy consumption due to processing (executing the code) and transmitting.

VII. Conclusion and Future Work

In this paper, we presented a work in progress on energy-efficient mechanisms based on data reduction for body sensor networks. We reviewed compressive sensing and adaptive sampling approaches that have been proposed in order to reduce the amount of data collected and transmitted over the network. We provided a discussion about the differences and the advantages of the different techniques and we formalized an open question concerning tha data compression in body sensor networks.

Our main objective for future work is to reduce the number of bits needed to represent the sensed data prior to transmission, while taking into consideration the trade-off between the computational cost and the compression ratio. Then, we intend to combine the compressive data model with an adaptive sampling technique to further reduce the collected data prior to transmission.

Acknowledgment

This work is partially funded with support from the National Council for Scientific Research in Lebanon, the Labex ACTION program (contract ANR-11-LABX-01-01), and the Lebanese University research program

References

[1] M. Magno, T. Polonelli, F. Casamassima, A. Gomez, E. Farella, and L. Benini, "Energy-efficient context aware power management with asynchronous protocol for body sensor network," *Mobile Networks and Applications*, pp. 1–11, 2016.

[2] S.-Y. Chen, C.-F. Lai, R.-H. Hwang, Y.-H. Lai, and M.-S. Wang, "An adaptive sensor data segments selection method for wearable health care services," *Journal of medical systems*, vol. 39, no. 12, p. 194, 2015.

[3] A. Wang, F. Lin, Z. Jin, and W. Xu, "A configurable energy-efficient compressed sensing architecture with its application on body sensor networks," *IEEE Transactions on Industrial Informatics*, vol. 12, no. 1, pp. 15–27, 2016.

[4] S. Li, L. Da Xu, and X. Wang, "Compressed sensing signal and data acquisition in wireless sensor networks and internet of things," *IEEE Transactions on Industrial Informatics*, vol. 9, no. 4, pp. 2177–2186, 2013.

[5] O. Faust, U. R. Acharya, J. Ma, L. C. Min, and T. Tamura, "Compressed sampling for heart rate monitoring," *Computer methods and programs in biomedicine*, vol. 108, no. 3, pp. 1191–1198, 2012.

[6] C. Habib, A. Makhoul, R. Darazi, and C. Salim, "Self-adaptive data collection and fusion for health monitoring based on body sensor networks," *IEEE Transactions on Industrial Informatics*, vol. 12, no. 6, pp. 2342–2352, 2016.

[7] ——, "Real-time sampling rate adaptation based on continuous risk level evaluation in wireless body sensor networks," August 2017.

[8] S. Li, L. Da Xu, and X. Wang, "A continuous biomedical signal acquisition system based on compressed sensing in body sensor networks," *IEEE transactions on industrial informatics*, vol. 9, no. 3, pp. 1764–1771, 2013.

[9] H. Mamaghanian, N. Khaled, D. Atienza, and P. Vandergheynst, "Compressed sensing for real-time energy-efficient ecg compression on wireless body sensor nodes," *IEEE Transactions on Biomedical Engineering*, vol. 58, no. 9, pp. 2456–2466, 2011.

[10] I. Akyildiz, W. Su, Y. Sankarasubramaniam, and E. Cayirci, "Wireless sensor networks: a survey," *Computer Networks*, vol. 38, no. 4, pp. 393 – 422, 2002.

[11] A. J. Jerri, "The shannon sampling theoremits various extensions and applications: A tutorial review," *Proceedings of the IEEE*, vol. 65, no. 11, pp. 1565–1596, 1977.

[12] T. Rault, A. Bouabdallah, and Y. Challal, "Energy efficiency in wireless sensor networks: A top-down survey," *Computer Networks*, vol. 67, pp. 104–122, 2014.

[13] X. Qi, M. Keally, G. Zhou, Y. Li, and Z. Ren, "Adasense: Adapting sampling rates for activity recognition in body sensor networks," *2013 IEEE 19th Real-Time and Embedded Technology and Applications Symposium (RTAS)*, pp. 163–172, 2013.

[14] A. Makhoul, H. Harb, and D. Laiymani, "Residual energy-based adaptive data collection approach for periodic sensor networks," *Ad Hoc Networks*, vol. 35, pp. 149–160, 2015.

[15] D. Laiymani and A. Makhoul, "Adaptive data collection approach for periodic sensor networks," *2013 9th International Wireless Communications and Mobile Computing Conference, IWCMC 2013, Sardinia, Italy, July 1-5, 2013*, pp. 1448–1453, 2013.